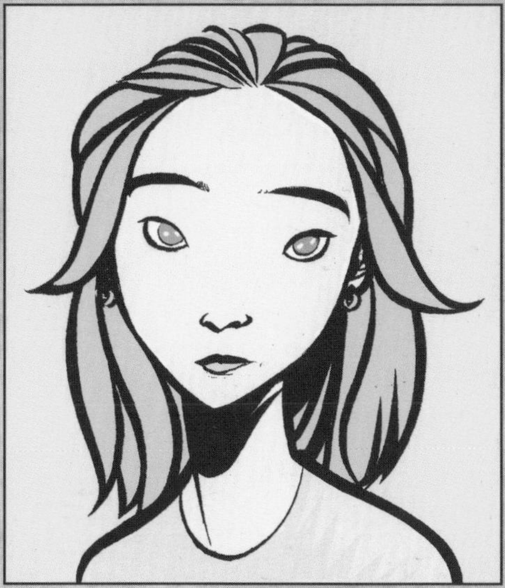

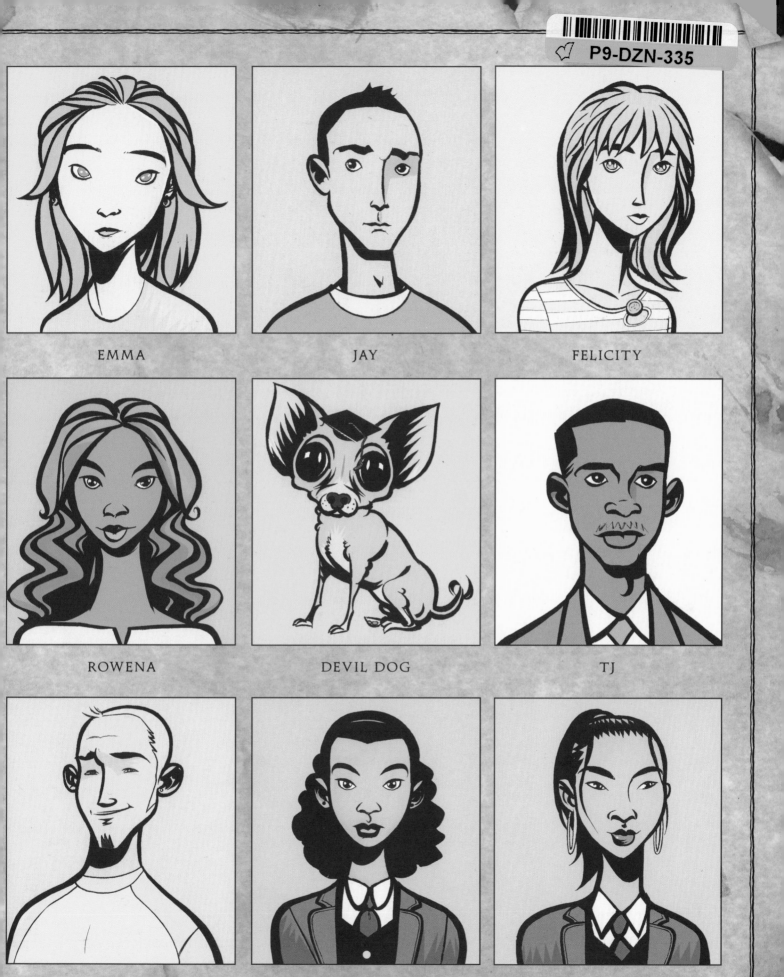

EMMA

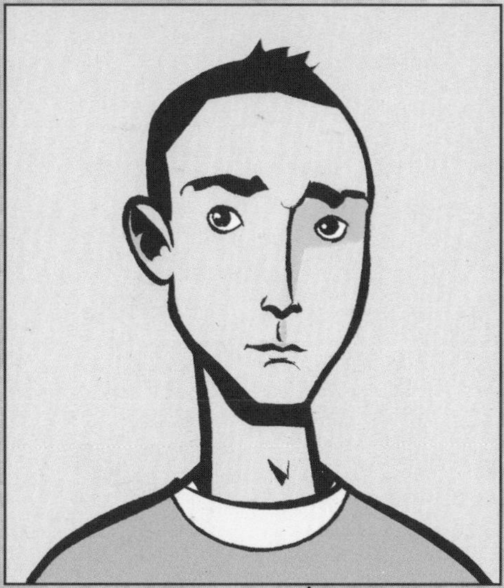

JAY

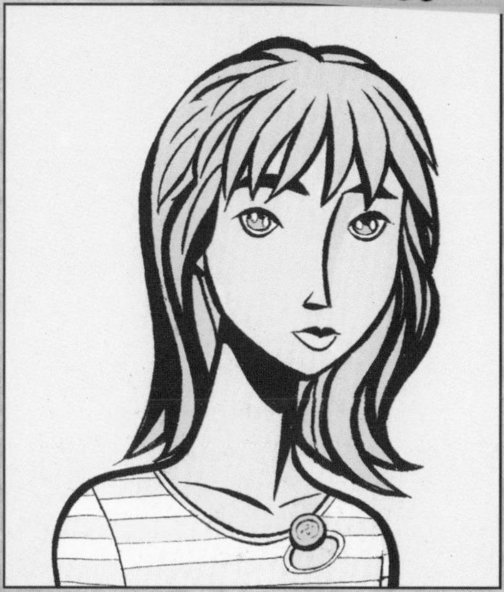

FELICITY

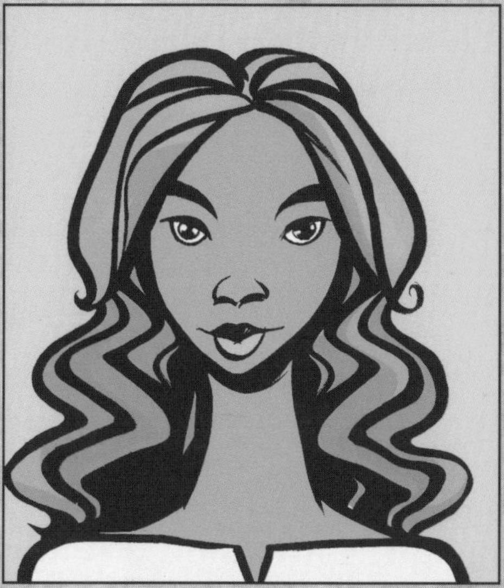

ROWENA

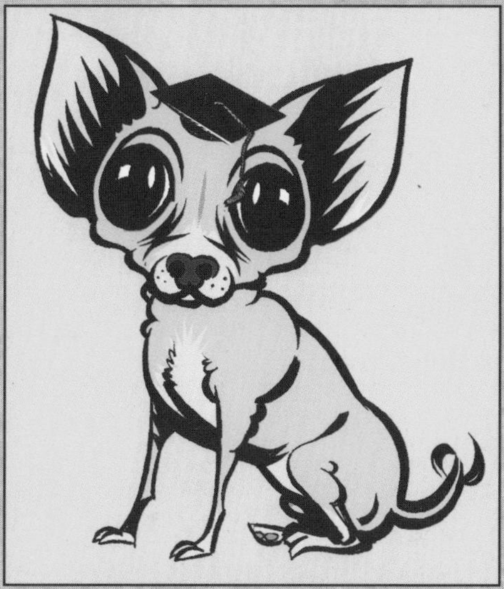

DEVIL DOG

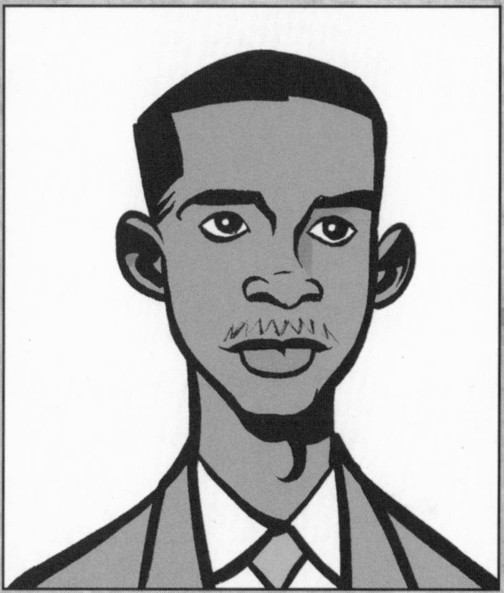

TJ

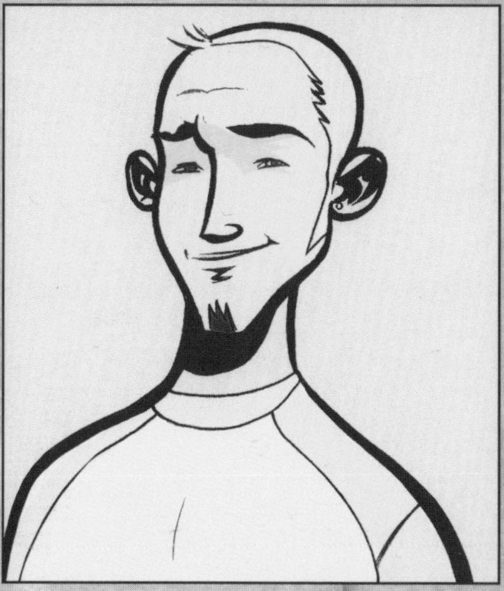

ALEX

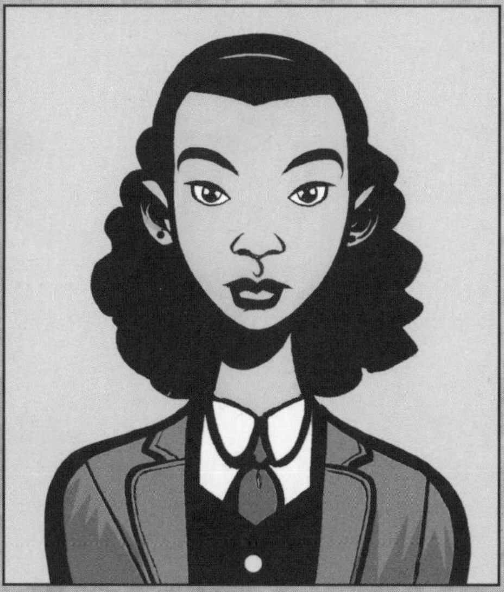

CLARA

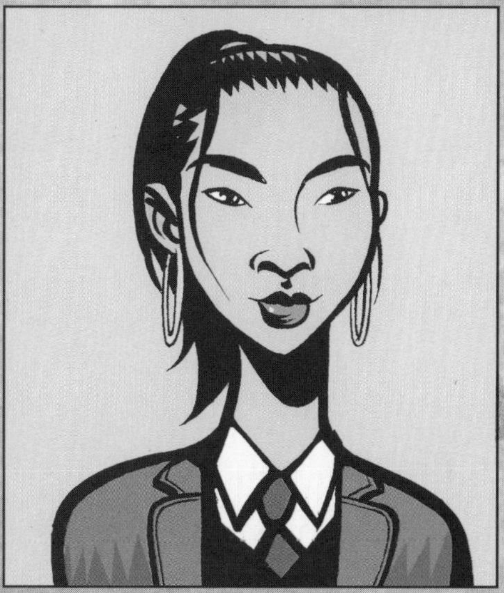

MILLIE

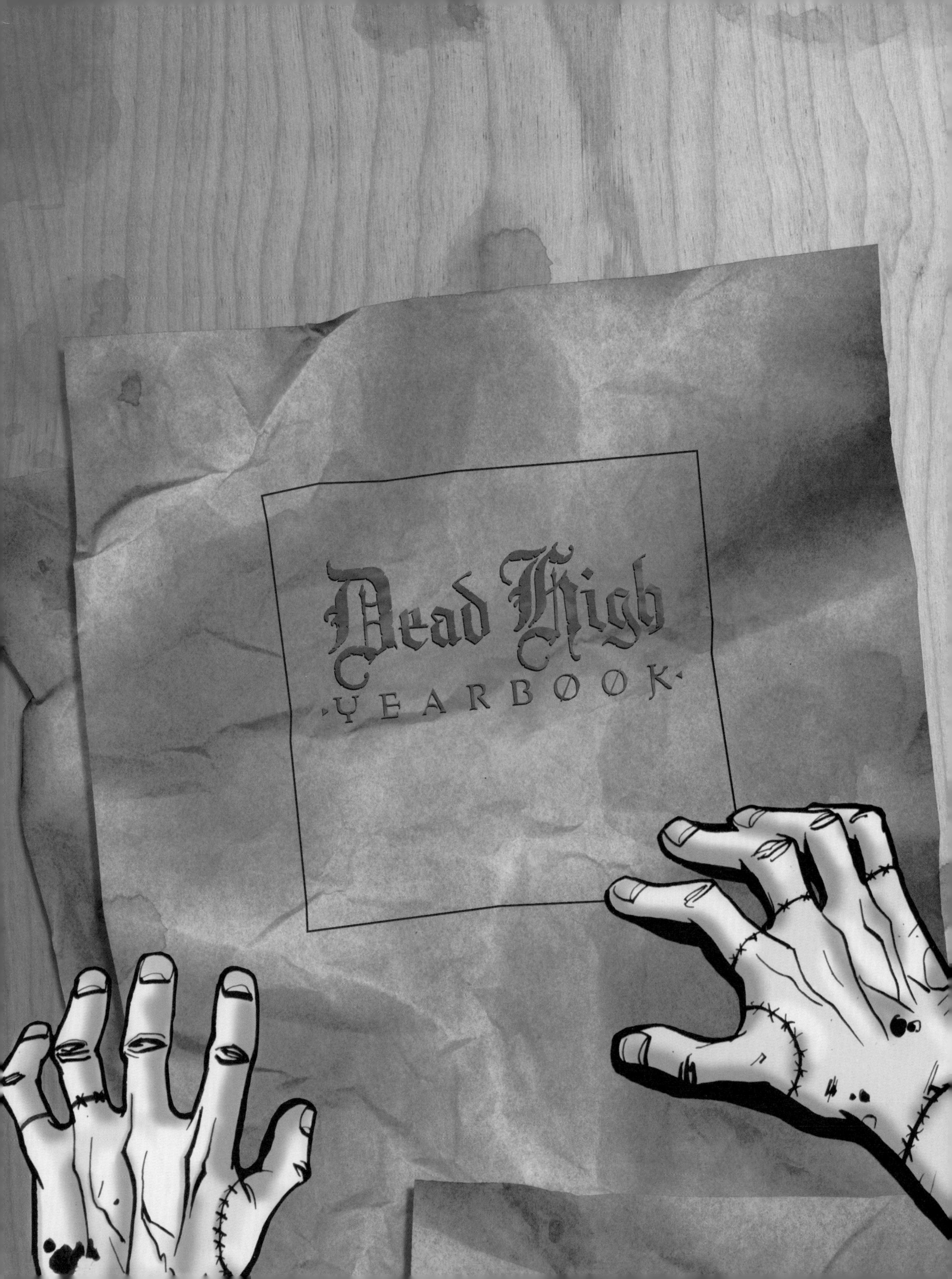
Dead High
YEARBOOK

+ GORE-IENTATION +
WELCOME TO DEAD HIGH
5

+ CHAPTER ONE +
FEAR PRESSURE
7

+ CHAPTER TWO +
WHAT'S GOT
INTO GRANDMA?
17

+ CHAPTER THREE +
DEVIL DOG
OF THE
DAMNED
26

Dead
YEAR

High BOOK 0

+ CHAPTER FOUR +
FANG YOU SO
VERY MUCH
35

+ CHAPTER FIVE +
HAVE A NICEY
ICEE LAST DAY
44

+ CHAPTER SIX +
WHO ARE YOU
HAVING FOR
DINNER?
53

+ CHAPTER SEVEN +
HEAD OF
THE CLASS
63

+ CHAPTER EIGHT +
GOOD-BYE AND
GOOD LUCK
71

+ DUTTON BOOKS +

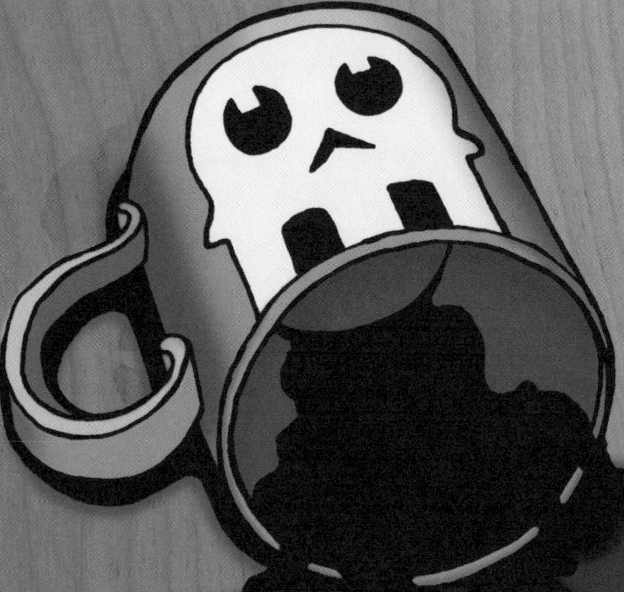

DUTTON BOOKS
A member of Penguin Group (USA) Inc.

Published by the Penguin Group
Penguin Group (USA) Inc., 375 Hudson Street, New York, New York 10014, U.S.A. • Penguin Group (Canada), 90 Eglinton Avenue East, Suite 700, Toronto, Ontario, Canada M4P 2Y3 (a division of Pearson Penguin Canada Inc.) • Penguin Books Ltd, 80 Strand, London WC2R 0RL, England • Penguin Ireland, 25 St Stephen's Green, Dublin 2, Ireland (a division of Penguin Books Ltd) • Penguin Group (Australia), 250 Camberwell Road, Camberwell, Victoria 3124, Australia (a division of Pearson Australia Group Pty Ltd) • Penguin Books India Pvt Ltd, 11 Community Centre, Panchsheel Park, New Delhi—110 017, India • Penguin Group (NZ), Cnr Airborne and Rosedale Roads, Albany, Auckland 1310, New Zealand (a division of Pearson New Zealand Ltd) • Penguin Books (South Africa) (Pty) Ltd, 24 Sturdee Avenue, Rosebank, Johannesburg 2196, South Africa • Penguin Books Ltd, Registered Offices: 80 Strand, London WC2R 0RL, England

CIP Data is available.

Published in the United States by Dutton Books,
a member of Penguin Group (USA) Inc.
345 Hudson Street, New York, New York 10014
www.penguin.com/youngreaders

Printed in China • First Edition
ISBN 978-0-525-47783-9
1 2 3 4 5 6 7 8 9 10

GORE-IENTATION:
WELCOME TO DEAD HIGH
AND SEGUES

Story by Ivan Velez
Art by Shawn Martinbrough
Colors and lettering by Wilson Ramos Jr.

FEAR PRESSURE

Story by John Rozum
Art by Wilfred Santiago
Colors by Dave McCaig
Lettering by Wilson Ramos Jr.

WHAT'S GOT INTO GRANDMA?

Story by Ho Che Anderson
Art by Brian Hurtt
Colors by Krista Ward
Lettering by Wilson Ramos Jr.

DEVIL DOG OF THE DAMNED

Story by Jennifer Camper
Art by ChrisCross
Colors by Jean Segarra-Rosa
Lettering by Wilson Ramos Jr.

FANG YOU SO VERY MUCH

Story by Wilfred Santiago
Art by Nicola Scott
Colors by Krista Ward
Lettering by Wilson Ramos Jr.

HAVE A NICEY
ICEE LAST DAY

Story by Mark McVeigh
Art by Pop Mhan
Colors by Krista Ward
Lettering by Wilson Ramos Jr.

WHO ARE YOU HAVING
FOR DINNER?

Story by Papo Martin
Art by Wilfred Santiago
Colors by Dave McCaig
Lettering by Wilson Ramos Jr.

HEAD OF THE CLASS

Story by Jacqueline Ching and Papo Martin
Art by Ho Che Anderson
Colors by Dave McCaig
Lettering by Wilson Ramos Jr.

GOOD-BYE AND GOOD LUCK

Story by Ivan Velez
Art by Shawn Martinbrough
Colors and lettering by Wilson Ramos Jr.

Edited by Mark McVeigh and Ivan Velez
Book design, title page art, and copyright page art by Jason Henry
Back cover art by ChrisCross
Endpaper art by Wilfred Santiago

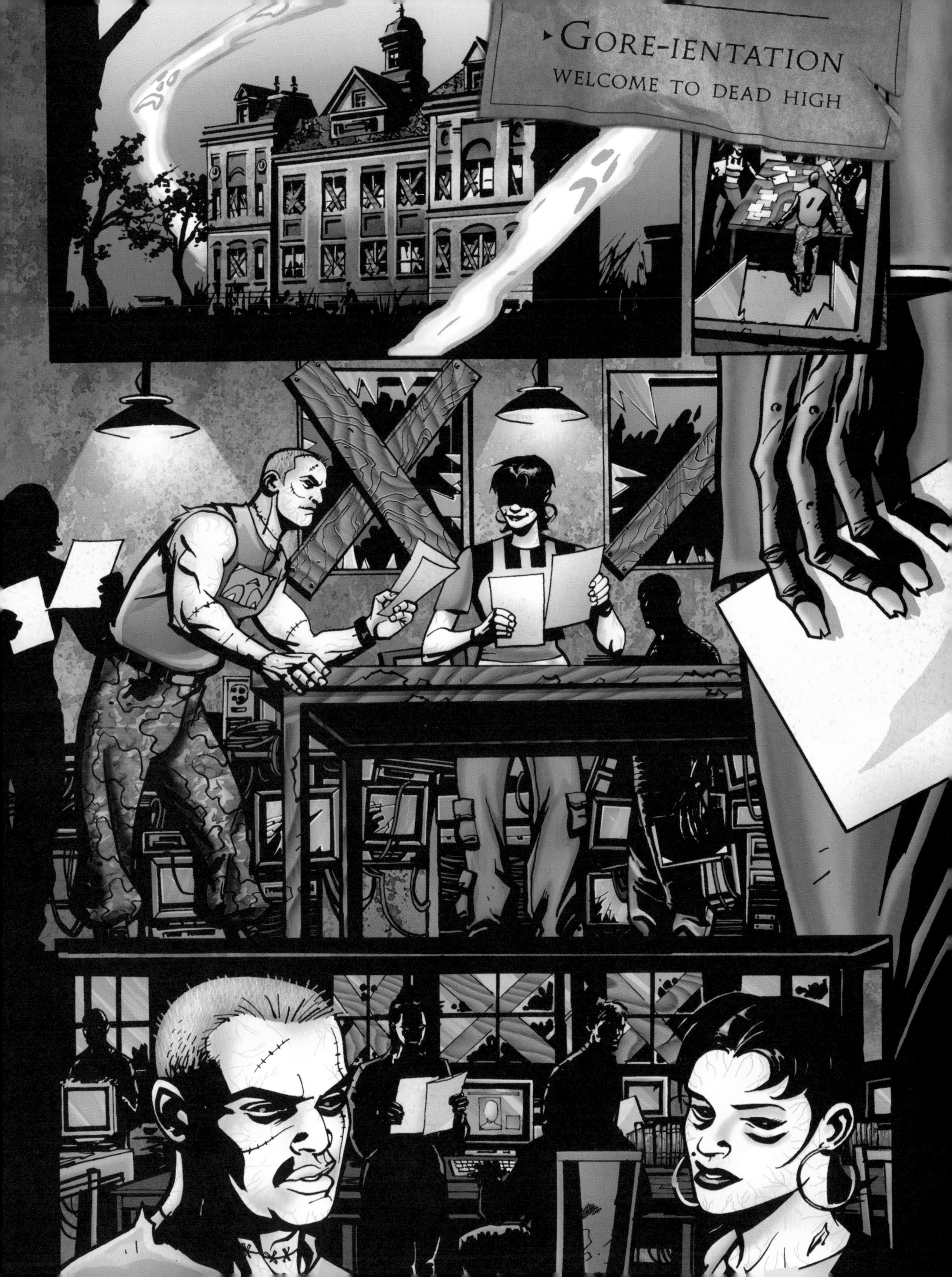
GORE-IENTATION
WELCOME TO DEAD HIGH

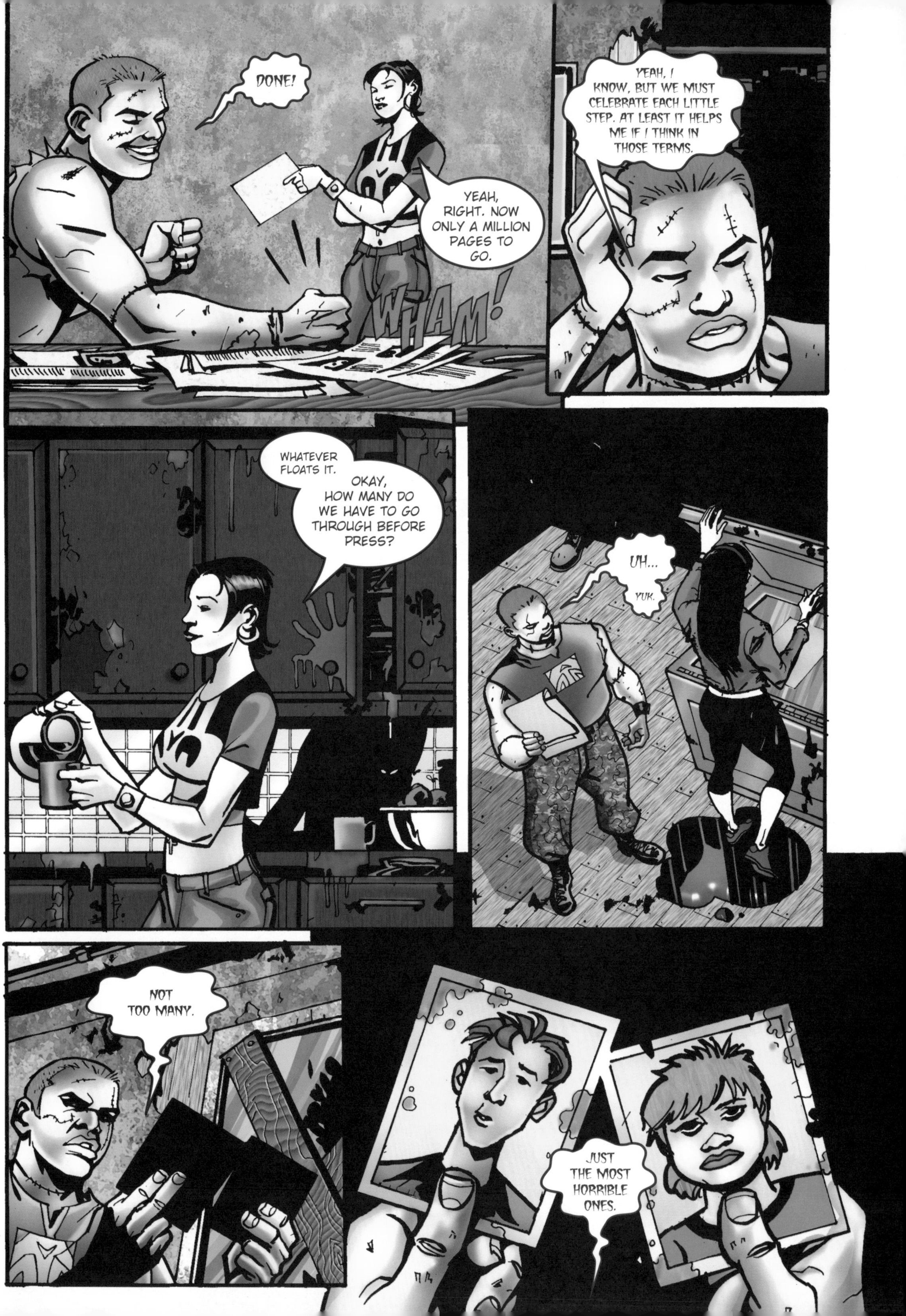
DONE!
YEAH, RIGHT. NOW ONLY A MILLION PAGES TO GO.
WHAM!
YEAH, I KNOW, BUT WE MUST CELEBRATE EACH LITTLE STEP. AT LEAST IT HELPS ME IF I THINK IN THOSE TERMS.
WHATEVER FLOATS IT.
OKAY, HOW MANY DO WE HAVE TO GO THROUGH BEFORE PRESS?
UH...
YUK.
NOT TOO MANY.
JUST THE MOST HORRIBLE ONES.

▸Fear Pressure

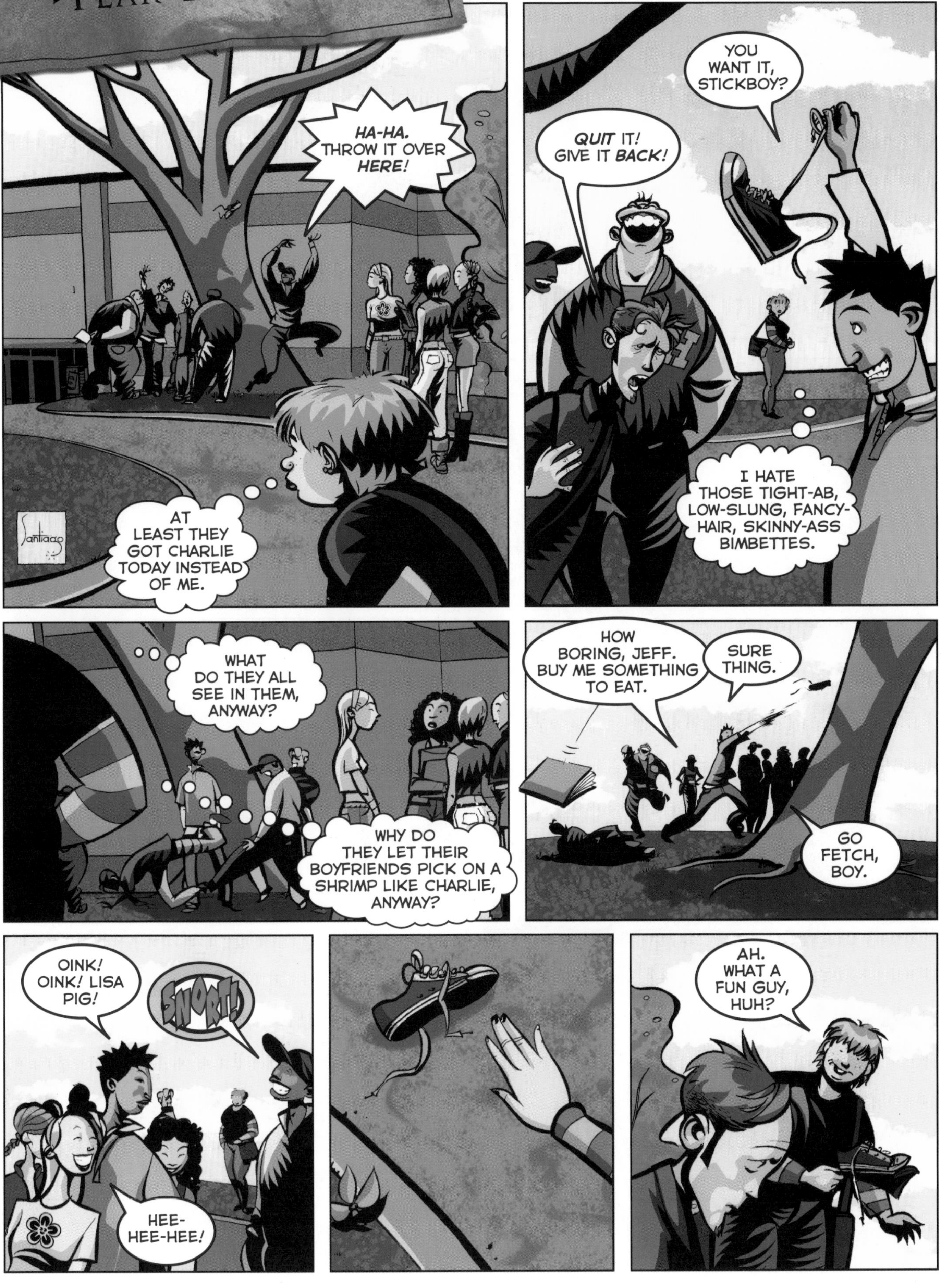

HA-HA. THROW IT OVER HERE!
AT LEAST THEY GOT CHARLIE TODAY INSTEAD OF ME.
Santiago
YOU WANT IT, STICKBOY?
QUIT IT! GIVE IT BACK!
I HATE THOSE TIGHT-AB, LOW-SLUNG, FANCY-HAIR, SKINNY-ASS BIMBETTES.
WHAT DO THEY ALL SEE IN THEM, ANYWAY?
WHY DO THEY LET THEIR BOYFRIENDS PICK ON A SHRIMP LIKE CHARLIE, ANYWAY?
HOW BORING, JEFF. BUY ME SOMETHING TO EAT.
SURE THING.
GO FETCH, BOY.
OINK! OINK! LISA PIG!
SNORT!
HEE-HEE-HEE!
AH. WHAT A FUN GUY, HUH?

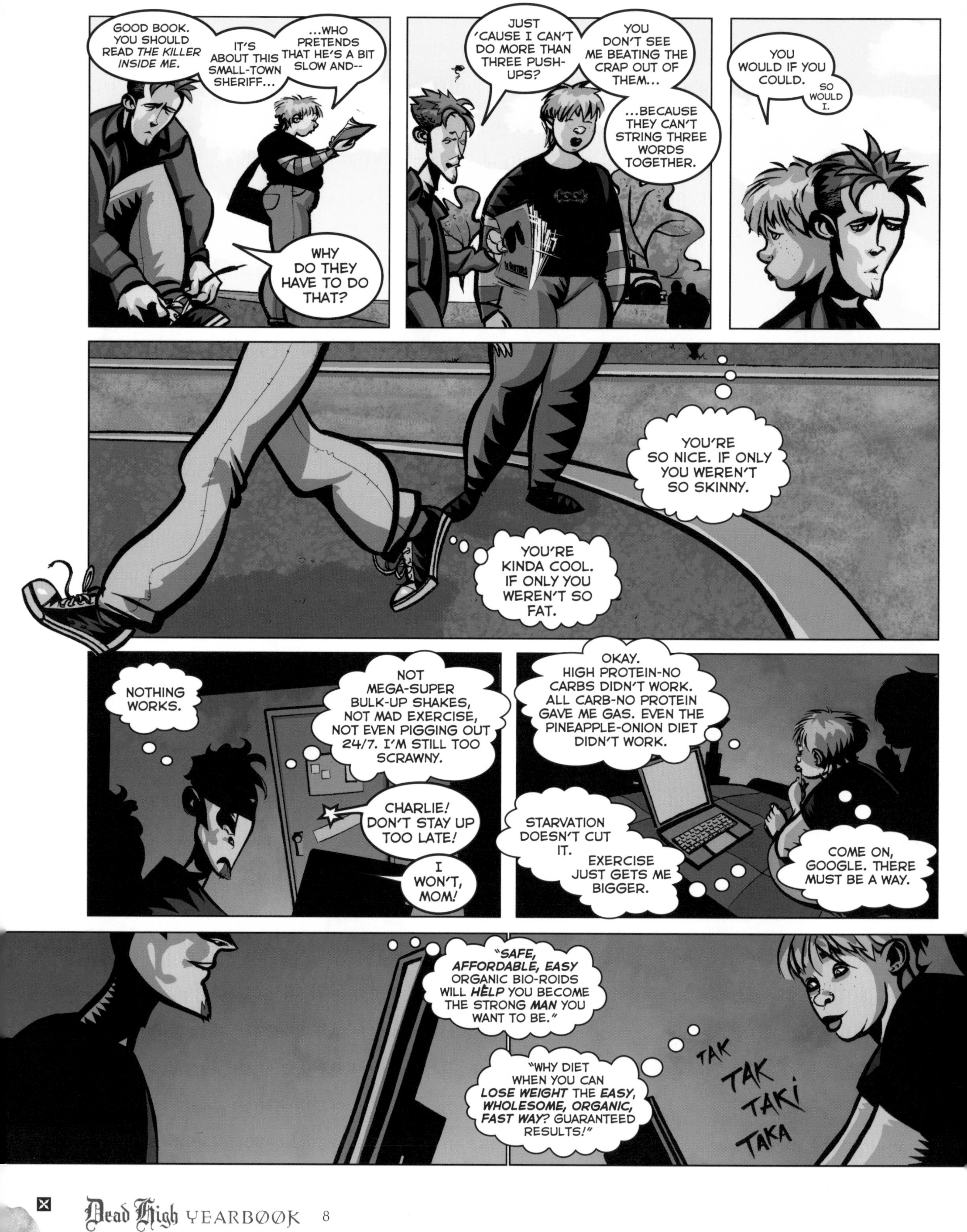
GOOD BOOK. YOU SHOULD READ *THE KILLER INSIDE ME.*
IT'S ABOUT THIS SMALL-TOWN SHERIFF...
...WHO PRETENDS THAT HE'S A BIT SLOW AND--
WHY DO THEY HAVE TO DO THAT?
JUST 'CAUSE I CAN'T DO MORE THAN THREE PUSH-UPS?
YOU DON'T SEE ME BEATING THE CRAP OUT OF THEM...
...BECAUSE THEY CAN'T STRING THREE WORDS TOGETHER.
YOU WOULD IF YOU COULD.
SO WOULD I.
YOU'RE SO NICE. IF ONLY YOU WEREN'T SO SKINNY.
YOU'RE KINDA COOL. IF ONLY YOU WEREN'T SO FAT.
NOTHING WORKS.
NOT MEGA-SUPER BULK-UP SHAKES, NOT MAD EXERCISE, NOT EVEN PIGGING OUT 24/7. I'M STILL TOO SCRAWNY.
CHARLIE! DON'T STAY UP TOO LATE!
I WON'T, MOM!
OKAY. HIGH PROTEIN-NO CARBS DIDN'T WORK. ALL CARB-NO PROTEIN GAVE ME GAS. EVEN THE PINEAPPLE-ONION DIET DIDN'T WORK.
STARVATION DOESN'T CUT IT.
EXERCISE JUST GETS ME BIGGER.
COME ON, GOOGLE. THERE MUST BE A WAY.
"***SAFE, AFFORDABLE, EASY*** ORGANIC BIO-ROIDS WILL ***HELP*** YOU BECOME THE STRONG ***MAN*** YOU WANT TO BE."
"WHY DIET WHEN YOU CAN ***LOSE WEIGHT*** THE ***EASY, WHOLESOME, ORGANIC, FAST WAY?*** GUARANTEED RESULTS!"
TAK
TAK
TAKi
TAKA

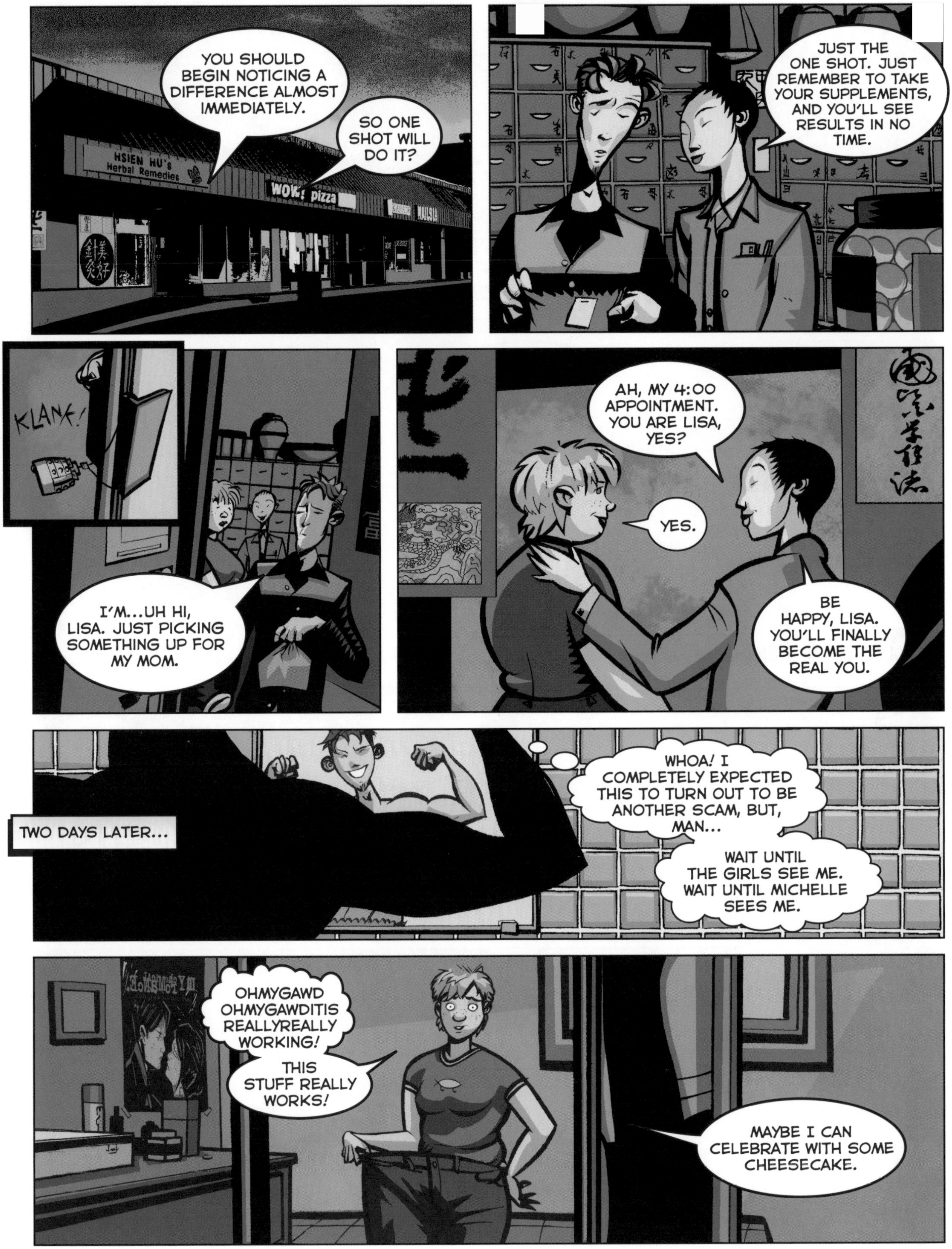
YOU SHOULD BEGIN NOTICING A DIFFERENCE ALMOST IMMEDIATELY.
SO ONE SHOT WILL DO IT?
HSIEN HU's Herbal Remedies
WOW! pizza
JUST THE ONE SHOT. JUST REMEMBER TO TAKE YOUR SUPPLEMENTS, AND YOU'LL SEE RESULTS IN NO TIME.
KLANK!
I'M...UH HI, LISA. JUST PICKING SOMETHING UP FOR MY MOM.
AH, MY 4:00 APPOINTMENT. YOU ARE LISA, YES?
YES.
BE HAPPY, LISA. YOU'LL FINALLY BECOME THE REAL YOU.
TWO DAYS LATER...
WHOA! I COMPLETELY EXPECTED THIS TO TURN OUT TO BE ANOTHER SCAM, BUT, MAN...
WAIT UNTIL THE GIRLS SEE ME. WAIT UNTIL MICHELLE SEES ME.
OHMYGAWD OHMYGAWDITIS REALLYREALLY WORKING!
THIS STUFF REALLY WORKS!
MAYBE I CAN CELEBRATE WITH SOME CHEESECAKE.

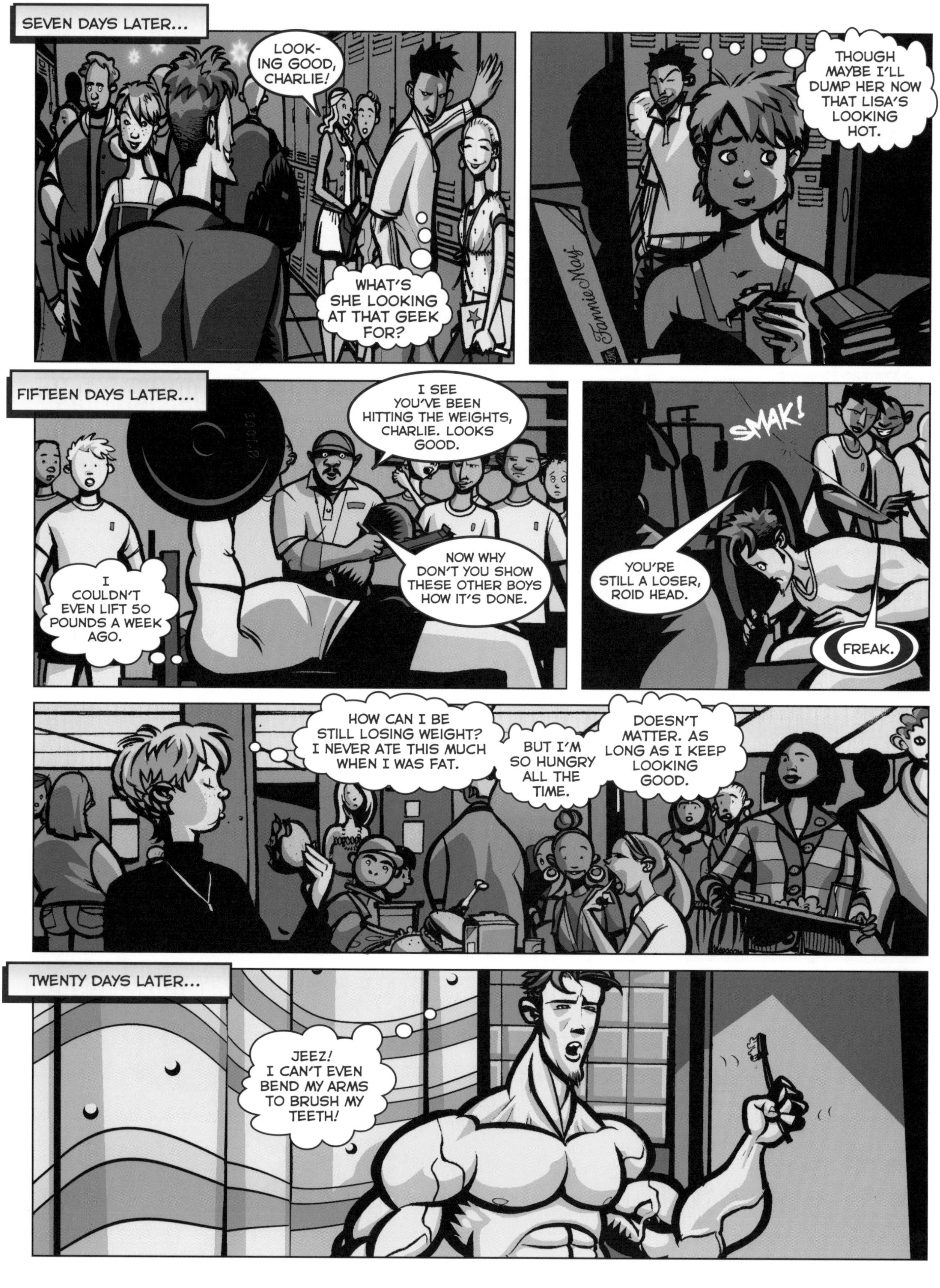
SEVEN DAYS LATER...
LOOK-ING GOOD, CHARLIE!
WHAT'S SHE LOOKING AT THAT GEEK FOR?
THOUGH MAYBE I'LL DUMP HER NOW THAT LISA'S LOOKING HOT.
FIFTEEN DAYS LATER...
I SEE YOU'VE BEEN HITTING THE WEIGHTS, CHARLIE. LOOKS GOOD.
I COULDN'T EVEN LIFT 50 POUNDS A WEEK AGO.
NOW WHY DON'T YOU SHOW THESE OTHER BOYS HOW IT'S DONE.
SMAK!
YOU'RE STILL A LOSER, ROID HEAD.
FREAK.
HOW CAN I BE STILL LOSING WEIGHT? I NEVER ATE THIS MUCH WHEN I WAS FAT.
BUT I'M SO HUNGRY ALL THE TIME.
DOESN'T MATTER. AS LONG AS I KEEP LOOKING GOOD.
TWENTY DAYS LATER...
JEEZ! I CAN'T EVEN BEND MY ARMS TO BRUSH MY TEETH!

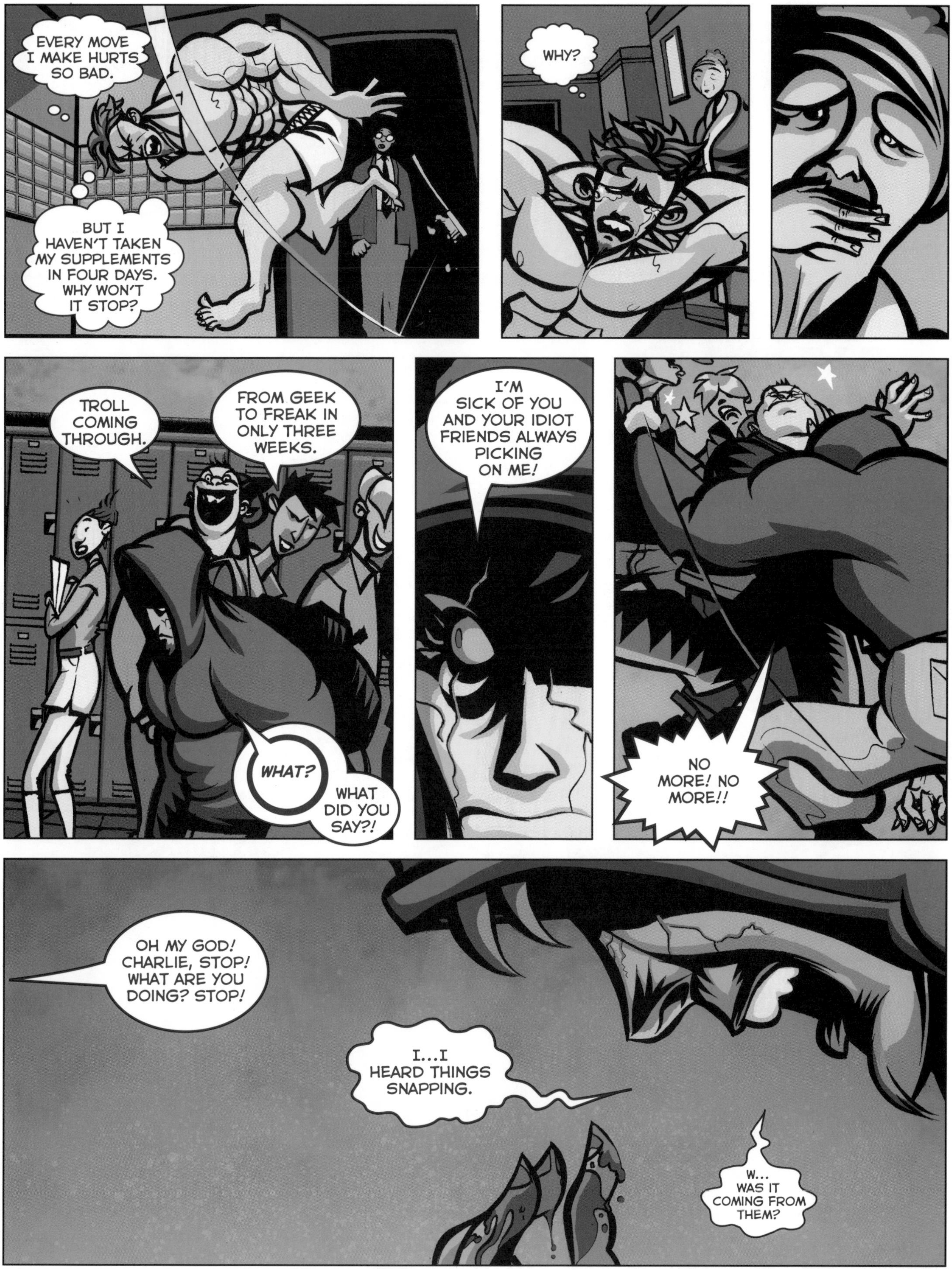
EVERY MOVE I MAKE HURTS SO BAD.
BUT I HAVEN'T TAKEN MY SUPPLEMENTS IN FOUR DAYS. WHY WON'T IT STOP?
WHY?
TROLL COMING THROUGH.
FROM GEEK TO FREAK IN ONLY THREE WEEKS.
WHAT?
WHAT DID YOU SAY?!
I'M SICK OF YOU AND YOUR IDIOT FRIENDS ALWAYS PICKING ON ME!
NO MORE! NO MORE!!
OH MY GOD! CHARLIE, STOP! WHAT ARE YOU DOING? STOP!
I...I HEARD THINGS SNAPPING.
W... WAS IT COMING FROM THEM?

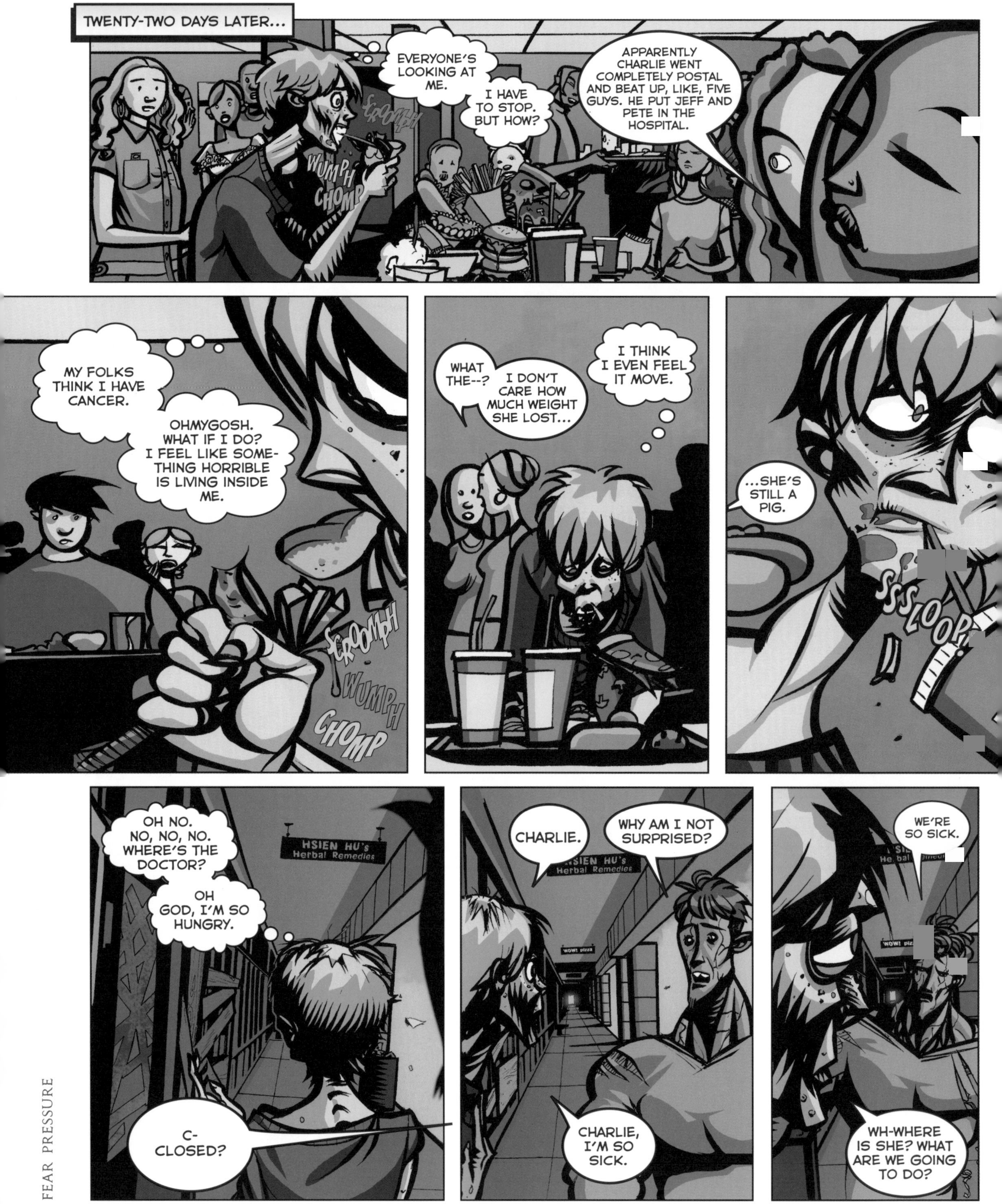

TWENTY-TWO DAYS LATER...
EVERYONE'S LOOKING AT ME.
I HAVE TO STOP. BUT HOW?
APPARENTLY CHARLIE WENT COMPLETELY POSTAL AND BEAT UP, LIKE, FIVE GUYS. HE PUT JEFF AND PETE IN THE HOSPITAL.
SCROOMPH
WUMPH
CHOMP
MY FOLKS THINK I HAVE CANCER.
OHMYGOSH. WHAT IF I DO? I FEEL LIKE SOME-THING HORRIBLE IS LIVING INSIDE ME.
SCROOMPH
WUMPH
CHOMP
WHAT THE--?
I DON'T CARE HOW MUCH WEIGHT SHE LOST...
I THINK I EVEN FEEL IT MOVE.
...SHE'S STILL A PIG.
SSSLOOP
OH NO. NO, NO, NO. WHERE'S THE DOCTOR?
HSIEN HU's Herbal Remedies
OH GOD, I'M SO HUNGRY.
C-CLOSED?
CHARLIE.
WHY AM I NOT SURPRISED?
CHARLIE, I'M SO SICK.
WE'RE SO SICK.
WH-WHERE IS SHE? WHAT ARE WE GOING TO DO?

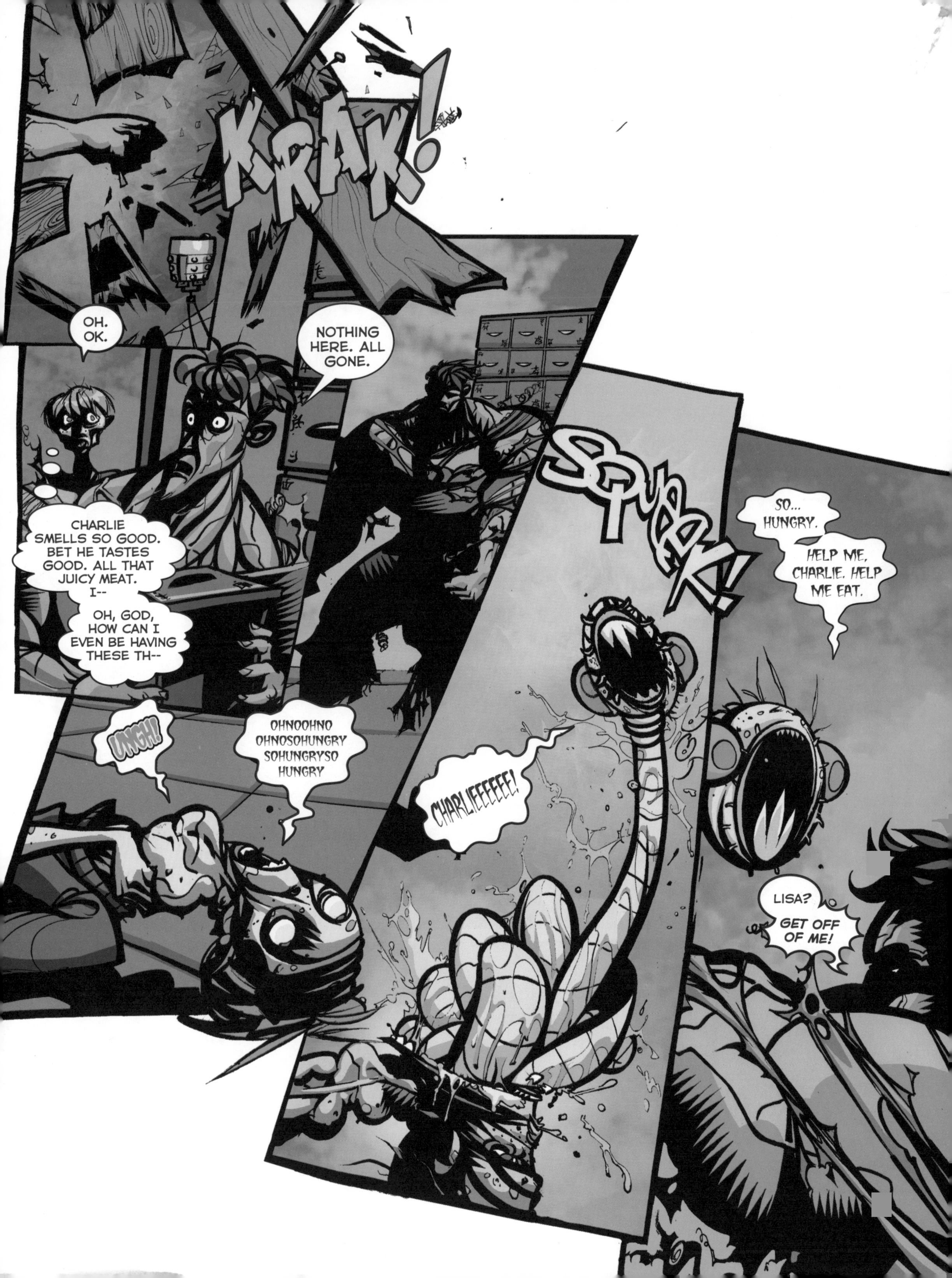
KRAK!
OH. OK.
NOTHING HERE. ALL GONE.
CHARLIE SMELLS SO GOOD. BET HE TASTES GOOD. ALL THAT JUICY MEAT. I--
OH, GOD, HOW CAN I EVEN BE HAVING THESE TH--
UNGH!
OHNOOHNO OHNOSOHUNGRY SOHUNGRYSO HUNGRY
SQUEEK!
CHARLIEEEEEEE!
SO... HUNGRY.
HELP ME, CHARLIE. HELP ME EAT.
LISA? GET OFF OF ME!

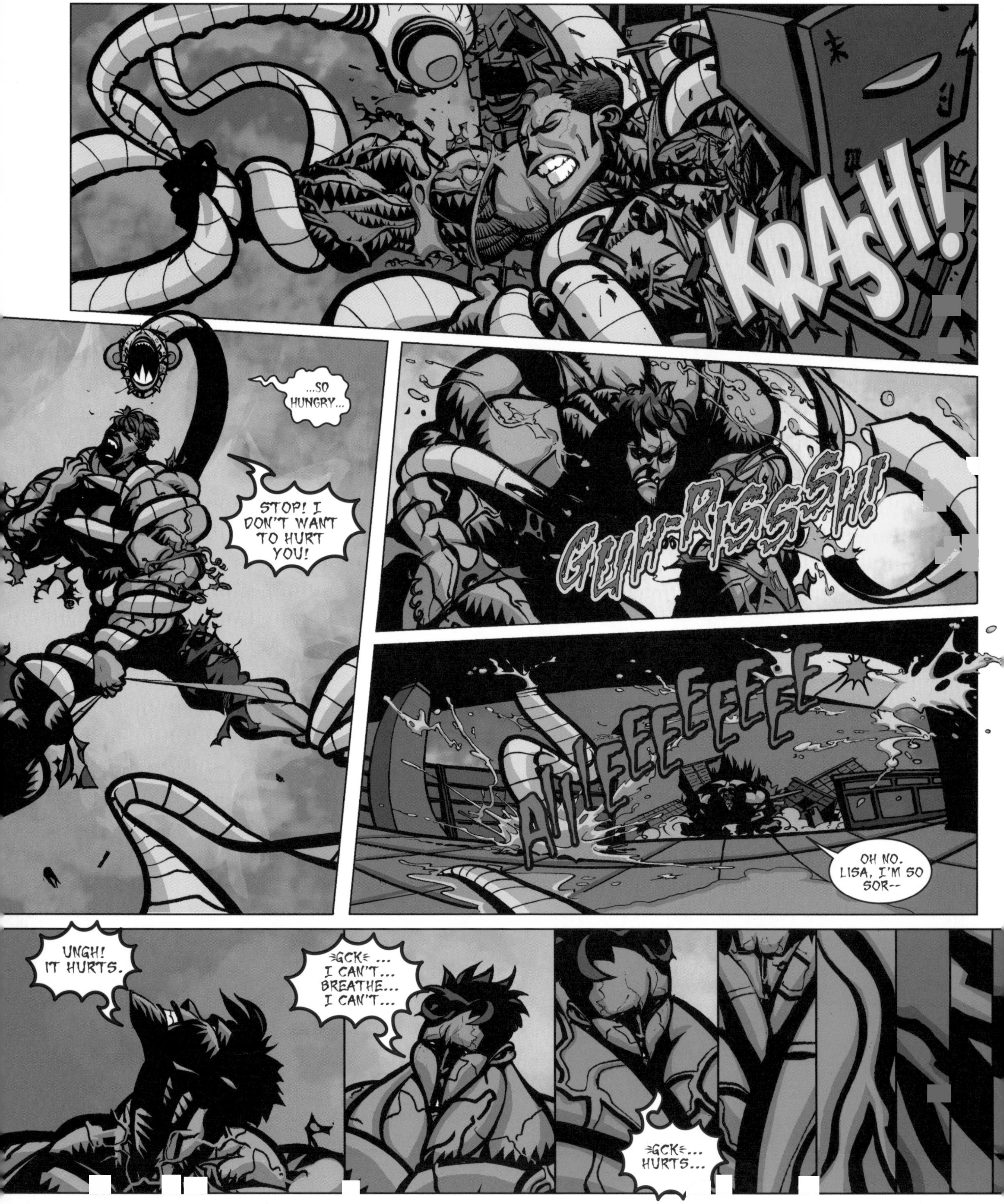
KRASH!
...SO HUNGRY...
STOP! I DON'T WANT TO HURT YOU!
GUH-RISSSH!
AIIEEEEEEEEE
OH NO. LISA, I'M SO SOR--
UNGH! IT HURTS.
GCK ... I CAN'T... BREATHE... I CAN'T...
GCK... HURTS...

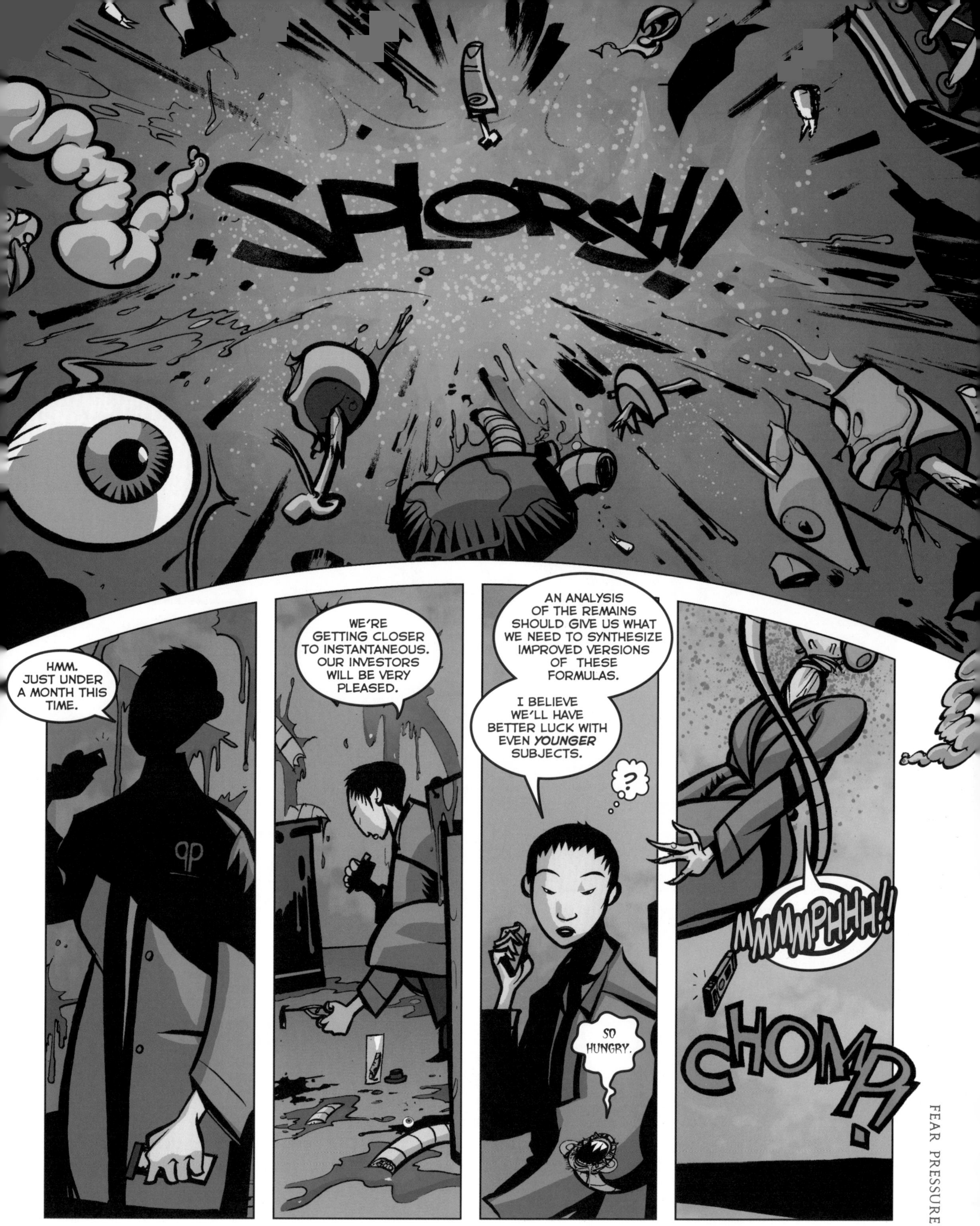
SPLORSH!!
HMM. JUST UNDER A MONTH THIS TIME.
WE'RE GETTING CLOSER TO INSTANTANEOUS. OUR INVESTORS WILL BE VERY PLEASED.
AN ANALYSIS OF THE REMAINS SHOULD GIVE US WHAT WE NEED TO SYNTHESIZE IMPROVED VERSIONS OF THESE FORMULAS.
I BELIEVE WE'LL HAVE BETTER LUCK WITH EVEN *YOUNGER* SUBJECTS.
?
SO HUNGRY.
MMMMPHHH!!
CHOMP!

FEAR PRESSURE

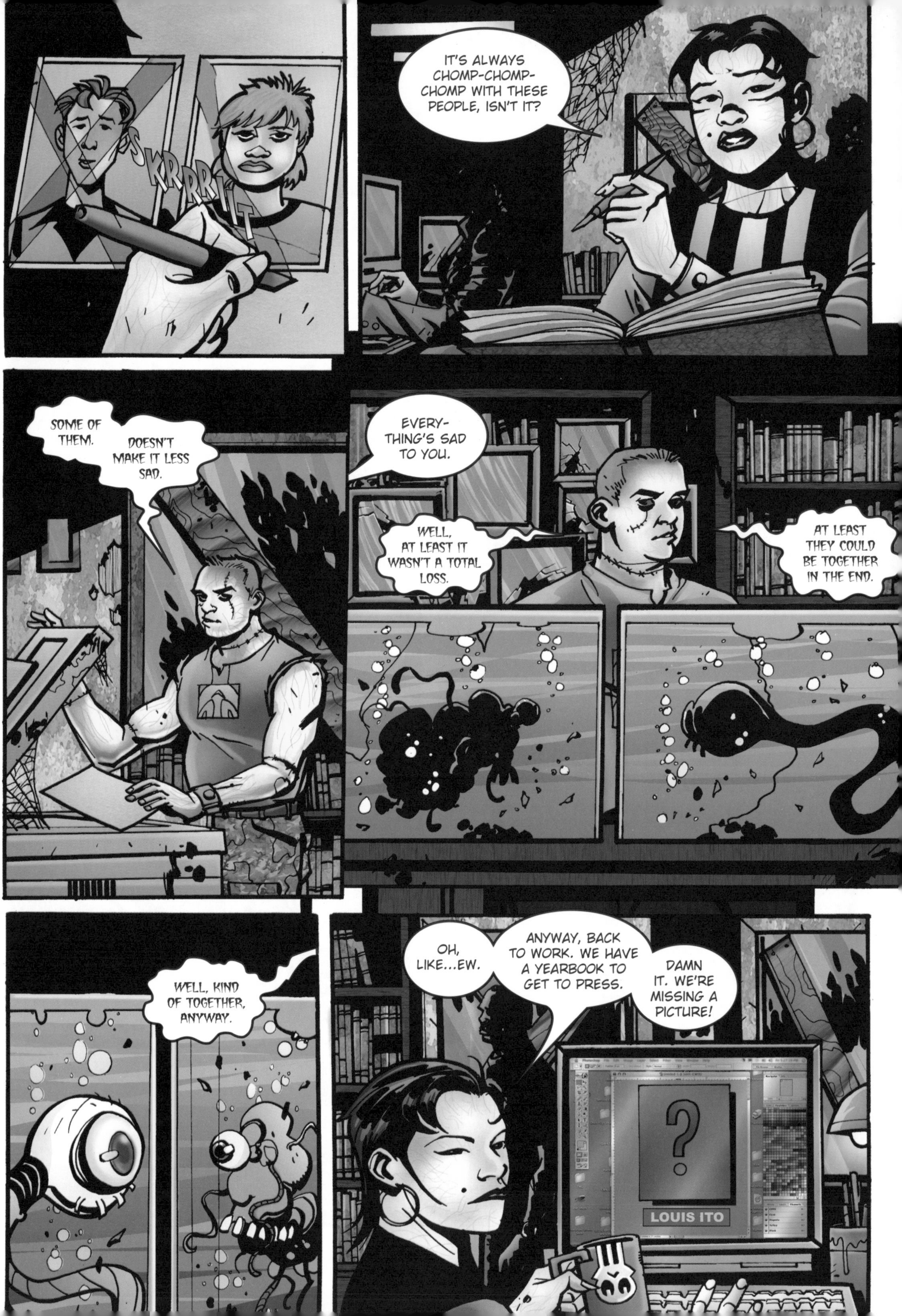
SKRRRIIIT
IT'S ALWAYS CHOMP-CHOMP-CHOMP WITH THESE PEOPLE, ISN'T IT?
SOME OF THEM.
DOESN'T MAKE IT LESS SAD.
EVERY-THING'S SAD TO YOU.
WELL, AT LEAST IT WASN'T A TOTAL LOSS.
AT LEAST THEY COULD BE TOGETHER IN THE END.
WELL, KIND OF TOGETHER, ANYWAY.
OH, LIKE...EW.
ANYWAY, BACK TO WORK. WE HAVE A YEARBOOK TO GET TO PRESS.
DAMN IT. WE'RE MISSING A PICTURE!
LOUIS ITO

What's Got Into Grandma?

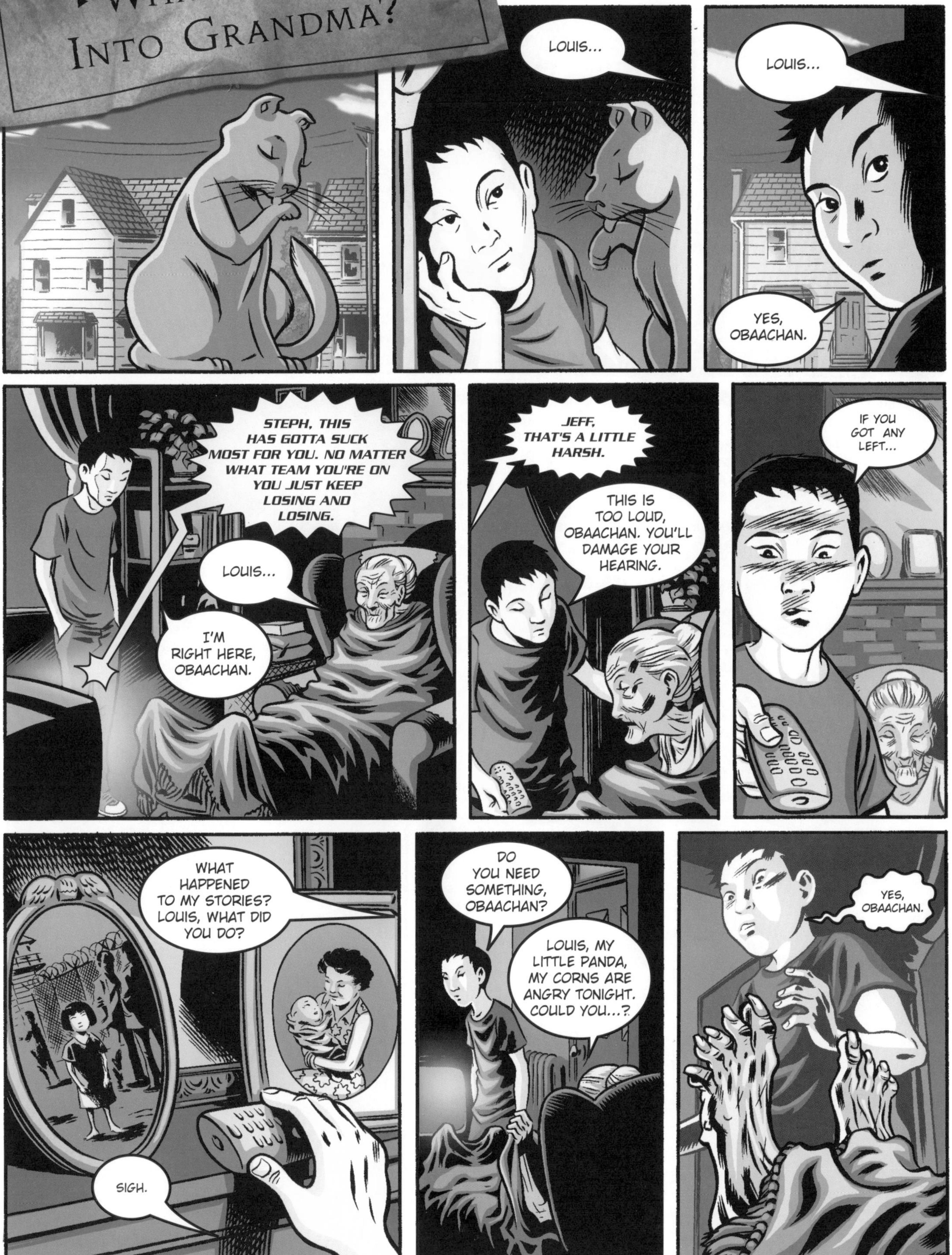
LOUIS...
LOUIS...
YES, OBAACHAN.
STEPH, THIS HAS GOTTA SUCK MOST FOR YOU. NO MATTER WHAT TEAM YOU'RE ON YOU JUST KEEP LOSING AND LOSING.
LOUIS...
I'M RIGHT HERE, OBAACHAN.
JEFF, THAT'S A LITTLE HARSH.
THIS IS TOO LOUD, OBAACHAN. YOU'LL DAMAGE YOUR HEARING.
IF YOU GOT ANY LEFT...
WHAT HAPPENED TO MY STORIES? LOUIS, WHAT DID YOU DO?
SIGH.
DO YOU NEED SOMETHING, OBAACHAN?
LOUIS, MY LITTLE PANDA, MY CORNS ARE ANGRY TONIGHT. COULD YOU...?
YES, OBAACHAN.

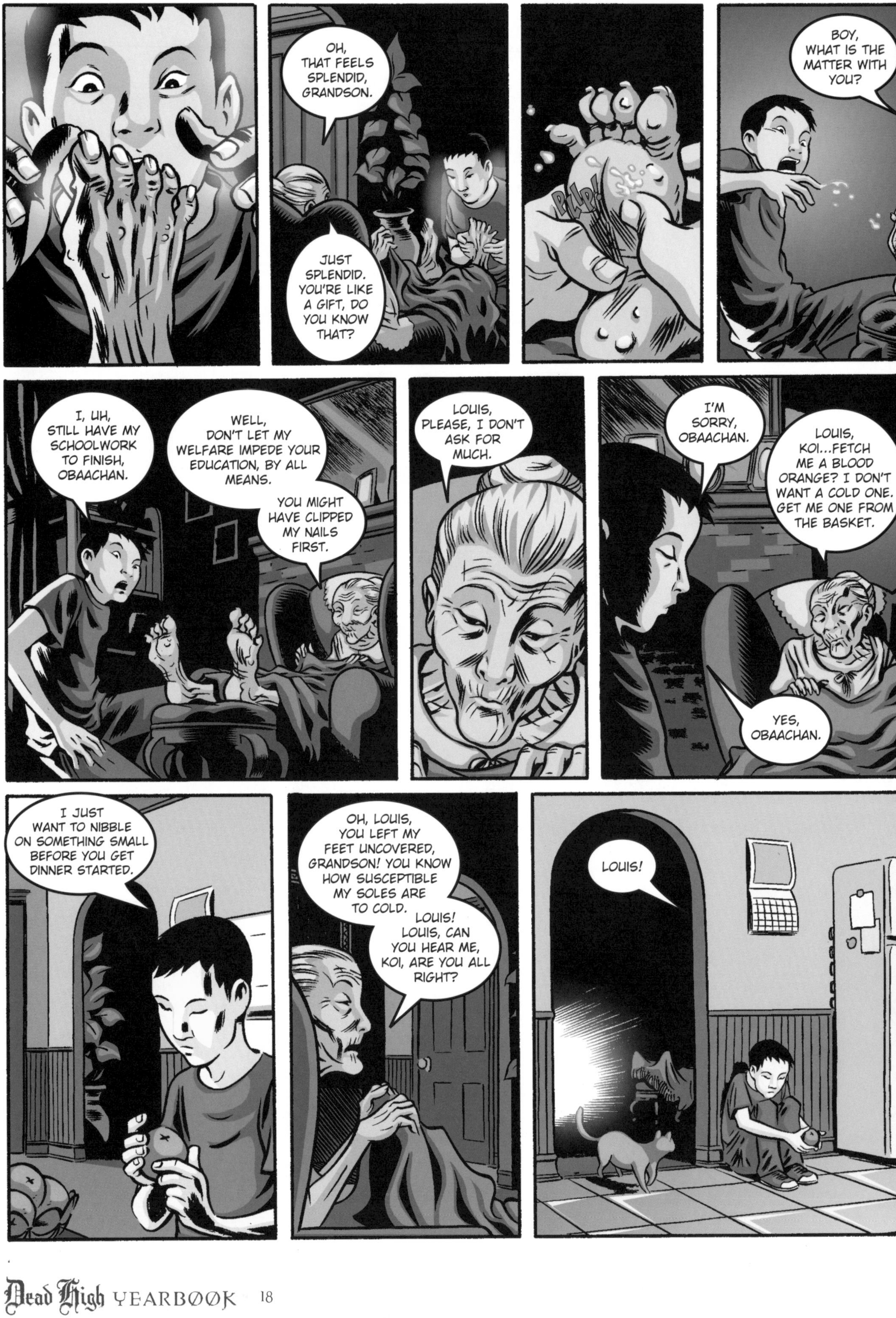
OH, THAT FEELS SPLENDID, GRANDSON.
JUST SPLENDID. YOU'RE LIKE A GIFT, DO YOU KNOW THAT?
PLLP!
BOY, WHAT IS THE MATTER WITH YOU?
I, UH, STILL HAVE MY SCHOOLWORK TO FINISH, OBAACHAN.
WELL, DON'T LET MY WELFARE IMPEDE YOUR EDUCATION, BY ALL MEANS.
YOU MIGHT HAVE CLIPPED MY NAILS FIRST.
LOUIS, PLEASE, I DON'T ASK FOR MUCH.
I'M SORRY, OBAACHAN.
LOUIS, KOI...FETCH ME A BLOOD ORANGE? I DON'T WANT A COLD ONE. GET ME ONE FROM THE BASKET.
YES, OBAACHAN.
I JUST WANT TO NIBBLE ON SOMETHING SMALL BEFORE YOU GET DINNER STARTED.
OH, LOUIS, YOU LEFT MY FEET UNCOVERED, GRANDSON! YOU KNOW HOW SUSCEPTIBLE MY SOLES ARE TO COLD.
LOUIS! LOUIS, CAN YOU HEAR ME, KOI, ARE YOU ALL RIGHT?
LOUIS!

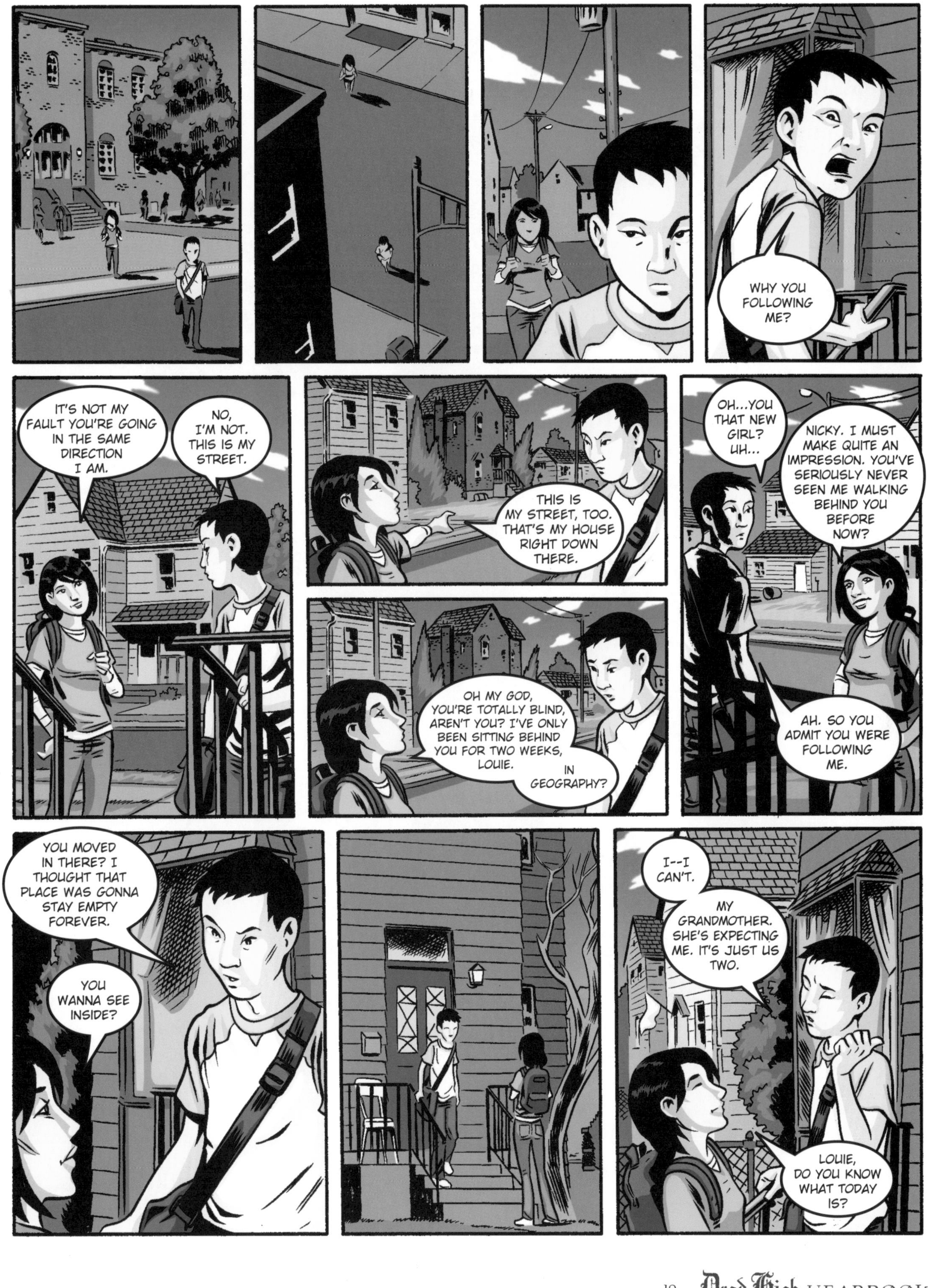
WHY YOU FOLLOWING ME?
IT'S NOT MY FAULT YOU'RE GOING IN THE SAME DIRECTION I AM.
NO, I'M NOT. THIS IS MY STREET.
THIS IS MY STREET, TOO. THAT'S MY HOUSE RIGHT DOWN THERE.
OH MY GOD, YOU'RE TOTALLY BLIND, AREN'T YOU? I'VE ONLY BEEN SITTING BEHIND YOU FOR TWO WEEKS, LOUIE.
IN GEOGRAPHY?
OH...YOU THAT NEW GIRL? UH...
NICKY. I MUST MAKE QUITE AN IMPRESSION. YOU'VE SERIOUSLY NEVER SEEN ME WALKING BEHIND YOU BEFORE NOW?
AH. SO YOU ADMIT YOU WERE FOLLOWING ME.
YOU MOVED IN THERE? I THOUGHT THAT PLACE WAS GONNA STAY EMPTY FOREVER.
YOU WANNA SEE INSIDE?
I--I CAN'T.
MY GRANDMOTHER. SHE'S EXPECTING ME. IT'S JUST US TWO.
LOUIE, DO YOU KNOW WHAT TODAY IS?

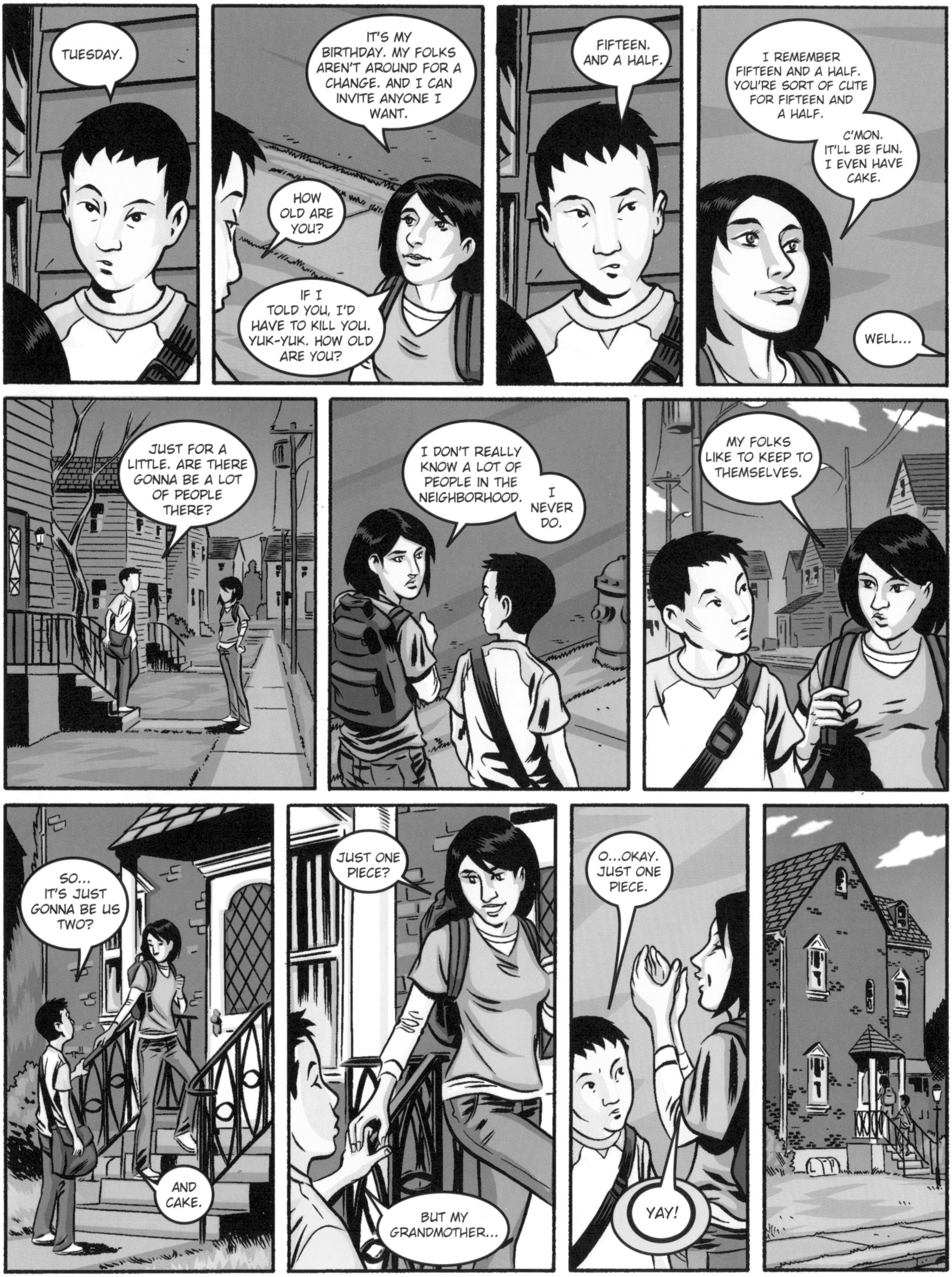
TUESDAY.
IT'S MY BIRTHDAY. MY FOLKS AREN'T AROUND FOR A CHANGE. AND I CAN INVITE ANYONE I WANT.
HOW OLD ARE YOU?
IF I TOLD YOU, I'D HAVE TO KILL YOU. YUK-YUK. HOW OLD ARE YOU?
FIFTEEN. AND A HALF.
I REMEMBER FIFTEEN AND A HALF. YOU'RE SORT OF CUTE FOR FIFTEEN AND A HALF.
C'MON. IT'LL BE FUN. I EVEN HAVE CAKE.
WELL...
JUST FOR A LITTLE. ARE THERE GONNA BE A LOT OF PEOPLE THERE?
I DON'T REALLY KNOW A LOT OF PEOPLE IN THE NEIGHBORHOOD.
I NEVER DO.
MY FOLKS LIKE TO KEEP TO THEMSELVES.
SO... IT'S JUST GONNA BE US TWO?
AND CAKE.
JUST ONE PIECE?
BUT MY GRANDMOTHER...
O...OKAY. JUST ONE PIECE.
YAY!

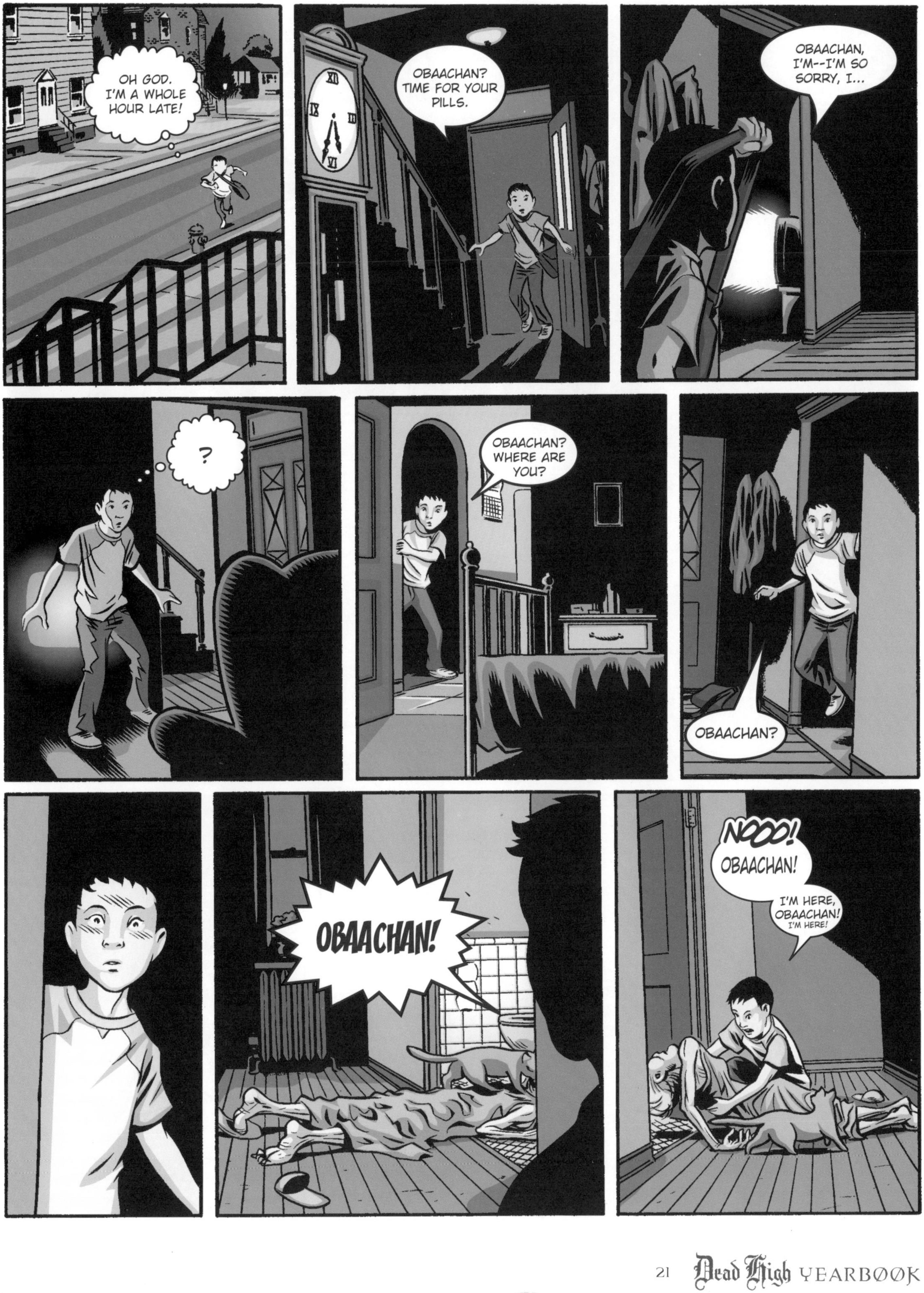
OH GOD. I'M A WHOLE HOUR LATE!
OBAACHAN? TIME FOR YOUR PILLS.
OBAACHAN, I'M--I'M SO SORRY, I...
?
OBAACHAN? WHERE ARE YOU?
OBAACHAN?
OBAACHAN!
NOOO! OBAACHAN!
I'M HERE, OBAACHAN! I'M HERE!

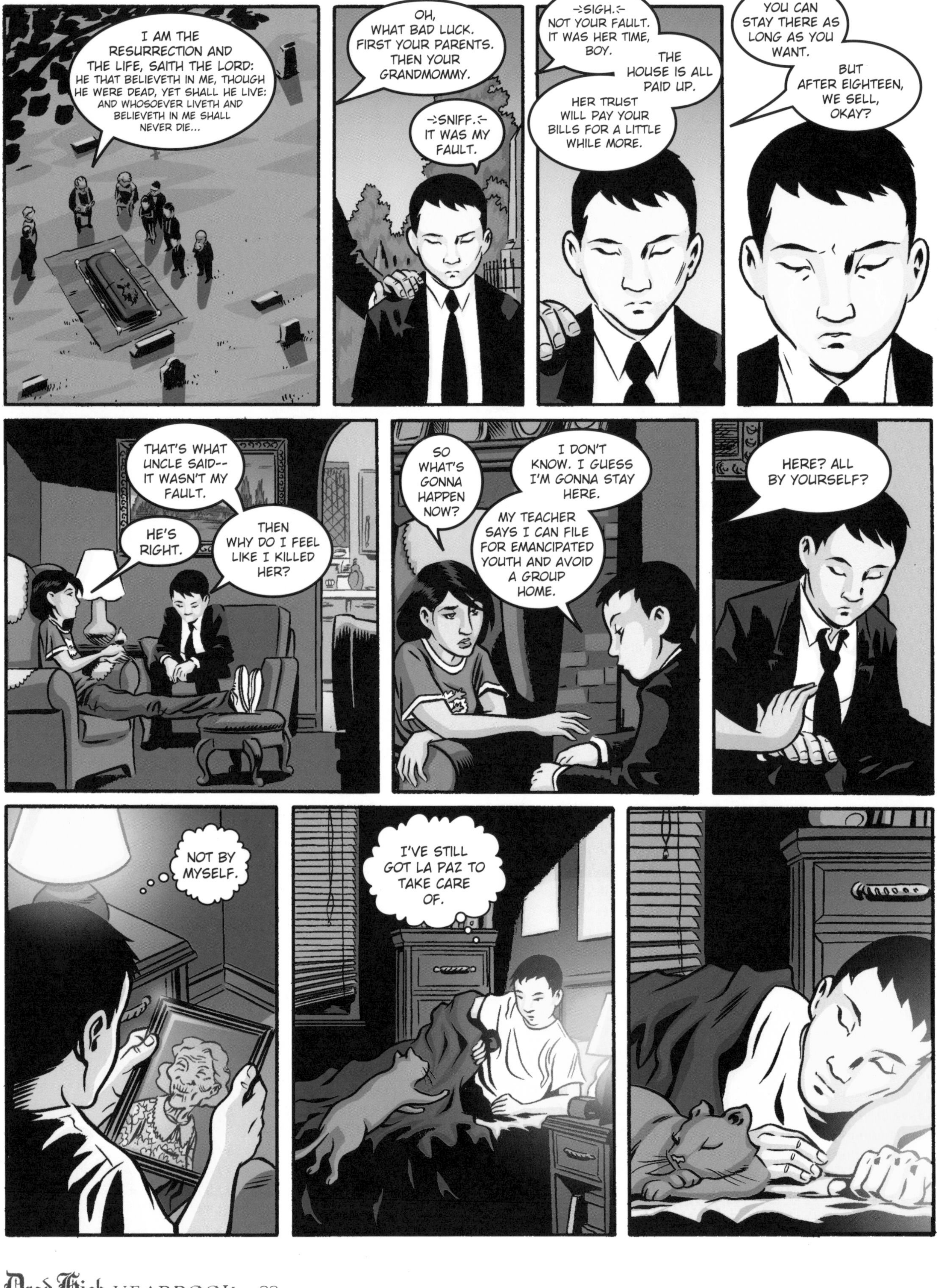
I AM THE RESURRECTION AND THE LIFE, SAITH THE LORD: HE THAT BELIEVETH IN ME, THOUGH HE WERE DEAD, YET SHALL HE LIVE: AND WHOSOEVER LIVETH AND BELIEVETH IN ME SHALL NEVER DIE...
OH, WHAT BAD LUCK. FIRST YOUR PARENTS. THEN YOUR GRANDMOMMY.
SNIFF. IT WAS MY FAULT.
SIGH. NOT YOUR FAULT. IT WAS HER TIME, BOY.
THE HOUSE IS ALL PAID UP.
HER TRUST WILL PAY YOUR BILLS FOR A LITTLE WHILE MORE.
YOU CAN STAY THERE AS LONG AS YOU WANT.
BUT AFTER EIGHTEEN, WE SELL, OKAY?
THAT'S WHAT UNCLE SAID-- IT WASN'T MY FAULT.
HE'S RIGHT.
THEN WHY DO I FEEL LIKE I KILLED HER?
SO WHAT'S GONNA HAPPEN NOW?
I DON'T KNOW. I GUESS I'M GONNA STAY HERE.
MY TEACHER SAYS I CAN FILE FOR EMANCIPATED YOUTH AND AVOID A GROUP HOME.
HERE? ALL BY YOURSELF?
NOT BY MYSELF.
I'VE STILL GOT LA PAZ TO TAKE CARE OF.

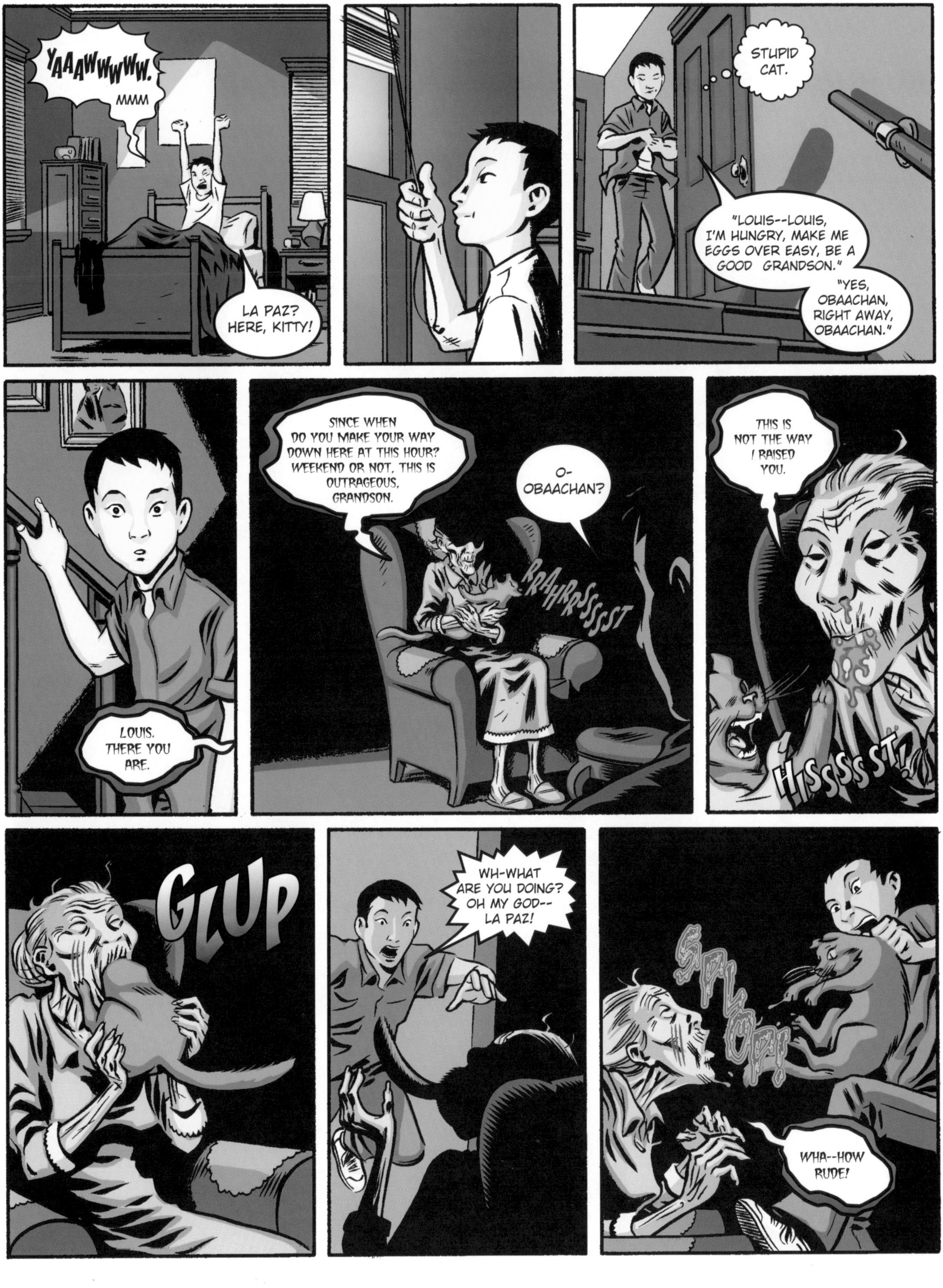
YAAAWWWWW.
MMM
LA PAZ? HERE, KITTY!
STUPID CAT.
"LOUIS--LOUIS, I'M HUNGRY, MAKE ME EGGS OVER EASY, BE A GOOD GRANDSON."
"YES, OBAACHAN, RIGHT AWAY, OBAACHAN."
LOUIS. THERE YOU ARE.
SINCE WHEN DO YOU MAKE YOUR WAY DOWN HERE AT THIS HOUR? WEEKEND OR NOT, THIS IS OUTRAGEOUS, GRANDSON.
O- OBAACHAN?
RRAHRRSSSSST
THIS IS NOT THE WAY I RAISED YOU.
HISSSSST!
GLUP
WH-WHAT ARE YOU DOING? OH MY GOD-- LA PAZ!
WHA--HOW RUDE!

WHAT'S GOT INTO GRANDMA?

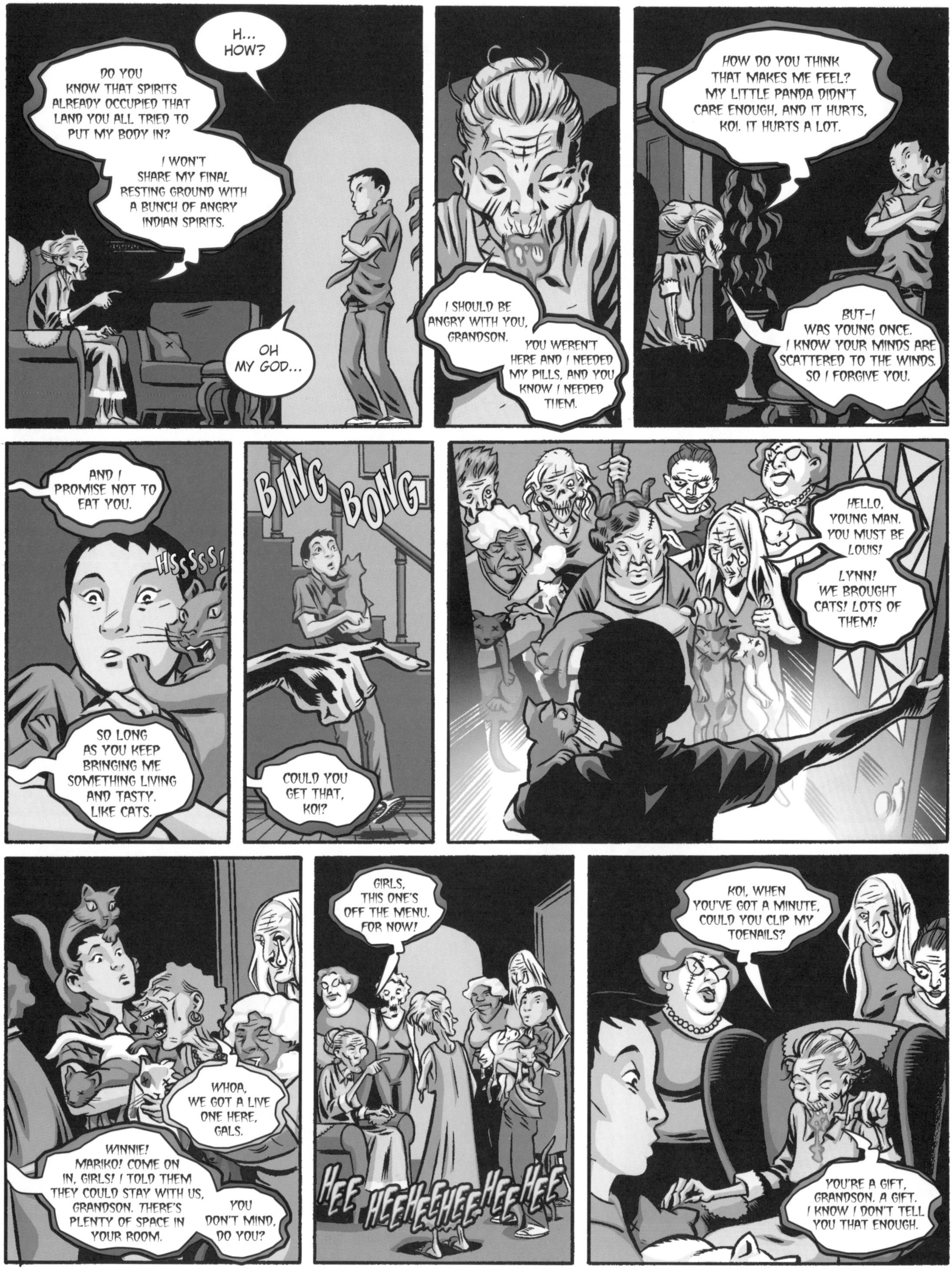
DO YOU KNOW THAT SPIRITS ALREADY OCCUPIED THAT LAND YOU ALL TRIED TO PUT MY BODY IN?
H... HOW?
I WON'T SHARE MY FINAL RESTING GROUND WITH A BUNCH OF ANGRY INDIAN SPIRITS.
OH MY GOD...
I SHOULD BE ANGRY WITH YOU, GRANDSON.
YOU WEREN'T HERE AND I NEEDED MY PILLS, AND YOU KNOW I NEEDED THEM.
HOW DO YOU THINK THAT MAKES ME FEEL? MY LITTLE PANDA DIDN'T CARE ENOUGH, AND IT HURTS, KOI. IT HURTS A LOT.
BUT--I WAS YOUNG ONCE. I KNOW YOUR MINDS ARE SCATTERED TO THE WINDS. SO I FORGIVE YOU.
AND I PROMISE NOT TO EAT YOU.
HSSSSS!
SO LONG AS YOU KEEP BRINGING ME SOMETHING LIVING AND TASTY. LIKE CATS.
BING BONG
COULD YOU GET THAT, KOI?
HELLO, YOUNG MAN. YOU MUST BE LOUIS!
LYNN! WE BROUGHT CATS! LOTS OF THEM!
WHOA, WE GOT A LIVE ONE HERE, GALS.
WINNIE! MARIKO! COME ON IN, GIRLS! I TOLD THEM THEY COULD STAY WITH US, GRANDSON. THERE'S PLENTY OF SPACE IN YOUR ROOM.
YOU DON'T MIND, DO YOU?
GIRLS, THIS ONE'S OFF THE MENU. FOR NOW!
HEE HEEHEEHEEHEE HEE HEE
KOI, WHEN YOU'VE GOT A MINUTE, COULD YOU CLIP MY TOENAILS?
YOU'RE A GIFT, GRANDSON. A GIFT. I KNOW I DON'T TELL YOU THAT ENOUGH.

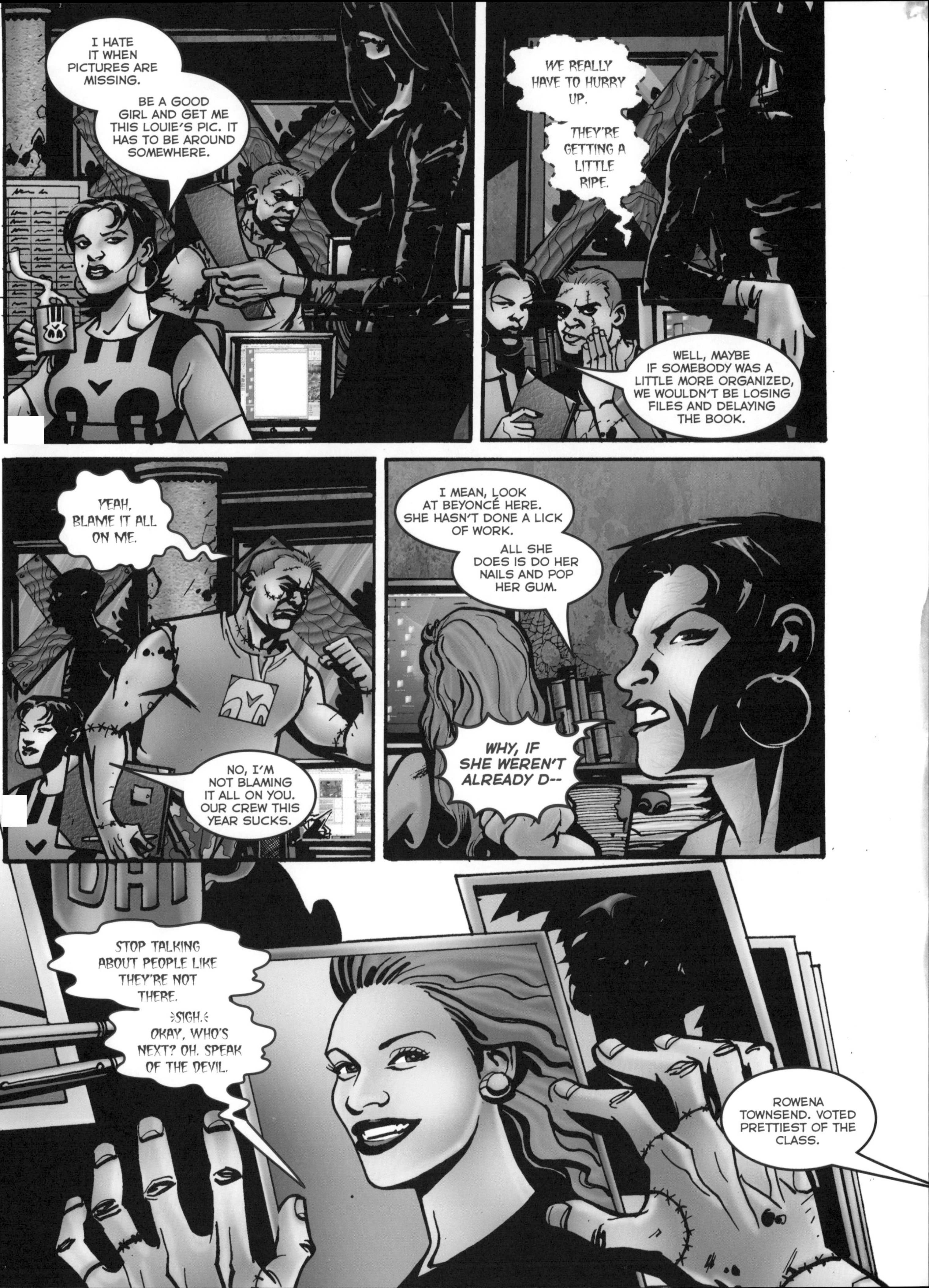
I HATE IT WHEN PICTURES ARE MISSING.
BE A GOOD GIRL AND GET ME THIS LOUIE'S PIC. IT HAS TO BE AROUND SOMEWHERE.
WE REALLY HAVE TO HURRY UP.
THEY'RE GETTING A LITTLE RIPE.
WELL, MAYBE IF SOMEBODY WAS A LITTLE MORE ORGANIZED, WE WOULDN'T BE LOSING FILES AND DELAYING THE BOOK.
YEAH, BLAME IT ALL ON ME.
NO, I'M NOT BLAMING IT ALL ON YOU. OUR CREW THIS YEAR SUCKS.
I MEAN, LOOK AT BEYONCÉ HERE. SHE HASN'T DONE A LICK OF WORK.
ALL SHE DOES IS DO HER NAILS AND POP HER GUM.
WHY, IF SHE WEREN'T ALREADY D--
STOP TALKING ABOUT PEOPLE LIKE THEY'RE NOT THERE.
SIGH.
OKAY, WHO'S NEXT? OH. SPEAK OF THE DEVIL.
ROWENA TOWNSEND. VOTED PRETTIEST OF THE CLASS.

Devil Dog of the Damned

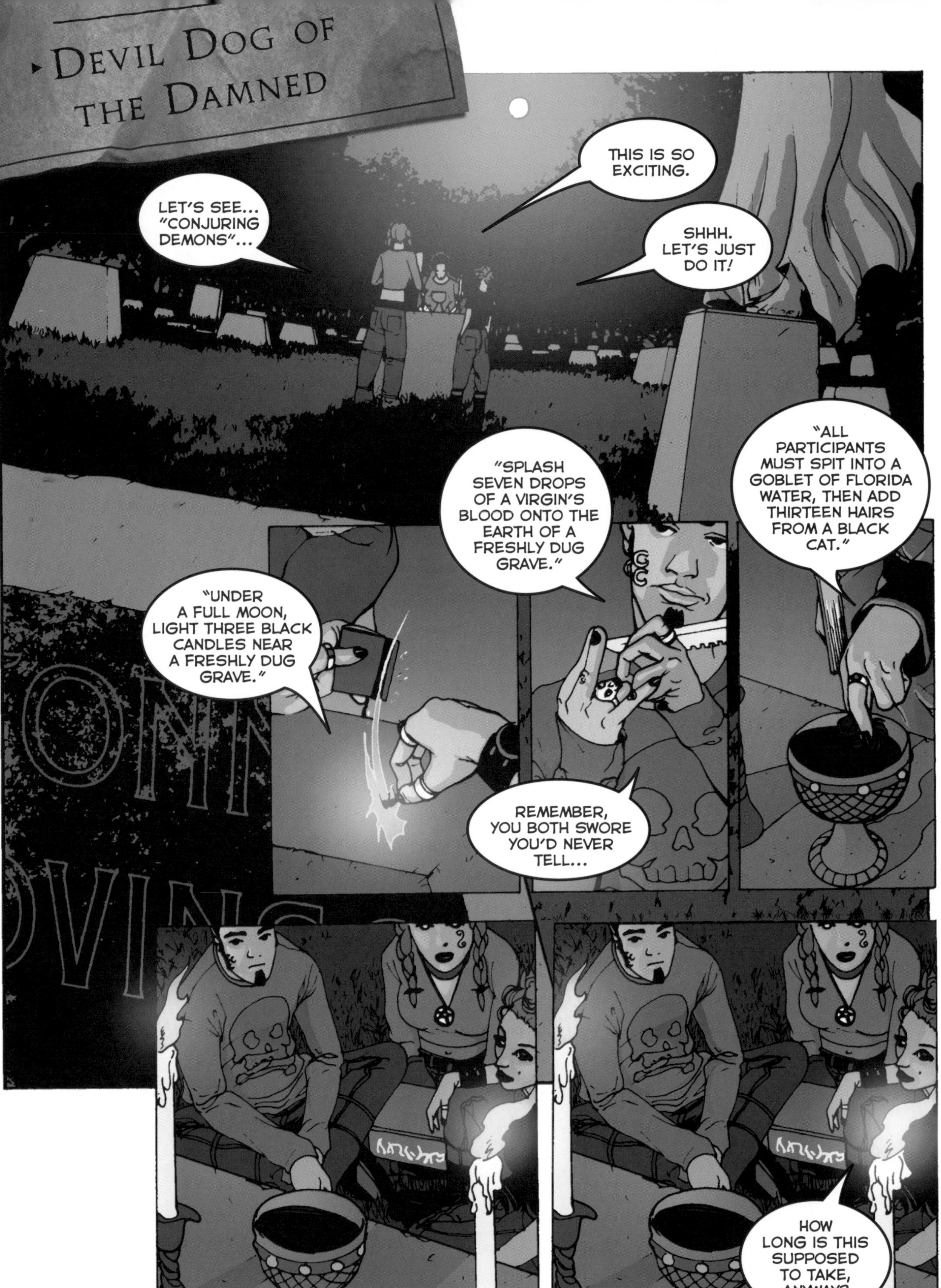

LET'S SEE... "CONJURING DEMONS"...
THIS IS SO EXCITING.
SHHH. LET'S JUST DO IT!
"UNDER A FULL MOON, LIGHT THREE BLACK CANDLES NEAR A FRESHLY DUG GRAVE."
"SPLASH SEVEN DROPS OF A VIRGIN'S BLOOD ONTO THE EARTH OF A FRESHLY DUG GRAVE."
"ALL PARTICIPANTS MUST SPIT INTO A GOBLET OF FLORIDA WATER, THEN ADD THIRTEEN HAIRS FROM A BLACK CAT."
REMEMBER, YOU BOTH SWORE YOU'D NEVER TELL...
HOW LONG IS THIS SUPPOSED TO TAKE, ANYWAY?

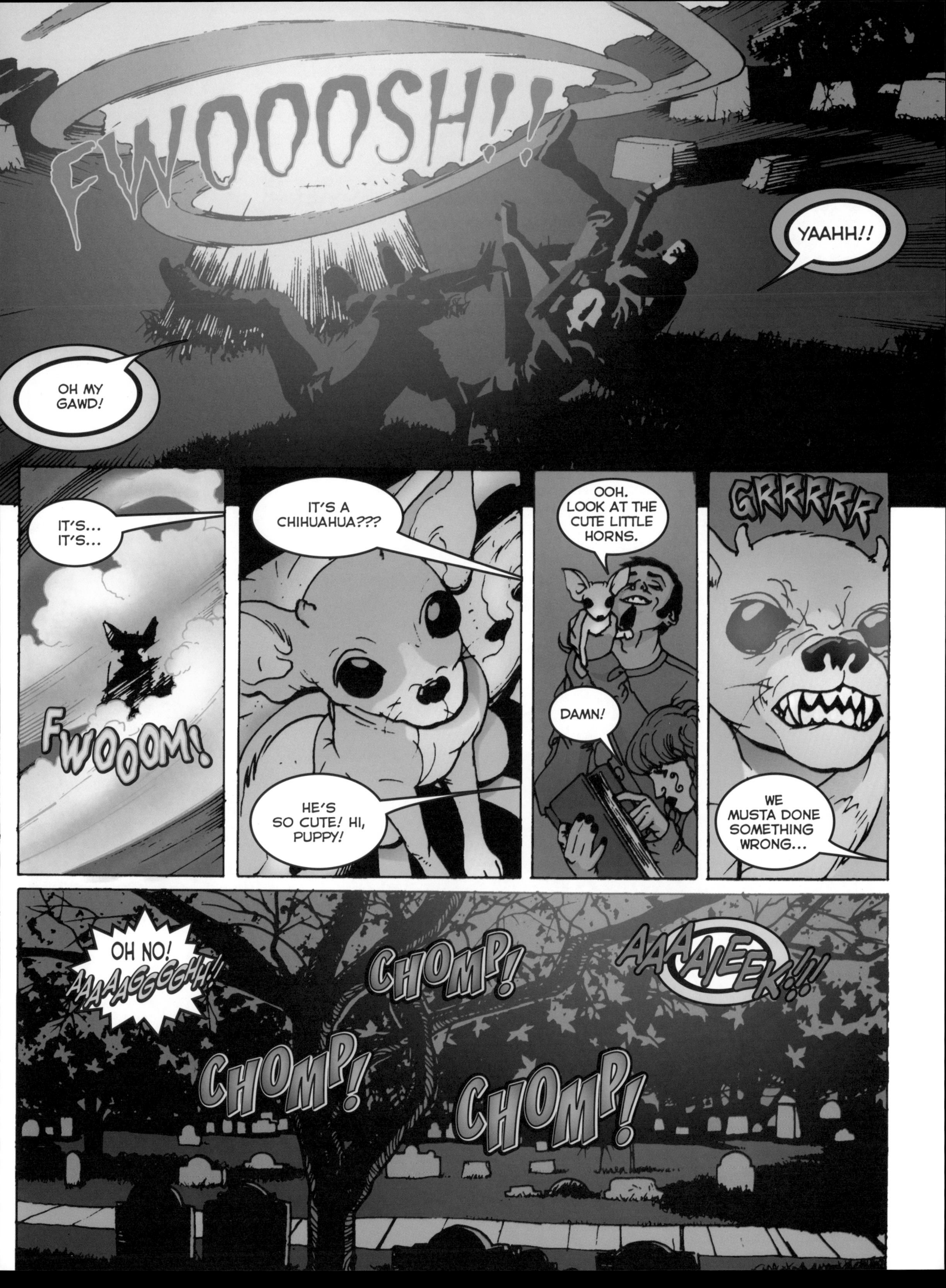
FWOOOSH!!
YAAHH!!
OH MY GAWD!
IT'S... IT'S...
FWOOOM!
IT'S A CHIHUAHUA???
HE'S SO CUTE! HI, PUPPY!
OOH. LOOK AT THE CUTE LITTLE HORNS.
DAMN!
GRRRRR
WE MUSTA DONE SOMETHING WRONG...
OH NO! AAAAAGGGGHH!!
CHOMP!
AAAAIEEEK!!!
CHOMP!
CHOMP!

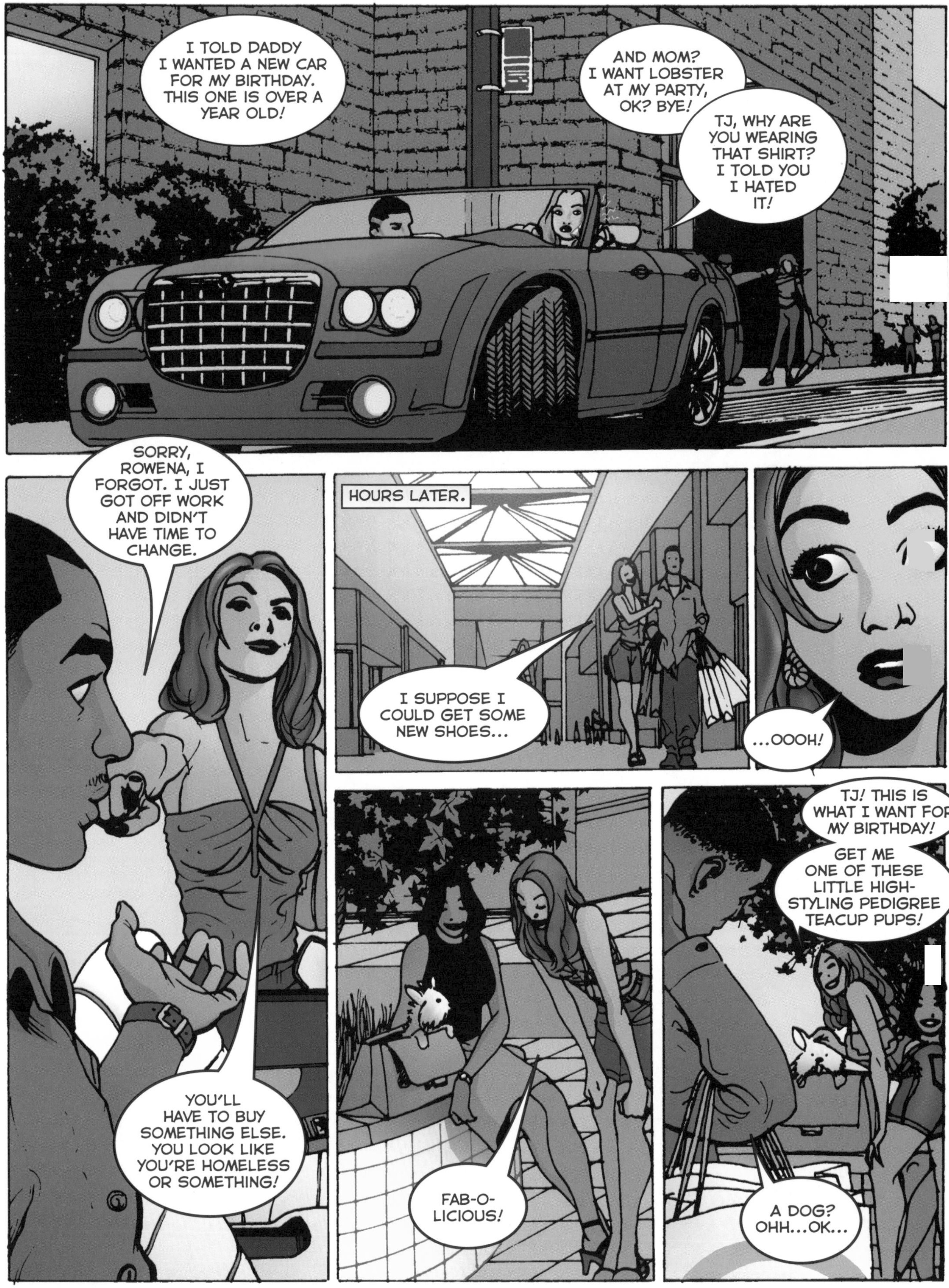

I TOLD DADDY I WANTED A NEW CAR FOR MY BIRTHDAY. THIS ONE IS OVER A YEAR OLD!
AND MOM? I WANT LOBSTER AT MY PARTY, OK? BYE!
TJ, WHY ARE YOU WEARING THAT SHIRT? I TOLD YOU I HATED IT!
SORRY, ROWENA, I FORGOT. I JUST GOT OFF WORK AND DIDN'T HAVE TIME TO CHANGE.
YOU'LL HAVE TO BUY SOMETHING ELSE. YOU LOOK LIKE YOU'RE HOMELESS OR SOMETHING!
HOURS LATER.
I SUPPOSE I COULD GET SOME NEW SHOES...
...OOOH!
FAB-O-LICIOUS!
TJ! THIS IS WHAT I WANT FOR MY BIRTHDAY!
GET ME ONE OF THESE LITTLE HIGH-STYLING PEDIGREE TEACUP PUPS!
A DOG? OHH...OK...

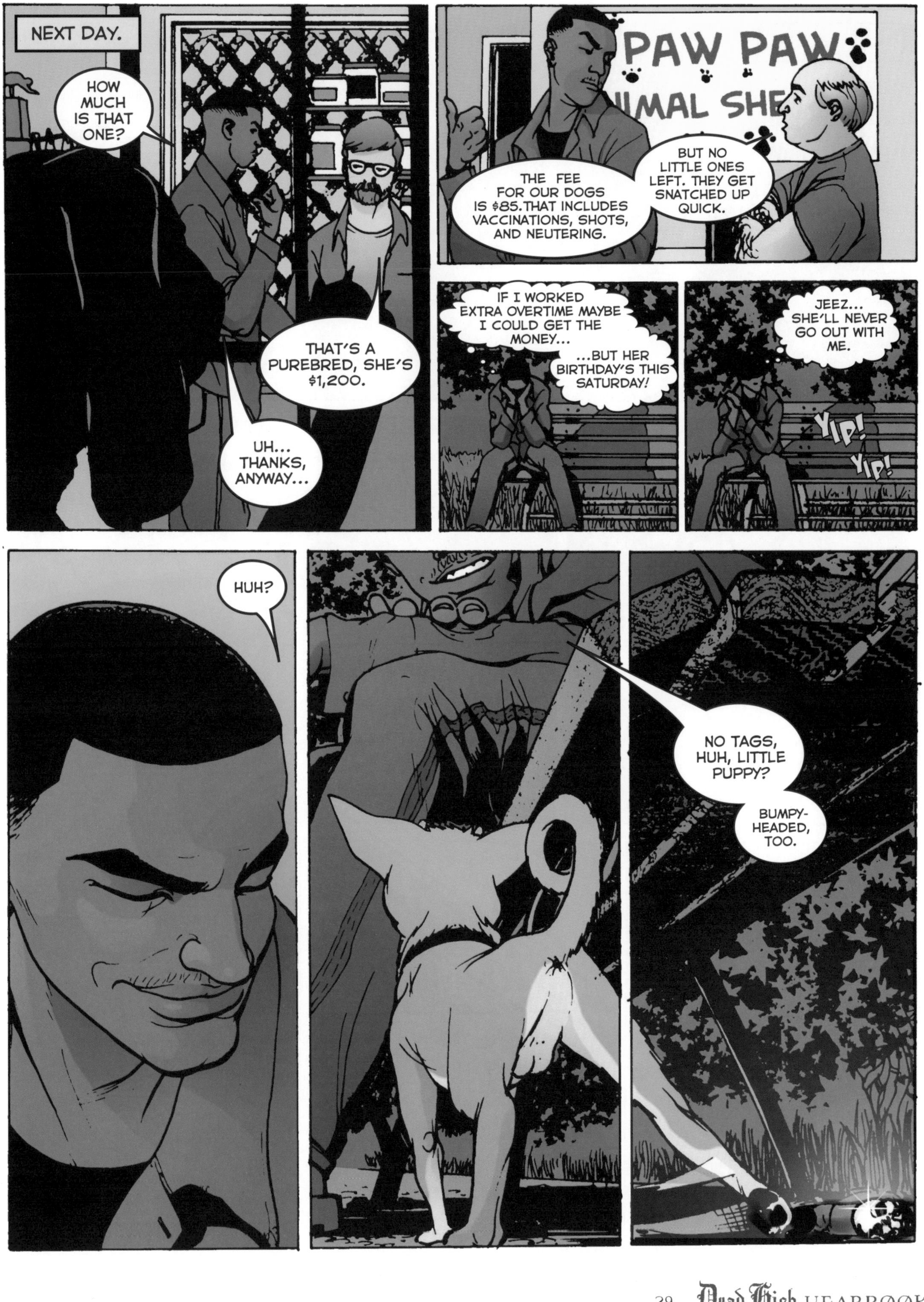
NEXT DAY.
HOW MUCH IS THAT ONE?
THAT'S A PUREBRED, SHE'S $1,200.
UH... THANKS, ANYWAY...
PAW PAW
IMAL SHE
THE FEE FOR OUR DOGS IS $85. THAT INCLUDES VACCINATIONS, SHOTS, AND NEUTERING.
BUT NO LITTLE ONES LEFT. THEY GET SNATCHED UP QUICK.
IF I WORKED EXTRA OVERTIME MAYBE I COULD GET THE MONEY...
...BUT HER BIRTHDAY'S THIS SATURDAY!
JEEZ... SHE'LL NEVER GO OUT WITH ME.
YIP!
YIP!
HUH?
NO TAGS, HUH, LITTLE PUPPY?
BUMPY-HEADED, TOO.

DEVIL DOG OF THE DAMNED

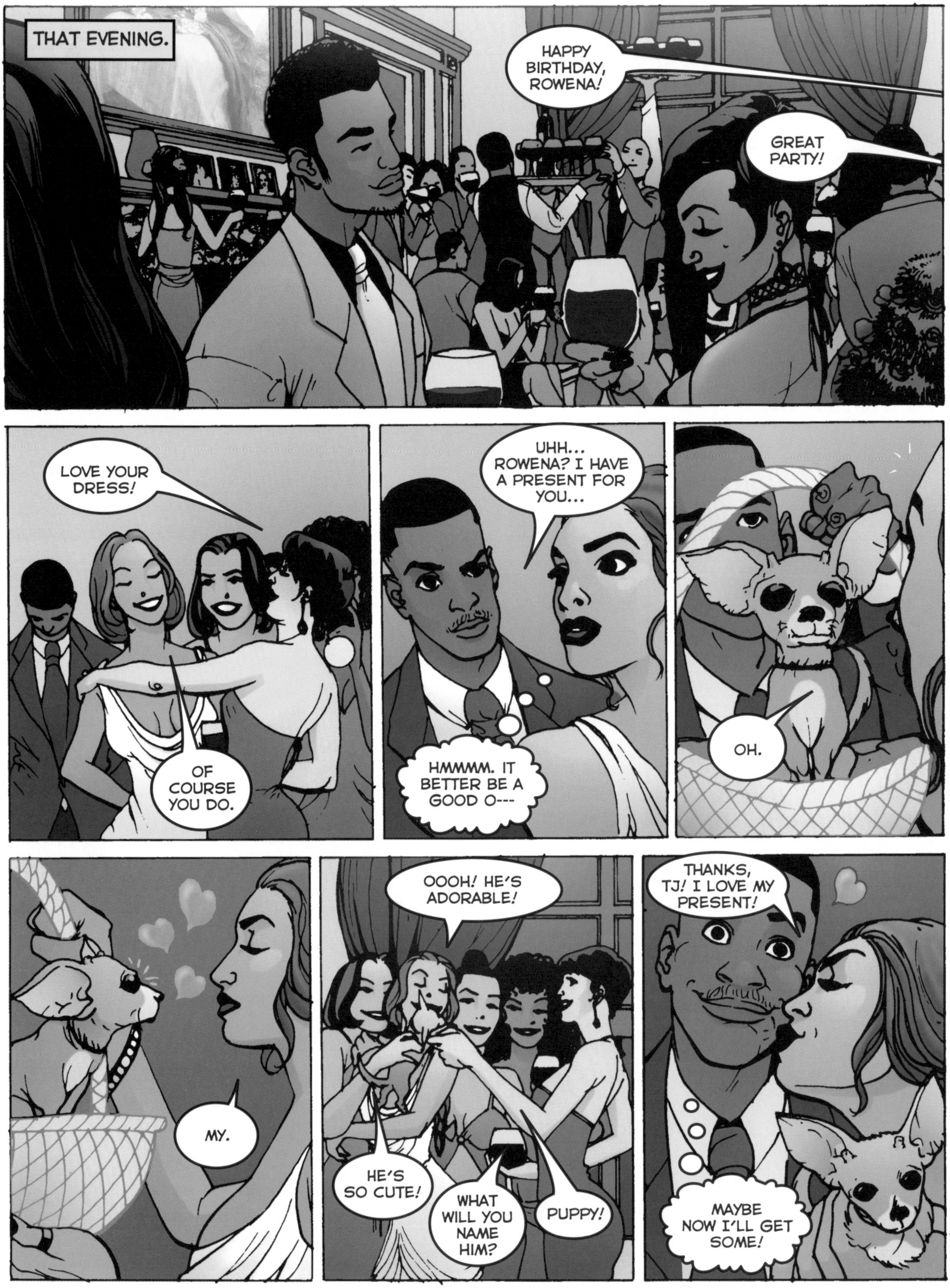

THAT EVENING.
HAPPY BIRTHDAY, ROWENA!
GREAT PARTY!
LOVE YOUR DRESS!
OF COURSE YOU DO.
UHH... ROWENA? I HAVE A PRESENT FOR YOU...
HMMMM. IT BETTER BE A GOOD O---
OH.
MY.
OOOH! HE'S ADORABLE!
HE'S SO CUTE!
WHAT WILL YOU NAME HIM?
PUPPY!
THANKS, TJ! I LOVE MY PRESENT!
MAYBE NOW I'LL GET SOME!

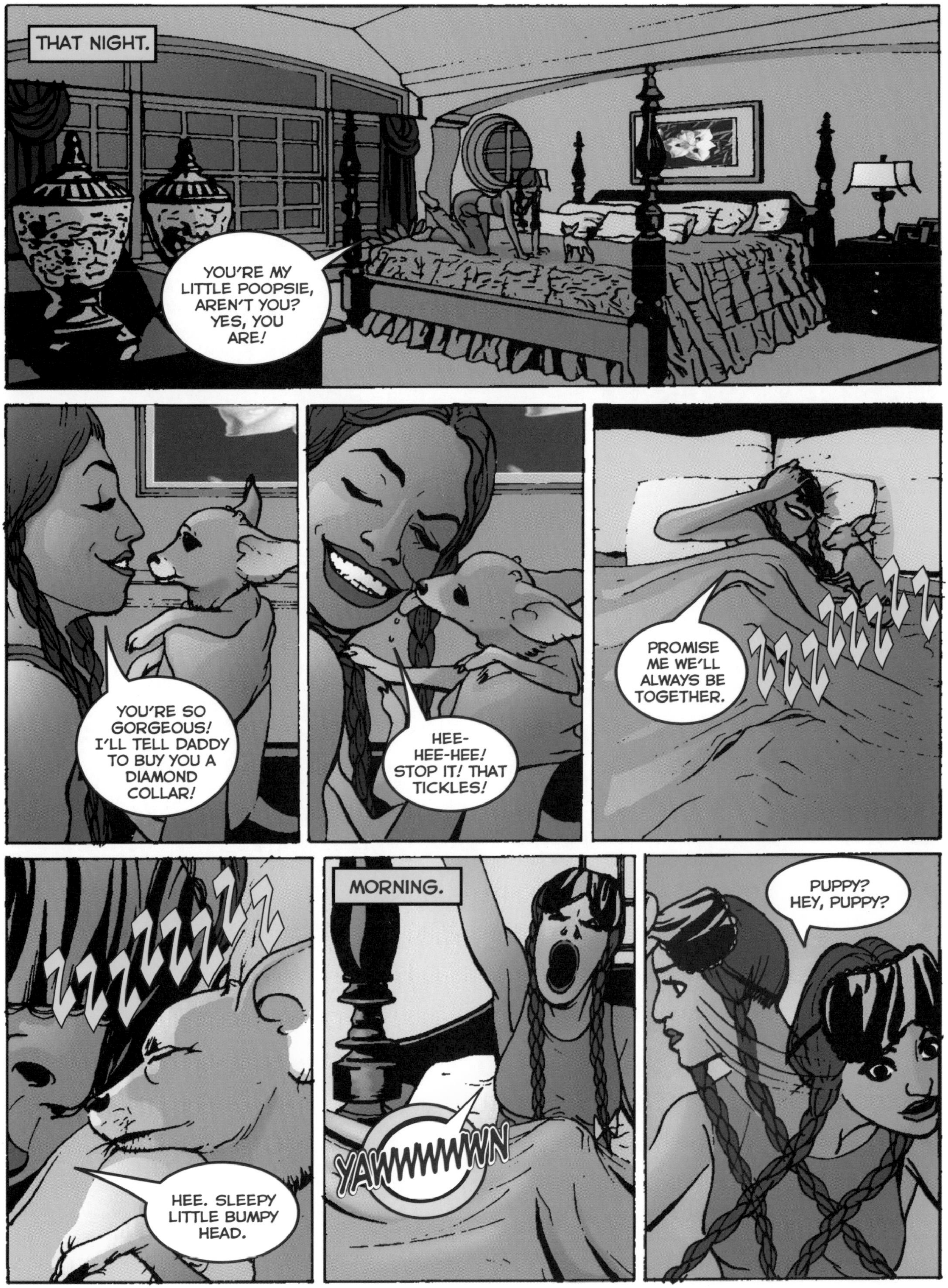
THAT NIGHT.
YOU'RE MY LITTLE POOPSIE, AREN'T YOU? YES, YOU ARE!
YOU'RE SO GORGEOUS! I'LL TELL DADDY TO BUY YOU A DIAMOND COLLAR!
HEE-HEE-HEE! STOP IT! THAT TICKLES!
PROMISE ME WE'LL ALWAYS BE TOGETHER.
ZZZZZZZZZZ
ZZZZZZZZZZ
HEE. SLEEPY LITTLE BUMPY HEAD.
MORNING.
YAWWWWWN
PUPPY? HEY, PUPPY?

DEVIL DOG OF THE DAMNED

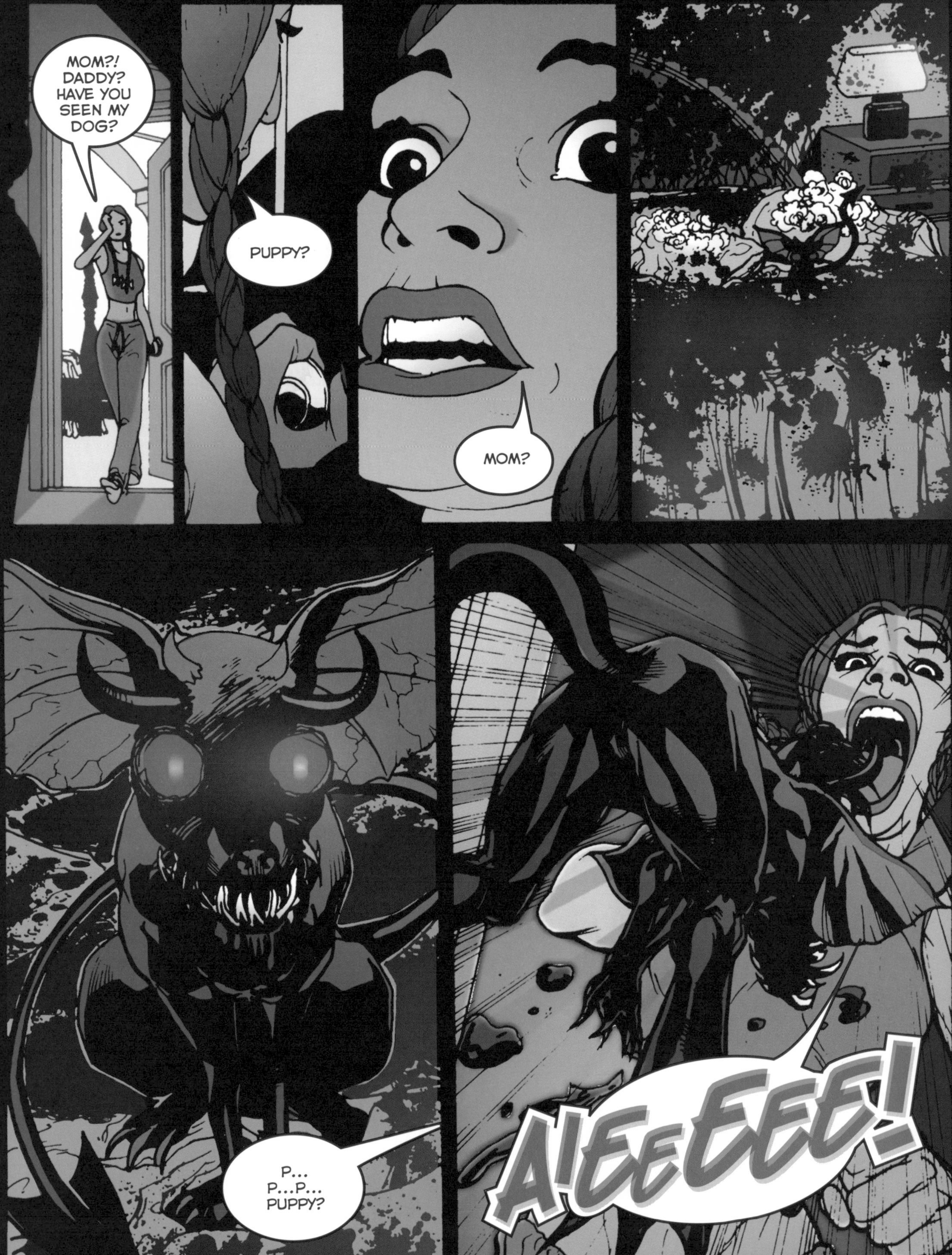
MOM?! DADDY? HAVE YOU SEEN MY DOG?
PUPPY?
MOM?
P... P...P... PUPPY?
AIEEEEE!

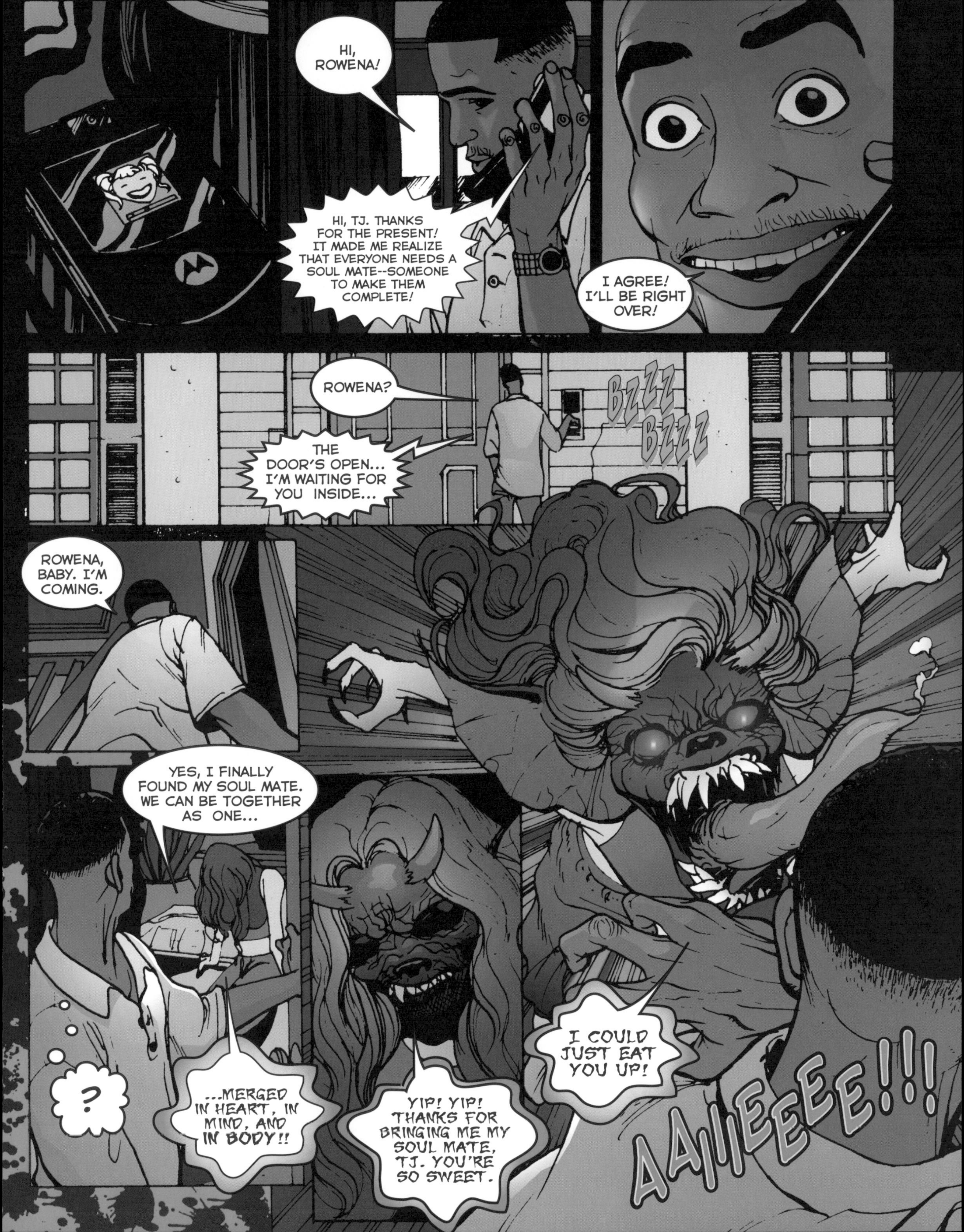
HI, ROWENA!
HI, TJ. THANKS FOR THE PRESENT! IT MADE ME REALIZE THAT EVERYONE NEEDS A SOUL MATE--SOMEONE TO MAKE THEM COMPLETE!
I AGREE! I'LL BE RIGHT OVER!
ROWENA?
THE DOOR'S OPEN... I'M WAITING FOR YOU INSIDE...
BZZZ BZZZ
ROWENA, BABY. I'M COMING.
YES, I FINALLY FOUND MY SOUL MATE. WE CAN BE TOGETHER AS ONE...
?
...MERGED IN HEART, IN MIND, AND IN BODY!!
YIP! YIP! THANKS FOR BRINGING ME MY SOUL MATE, TJ. YOU'RE SO SWEET.
I COULD JUST EAT YOU UP!
AAIIEEEE!!!

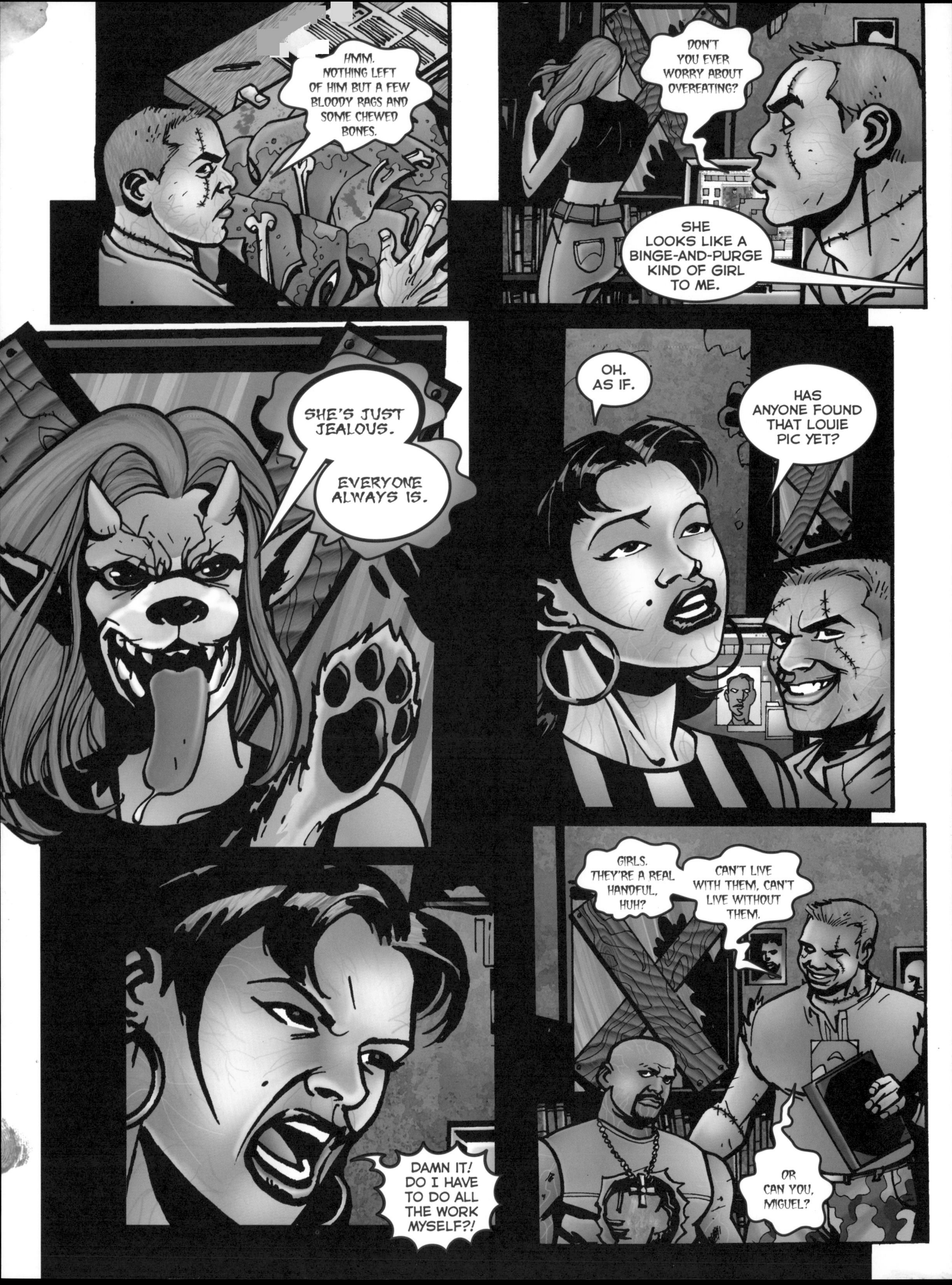
HMM. NOTHING LEFT OF HIM BUT A FEW BLOODY RAGS AND SOME CHEWED BONES.
DON'T YOU EVER WORRY ABOUT OVEREATING?
SHE LOOKS LIKE A BINGE-AND-PURGE KIND OF GIRL TO ME.
SHE'S JUST JEALOUS.
EVERYONE ALWAYS IS.
OH. AS IF.
HAS ANYONE FOUND THAT LOUIE PIC YET?
DAMN IT! DO I HAVE TO DO ALL THE WORK MYSELF?!
GIRLS. THEY'RE A REAL HANDFUL, HUH?
CAN'T LIVE WITH THEM, CAN'T LIVE WITHOUT THEM.
OR CAN YOU, MIGUEL?

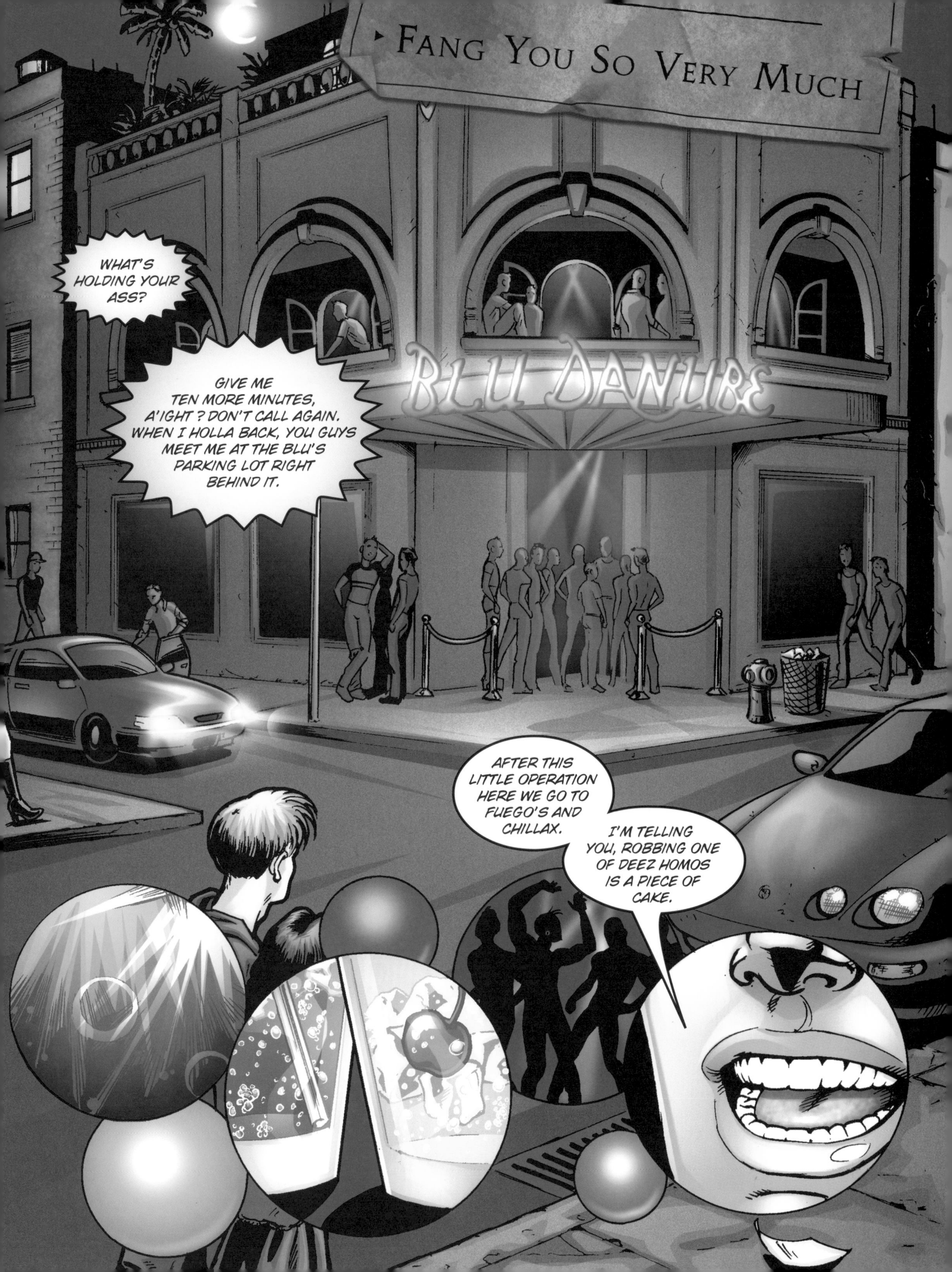

FANG YOU SO VERY MUCH
WHAT'S HOLDING YOUR ASS?
GIVE ME TEN MORE MINUTES, A'IGHT ? DON'T CALL AGAIN. WHEN I HOLLA BACK, YOU GUYS MEET ME AT THE BLU'S PARKING LOT RIGHT BEHIND IT.
BLU DANUBE
AFTER THIS LITTLE OPERATION HERE WE GO TO FUEGO'S AND CHILLAX.
I'M TELLING YOU, ROBBING ONE OF DEEZ HOMOS IS A PIECE OF CAKE.

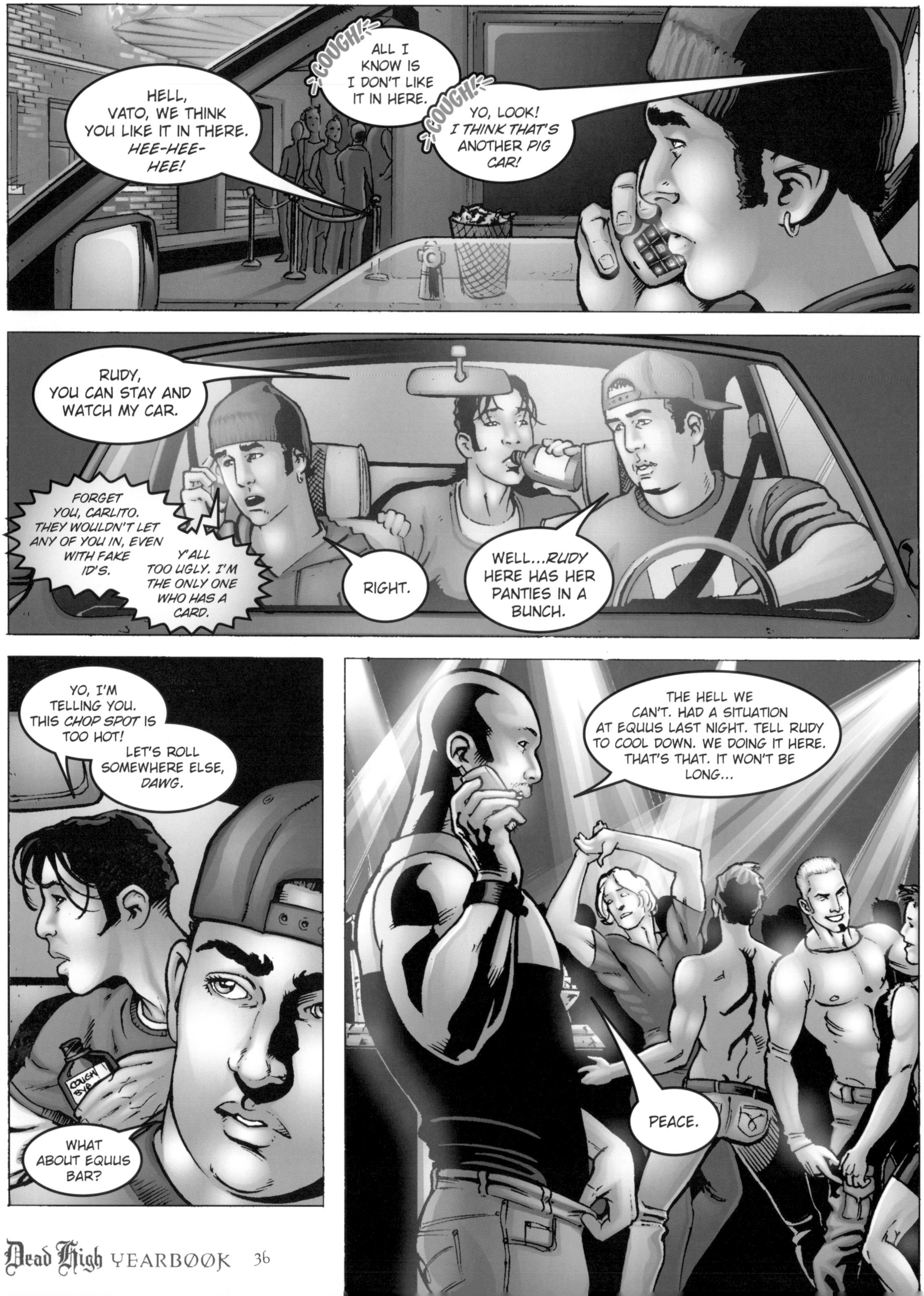
HELL, VATO, WE THINK YOU LIKE IT IN THERE. HEE-HEE-HEE!
COUGH!
ALL I KNOW IS I DON'T LIKE IT IN HERE.
COUGH!
YO, LOOK! I THINK THAT'S ANOTHER PIG CAR!
RUDY, YOU CAN STAY AND WATCH MY CAR.
FORGET YOU, CARLITO. THEY WOULDN'T LET ANY OF YOU IN, EVEN WITH FAKE ID'S.
Y'ALL TOO UGLY. I'M THE ONLY ONE WHO HAS A CARD.
RIGHT.
WELL...RUDY HERE HAS HER PANTIES IN A BUNCH.
YO, I'M TELLING YOU. THIS CHOP SPOT IS TOO HOT!
LET'S ROLL SOMEWHERE ELSE, DAWG.
COUGH SYP
WHAT ABOUT EQUUS BAR?
THE HELL WE CAN'T. HAD A SITUATION AT EQUUS LAST NIGHT. TELL RUDY TO COOL DOWN. WE DOING IT HERE. THAT'S THAT. IT WON'T BE LONG...
PEACE.

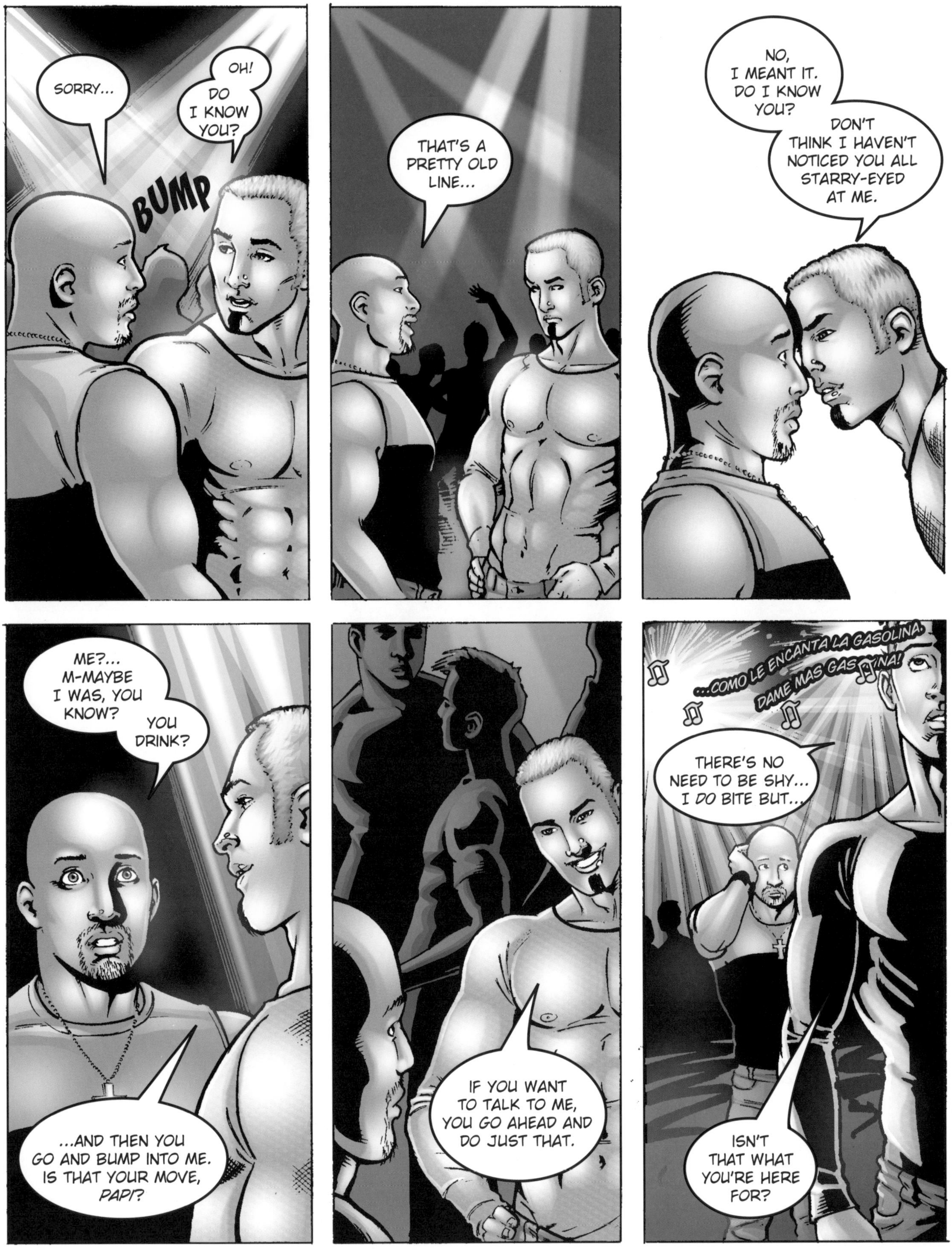
SORRY...
OH! DO I KNOW YOU?
BUMP
THAT'S A PRETTY OLD LINE...
NO, I MEANT IT. DO I KNOW YOU?
DON'T THINK I HAVEN'T NOTICED YOU ALL STARRY-EYED AT ME.
ME?... M-MAYBE I WAS, YOU KNOW?
YOU DRINK?
...AND THEN YOU GO AND BUMP INTO ME. IS THAT YOUR MOVE, PAPI?
IF YOU WANT TO TALK TO ME, YOU GO AHEAD AND DO JUST THAT.
...COMO LE ENCANTA LA GASOLINA,
DAME MAS GASOLINA!
THERE'S NO NEED TO BE SHY... I DO BITE BUT...
ISN'T THAT WHAT YOU'RE HERE FOR?

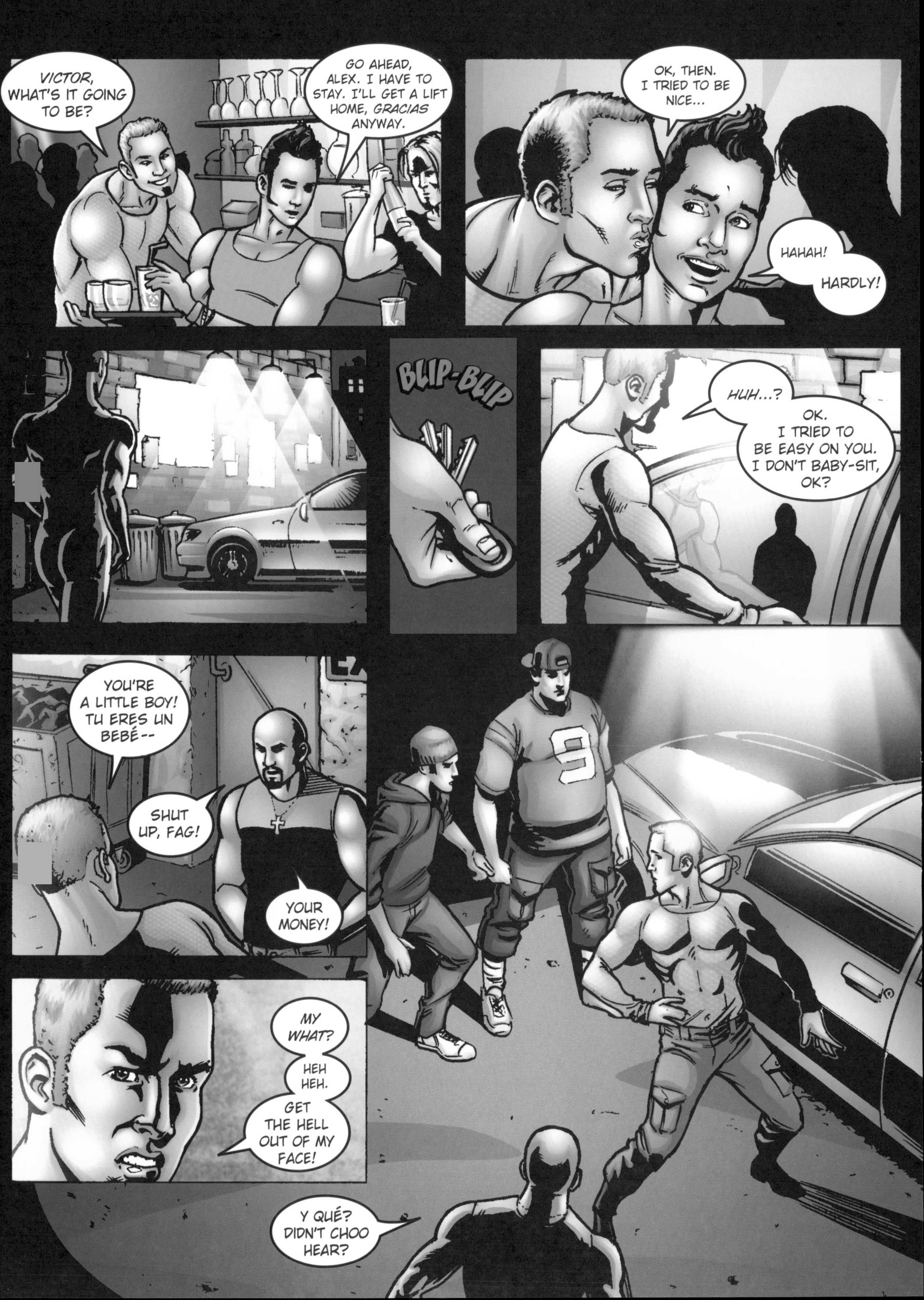
VICTOR, WHAT'S IT GOING TO BE?
GO AHEAD, ALEX. I HAVE TO STAY. I'LL GET A LIFT HOME, GRACIAS ANYWAY.
OK, THEN. I TRIED TO BE NICE...
HAHAH!
HARDLY!
BLIP-BLIP
HUH...?
OK. I TRIED TO BE EASY ON YOU. I DON'T BABY-SIT, OK?
YOU'RE A LITTLE BOY! TU ERES UN BEBÉ--
SHUT UP, FAG!
YOUR MONEY!
MY WHAT?
HEH HEH.
GET THE HELL OUT OF MY FACE!
Y QUÉ? DIDN'T CHOO HEAR?

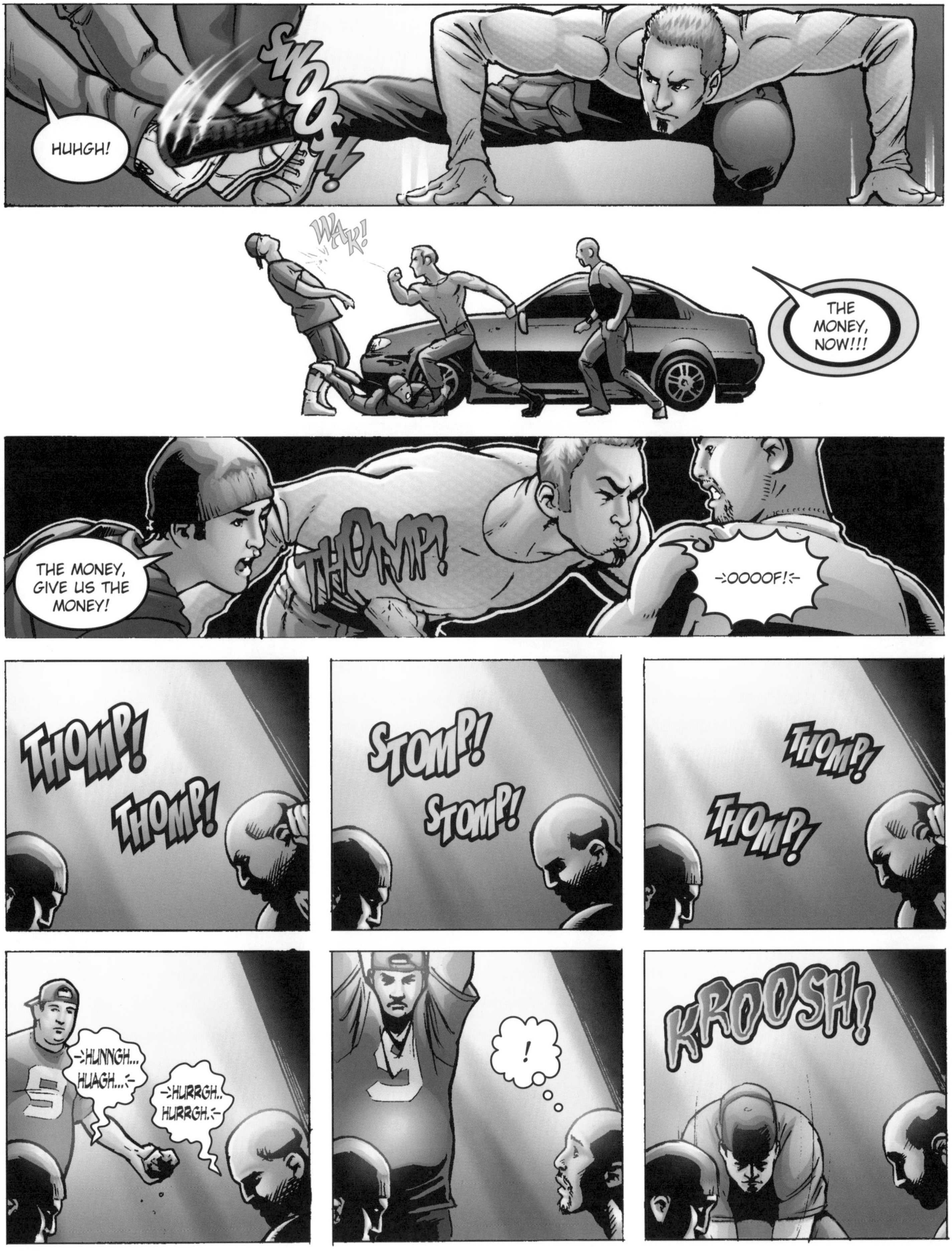
SWOOSH!
HUHGH!
WAK!
THE MONEY, NOW!!!
THE MONEY, GIVE US THE MONEY!
THOMP!
-OOOOF!-
THOMP!
THOMP!
STOMP!
STOMP!
THOMP!
THOMP!
-HUNNGH... HUAGH...-
-HURRGH.. HURRGH.-
!
KROOSH!

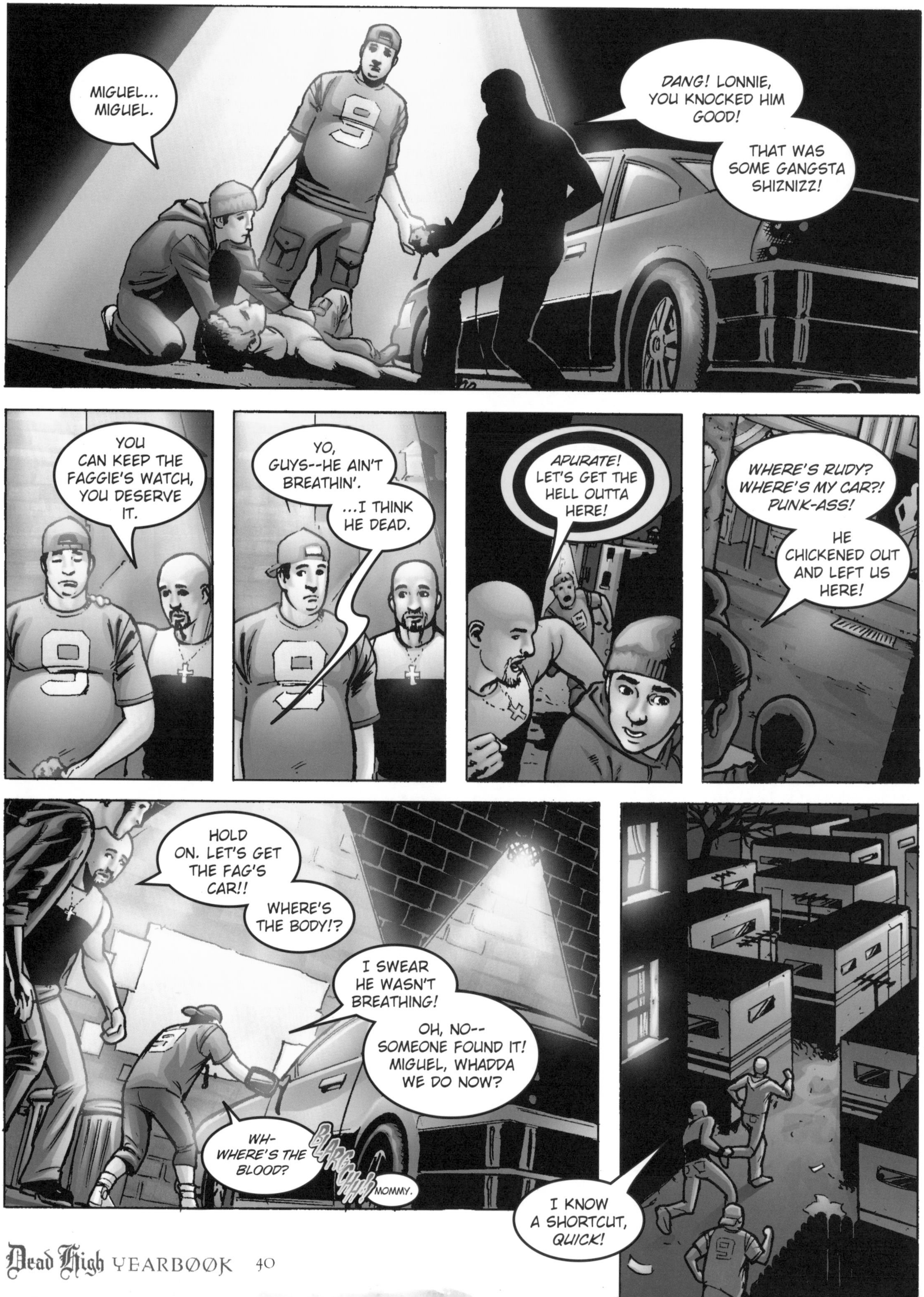
MIGUEL... MIGUEL.
DANG! LONNIE, YOU KNOCKED HIM GOOD!
THAT WAS SOME GANGSTA SHIZNIZZ!
YOU CAN KEEP THE FAGGIE'S WATCH, YOU DESERVE IT.
YO, GUYS--HE AIN'T BREATHIN'.
...I THINK HE DEAD.
APURATE! LET'S GET THE HELL OUTTA HERE!
WHERE'S RUDY? WHERE'S MY CAR?! PUNK-ASS!
HE CHICKENED OUT AND LEFT US HERE!
HOLD ON. LET'S GET THE FAG'S CAR!!
WHERE'S THE BODY!?
I SWEAR HE WASN'T BREATHING!
OH, NO-- SOMEONE FOUND IT! MIGUEL, WHADDA WE DO NOW?
WH- WHERE'S THE BLOOD?
BLARGHHH!
MOMMY.
I KNOW A SHORTCUT, QUICK!

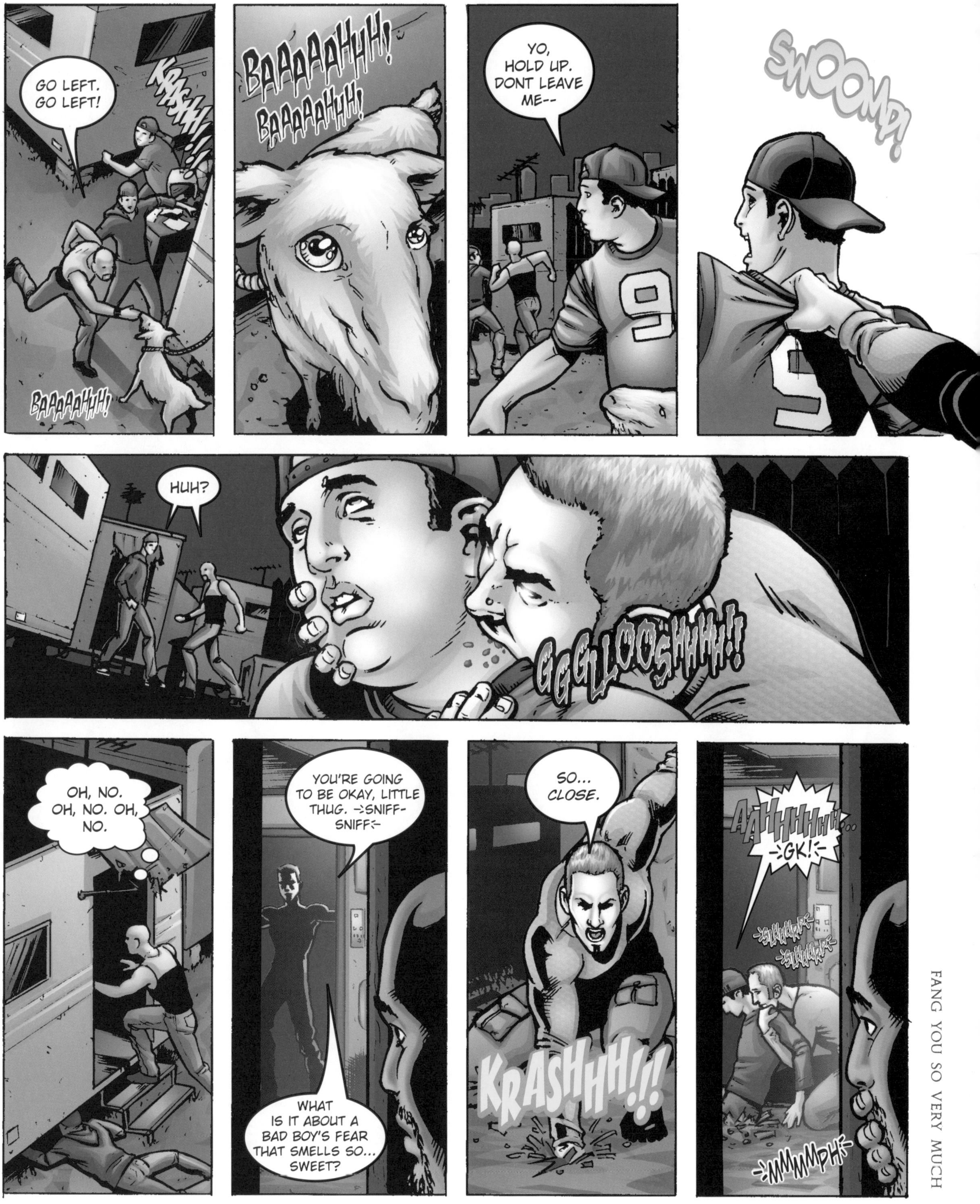
GO LEFT. GO LEFT!
KRASHH!!
BAAAAAHHH!
BAAAAAHHH!
BAAAAAHHH!
YO, HOLD UP. DONT LEAVE ME--
SWOOMP!
HUH?
GGGLOOSHHH!!
OH, NO. OH, NO. OH, NO.
YOU'RE GOING TO BE OKAY, LITTLE THUG. -SNIFF- SNIFF-
WHAT IS IT ABOUT A BAD BOY'S FEAR THAT SMELLS SO... SWEET?
SO... CLOSE.
KRASHHH!!!
AAHHHHHH...
-GK!-
MMMMPH

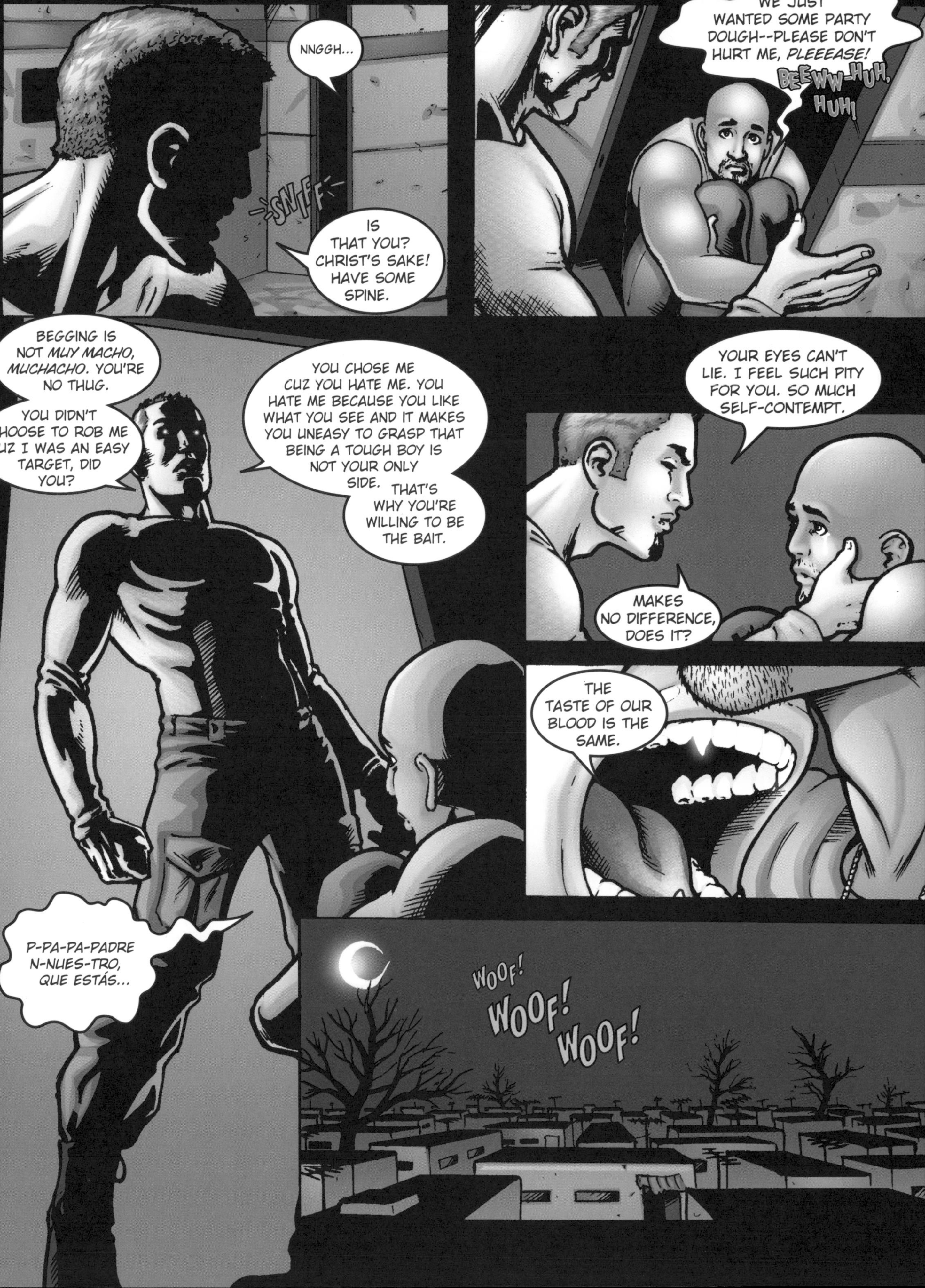
NNGGH...
-SNIFF-
IS THAT YOU? CHRIST'S SAKE! HAVE SOME SPINE.
WE JUST WANTED SOME PARTY DOUGH--PLEASE DON'T HURT ME, *PLEEEASE!*
BEEWW-HUH, HUH!
BEGGING IS NOT *MUY MACHO, MUCHACHO*. YOU'RE NO THUG.
YOU DIDN'T CHOOSE TO ROB ME CUZ I WAS AN EASY TARGET, DID YOU?
YOU CHOSE ME CUZ YOU HATE ME. YOU HATE ME BECAUSE YOU LIKE WHAT YOU SEE AND IT MAKES YOU UNEASY TO GRASP THAT BEING A TOUGH BOY IS NOT YOUR ONLY SIDE.
THAT'S WHY YOU'RE WILLING TO BE THE BAIT.
P-PA-PA-PADRE N-NUES-TRO, QUE ESTÁS...
YOUR EYES CAN'T LIE. I FEEL SUCH PITY FOR YOU. SO MUCH SELF-CONTEMPT.
MAKES NO DIFFERENCE, DOES IT?
THE TASTE OF OUR BLOOD IS THE SAME.
WOOF! WOOF! WOOF!

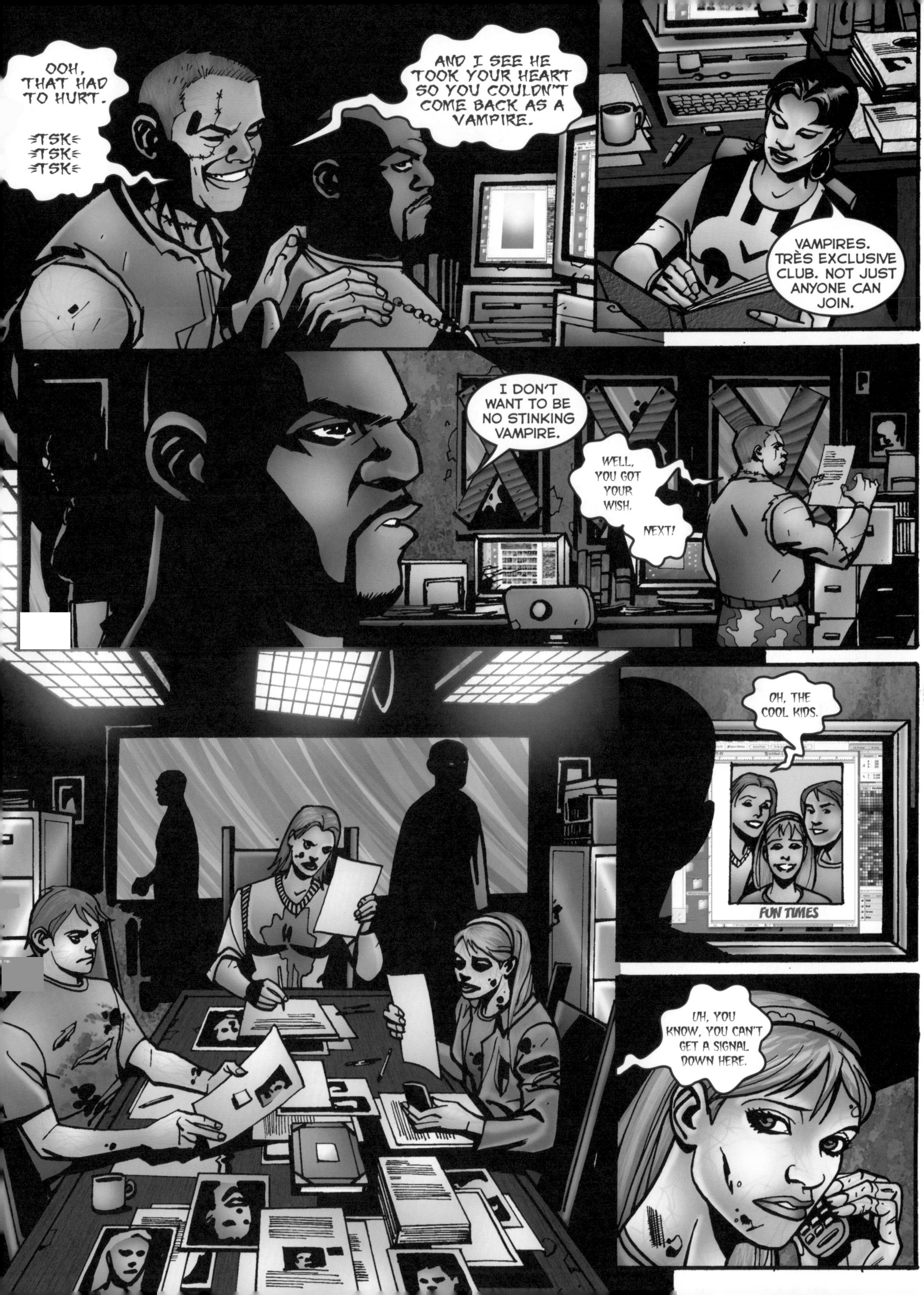
OOH, THAT HAD TO HURT.
TSK TSK TSK
AND I SEE HE TOOK YOUR HEART SO YOU COULDN'T COME BACK AS A VAMPIRE.
VAMPIRES. TRÈS EXCLUSIVE CLUB. NOT JUST ANYONE CAN JOIN.
I DON'T WANT TO BE NO STINKING VAMPIRE.
WELL, YOU GOT YOUR WISH.
NEXT!
OH, THE COOL KIDS.
FUN TIMES
UH, YOU KNOW, YOU CAN'T GET A SIGNAL DOWN HERE.

Have a Nicey Icee Last Day

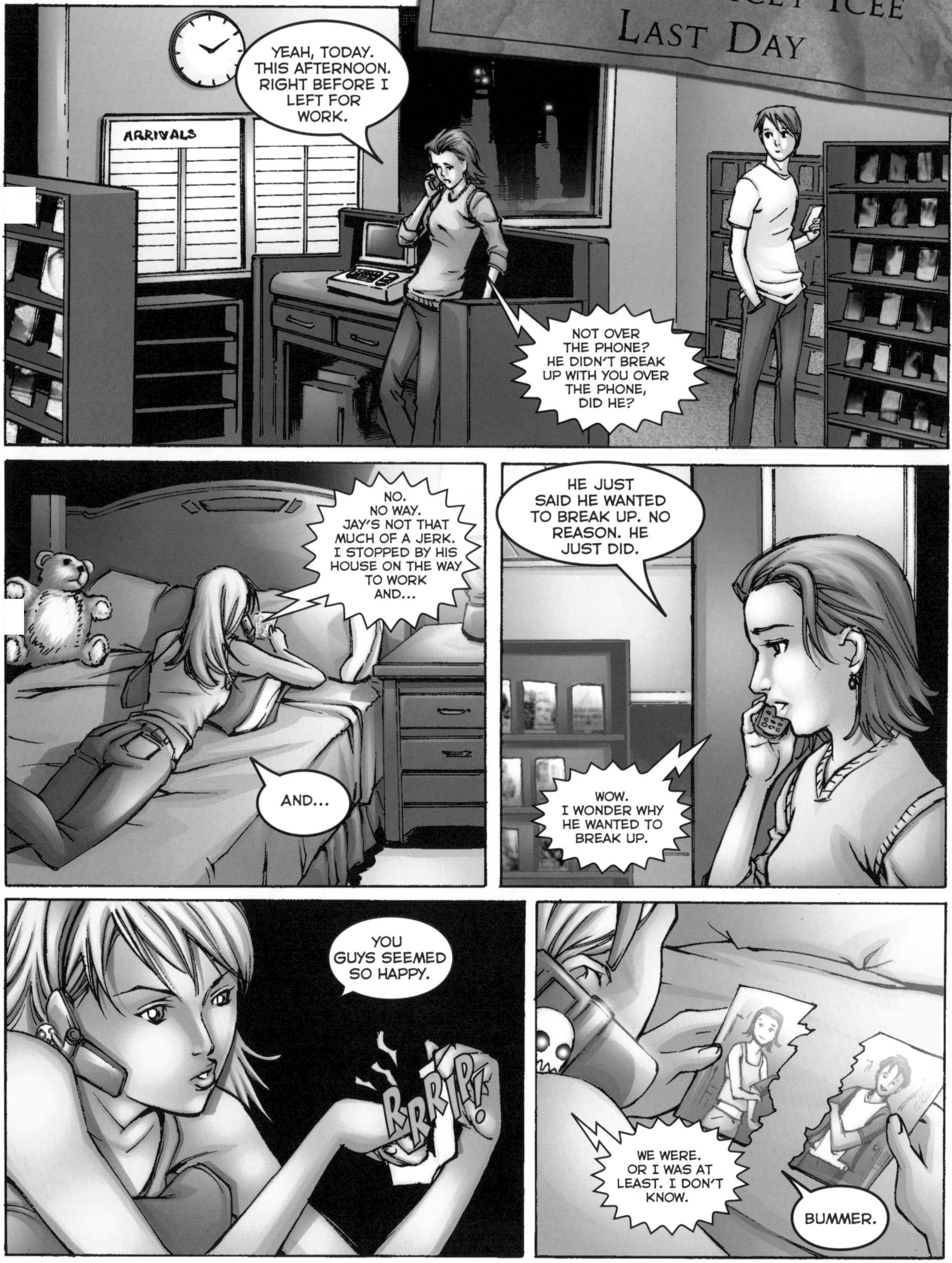

ARRIVALS
YEAH, TODAY. THIS AFTERNOON. RIGHT BEFORE I LEFT FOR WORK.
NOT OVER THE PHONE? HE DIDN'T BREAK UP WITH YOU OVER THE PHONE, DID HE?
NO. NO WAY. JAY'S NOT THAT MUCH OF A JERK. I STOPPED BY HIS HOUSE ON THE WAY TO WORK AND...
AND...
HE JUST SAID HE WANTED TO BREAK UP. NO REASON. HE JUST DID.
WOW. I WONDER WHY HE WANTED TO BREAK UP.
YOU GUYS SEEMED SO HAPPY.
RRRIP!
WE WERE. OR I WAS AT LEAST. I DON'T KNOW.
BUMMER.

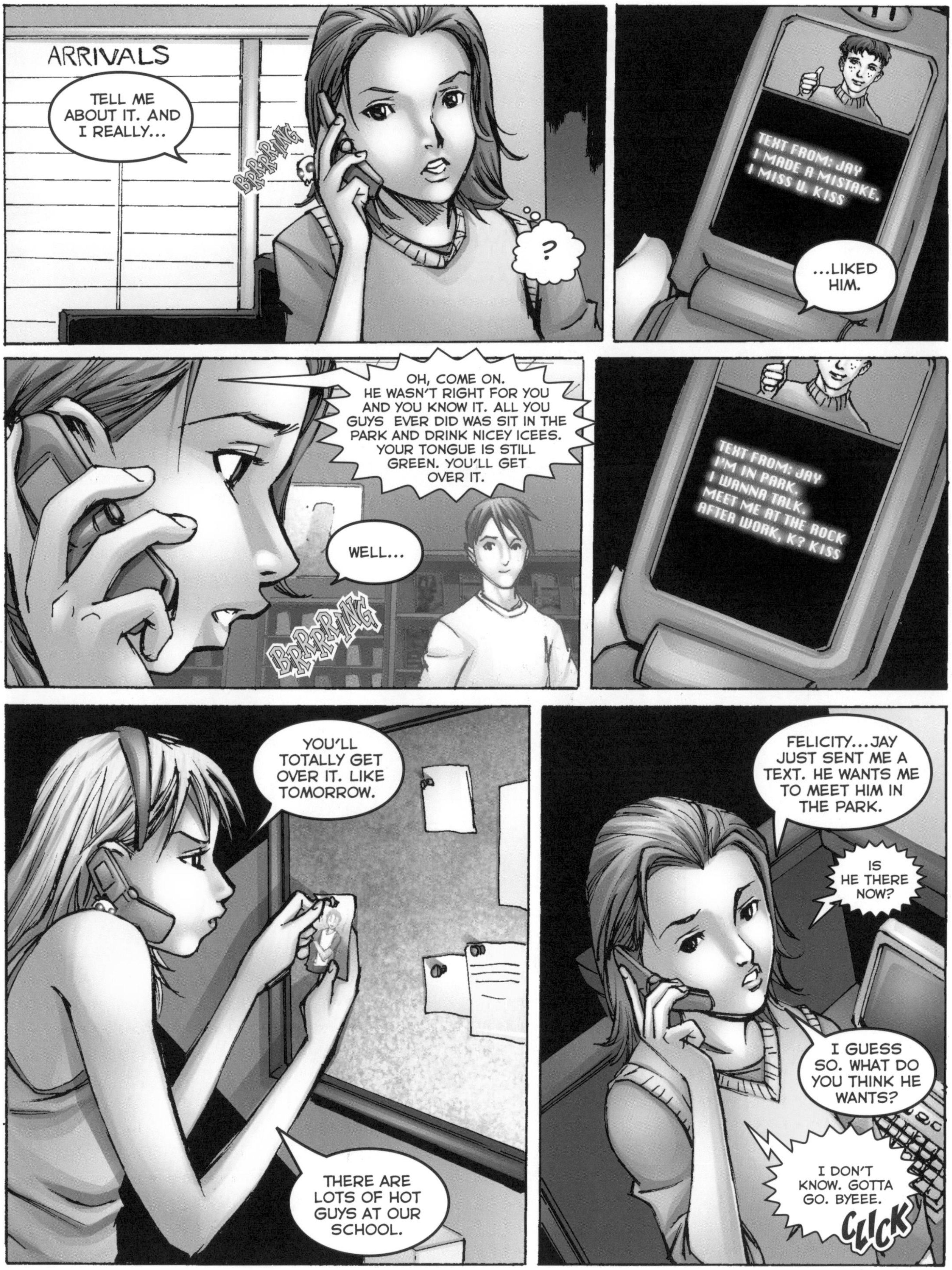
ARRIVALS
TELL ME ABOUT IT. AND I REALLY...
BRRRRING
?
TEXT FROM: JAY I MADE A MISTAKE. I MISS U. KISS
...LIKED HIM.
OH, COME ON. HE WASN'T RIGHT FOR YOU AND YOU KNOW IT. ALL YOU GUYS EVER DID WAS SIT IN THE PARK AND DRINK NICEY ICEES. YOUR TONGUE IS STILL GREEN. YOU'LL GET OVER IT.
WELL...
BRRRRING
TEXT FROM: JAY I'M IN PARK. I WANNA TALK. MEET ME AT THE ROCK AFTER WORK, K? KISS
YOU'LL TOTALLY GET OVER IT. LIKE TOMORROW.
THERE ARE LOTS OF HOT GUYS AT OUR SCHOOL.
FELICITY...JAY JUST SENT ME A TEXT. HE WANTS ME TO MEET HIM IN THE PARK.
IS HE THERE NOW?
I GUESS SO. WHAT DO YOU THINK HE WANTS?
I DON'T KNOW. GOTTA GO. BYEEE.
CLICK

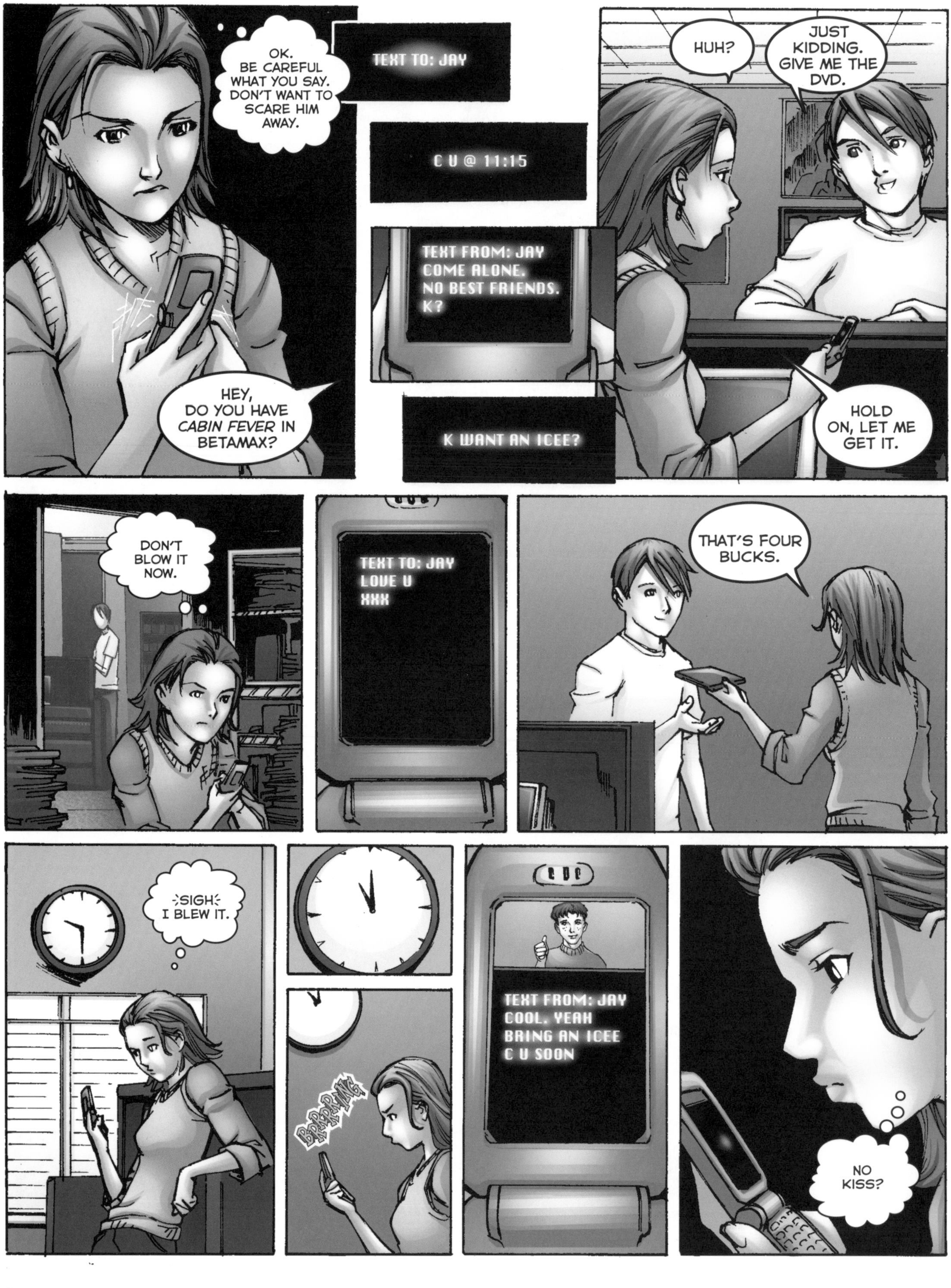

OK. BE CAREFUL WHAT YOU SAY. DON'T WANT TO SCARE HIM AWAY.
HEY, DO YOU HAVE *CABIN FEVER* IN BETAMAX?
TEXT TO: JAY
C U @ 11:15
TEXT FROM: JAY COME ALONE. NO BEST FRIENDS. K?
K WANT AN ICEE?
HUH?
JUST KIDDING. GIVE ME THE DVD.
HOLD ON, LET ME GET IT.
DON'T BLOW IT NOW.
TEXT TO: JAY LOVE U XXX
THAT'S FOUR BUCKS.
SIGH I BLEW IT.
BRRRRING
TEXT FROM: JAY COOL. YEAH BRING AN ICEE C U SOON
NO KISS?

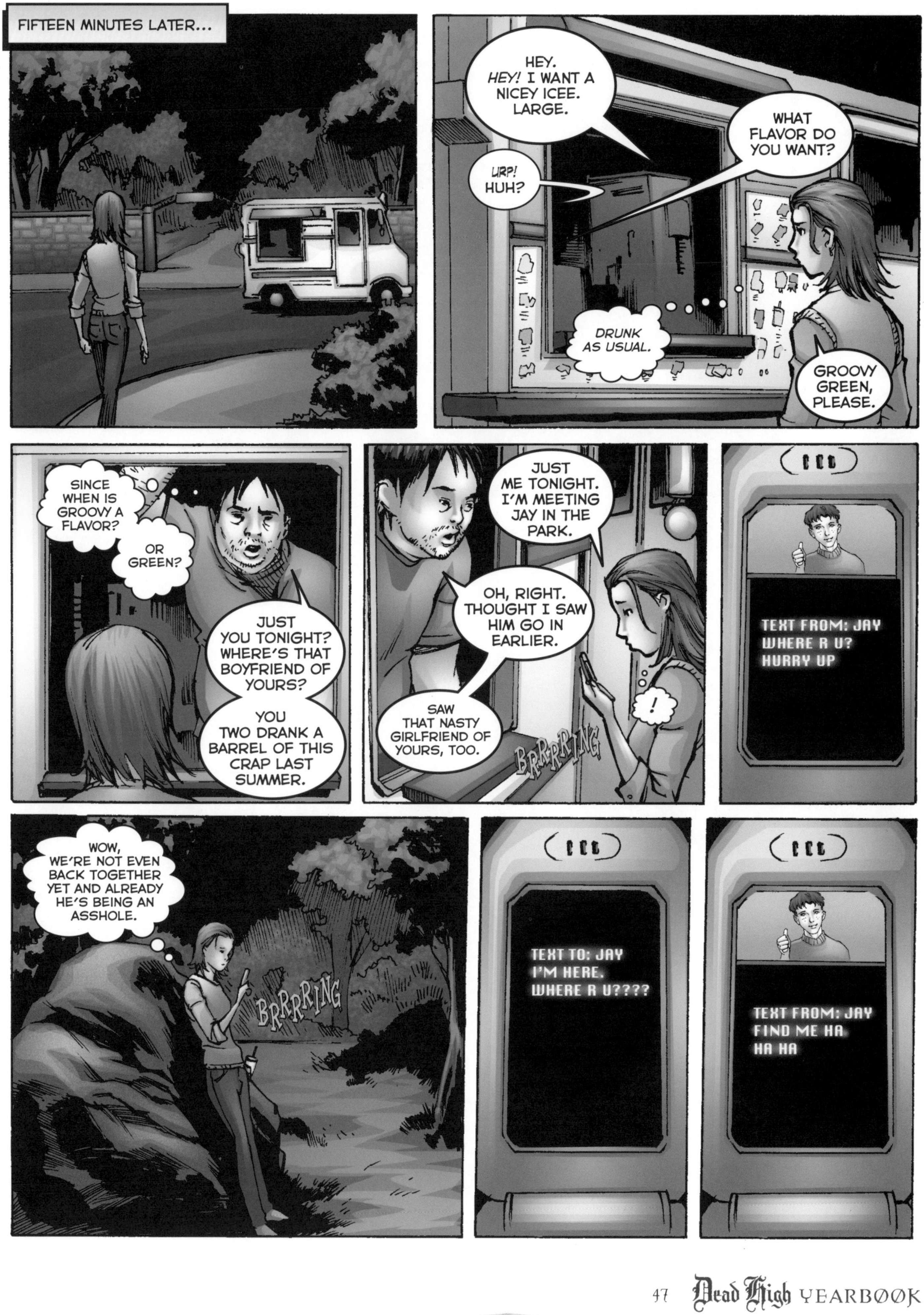

FIFTEEN MINUTES LATER...
HEY. HEY! I WANT A NICEY ICEE. LARGE.
URP! HUH?
WHAT FLAVOR DO YOU WANT?
DRUNK AS USUAL.
GROOVY GREEN, PLEASE.
SINCE WHEN IS GROOVY A FLAVOR?
OR GREEN?
JUST YOU TONIGHT? WHERE'S THAT BOYFRIEND OF YOURS?
YOU TWO DRANK A BARREL OF THIS CRAP LAST SUMMER.
JUST ME TONIGHT. I'M MEETING JAY IN THE PARK.
OH, RIGHT. THOUGHT I SAW HIM GO IN EARLIER.
SAW THAT NASTY GIRLFRIEND OF YOURS, TOO.
!
BRRRRING
TEXT FROM: JAY
WHERE R U?
HURRY UP
WOW, WE'RE NOT EVEN BACK TOGETHER YET AND ALREADY HE'S BEING AN ASSHOLE.
BRRRRING
TEXT TO: JAY
I'M HERE.
WHERE R U????
TEXT FROM: JAY
FIND ME HA.
HA HA

HAVE A NICEY ICEE LAST DAY

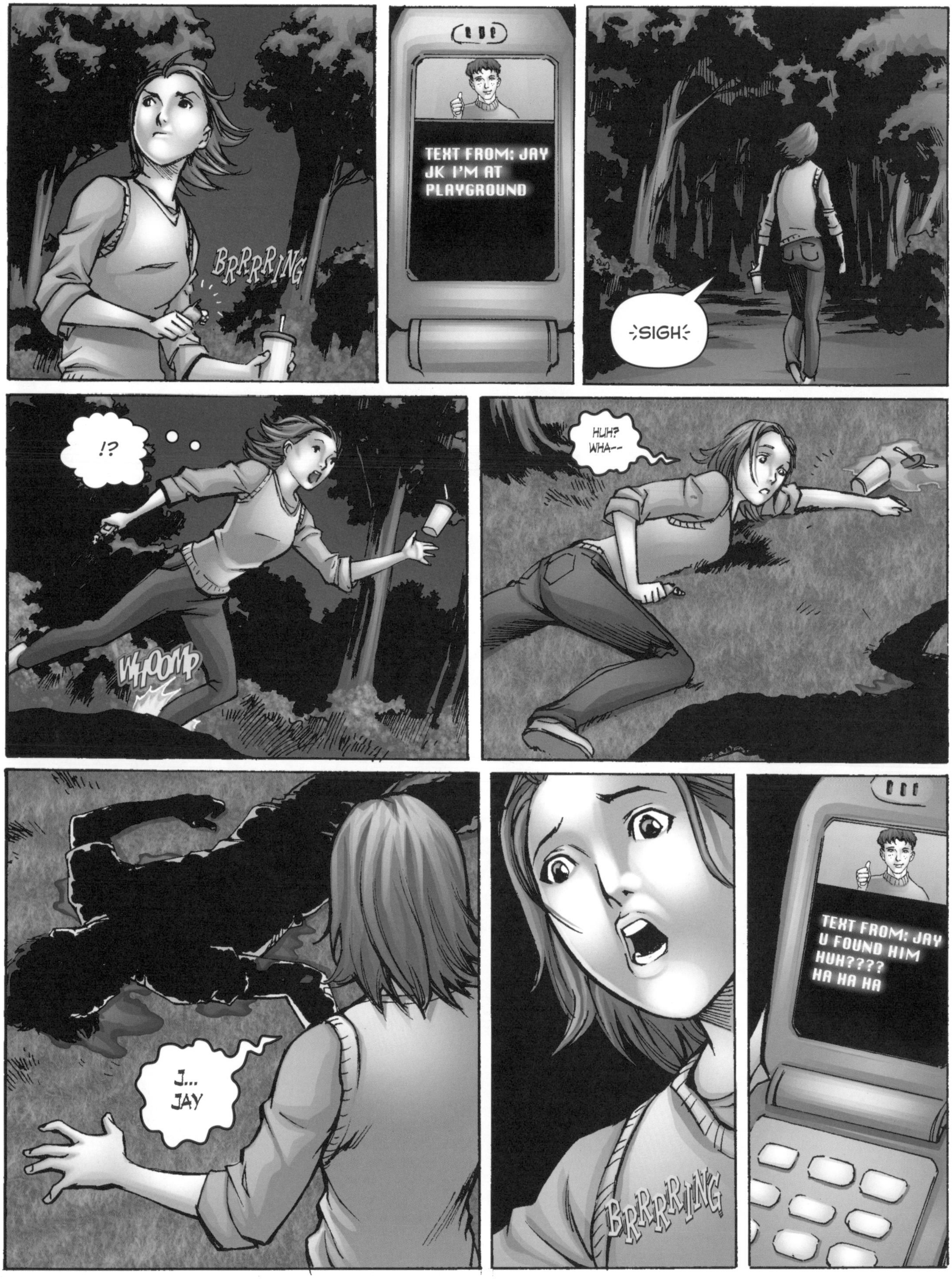
BRRRRING
TEXT FROM: JAY
JK I'M AT
PLAYGROUND
SIGH
!?
WHOOMP
HUH?
WHA--
J...
JAY
BRRRRING
TEXT FROM: JAY
U FOUND HIM
HUH????
HA HA HA

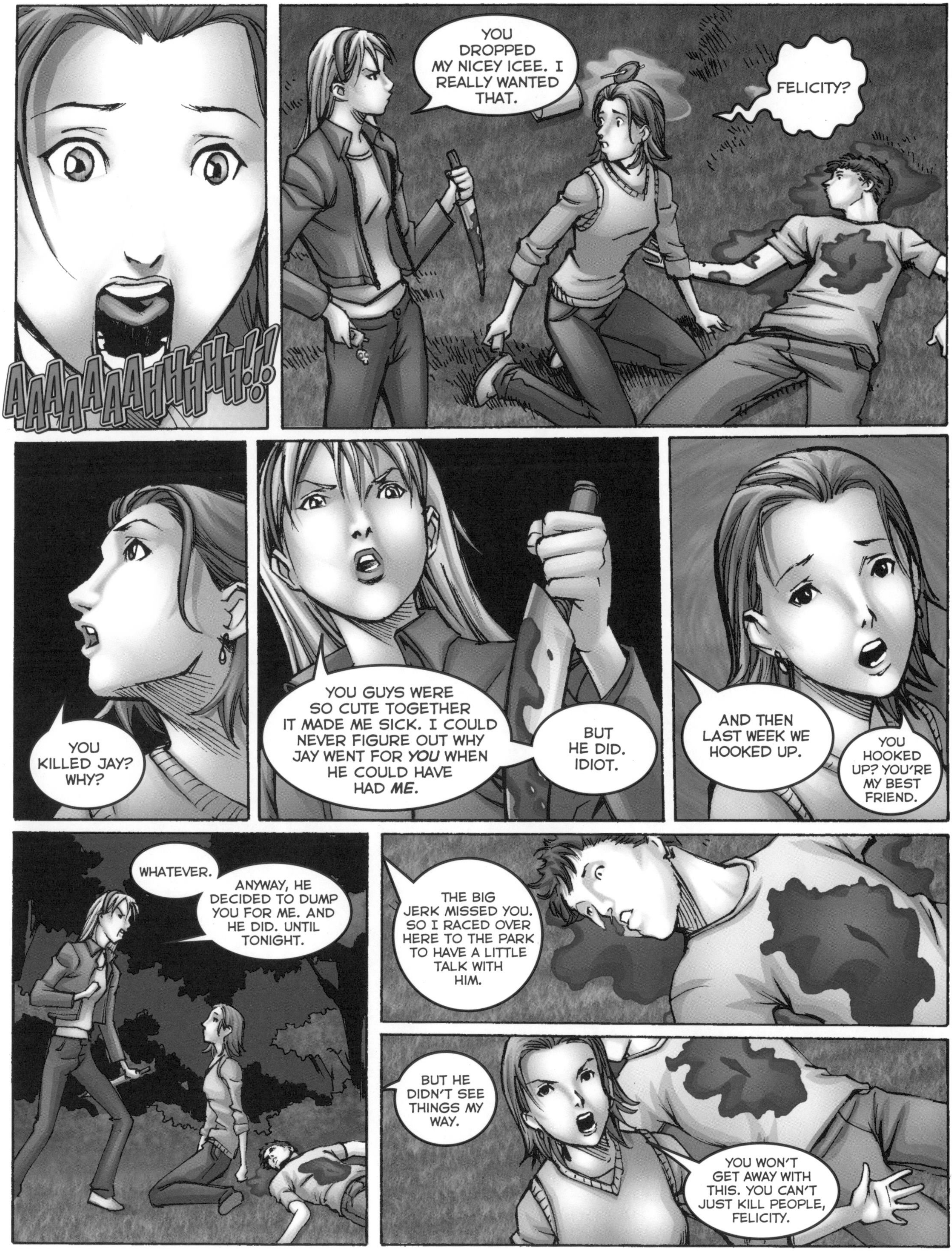
AAAAAAAHHHHH!!!
YOU DROPPED MY NICEY ICEE. I REALLY WANTED THAT.
FELICITY?
YOU KILLED JAY? WHY?
YOU GUYS WERE SO CUTE TOGETHER IT MADE ME SICK. I COULD NEVER FIGURE OUT WHY JAY WENT FOR *YOU* WHEN HE COULD HAVE HAD ***ME.***
BUT HE DID. IDIOT.
AND THEN LAST WEEK WE HOOKED UP.
YOU HOOKED UP? YOU'RE MY BEST FRIEND.
WHATEVER.
ANYWAY, HE DECIDED TO DUMP YOU FOR ME. AND HE DID. UNTIL TONIGHT.
THE BIG JERK MISSED YOU. SO I RACED OVER HERE TO THE PARK TO HAVE A LITTLE TALK WITH HIM.
BUT HE DIDN'T SEE THINGS MY WAY.
YOU WON'T GET AWAY WITH THIS. YOU CAN'T JUST KILL PEOPLE, FELICITY.

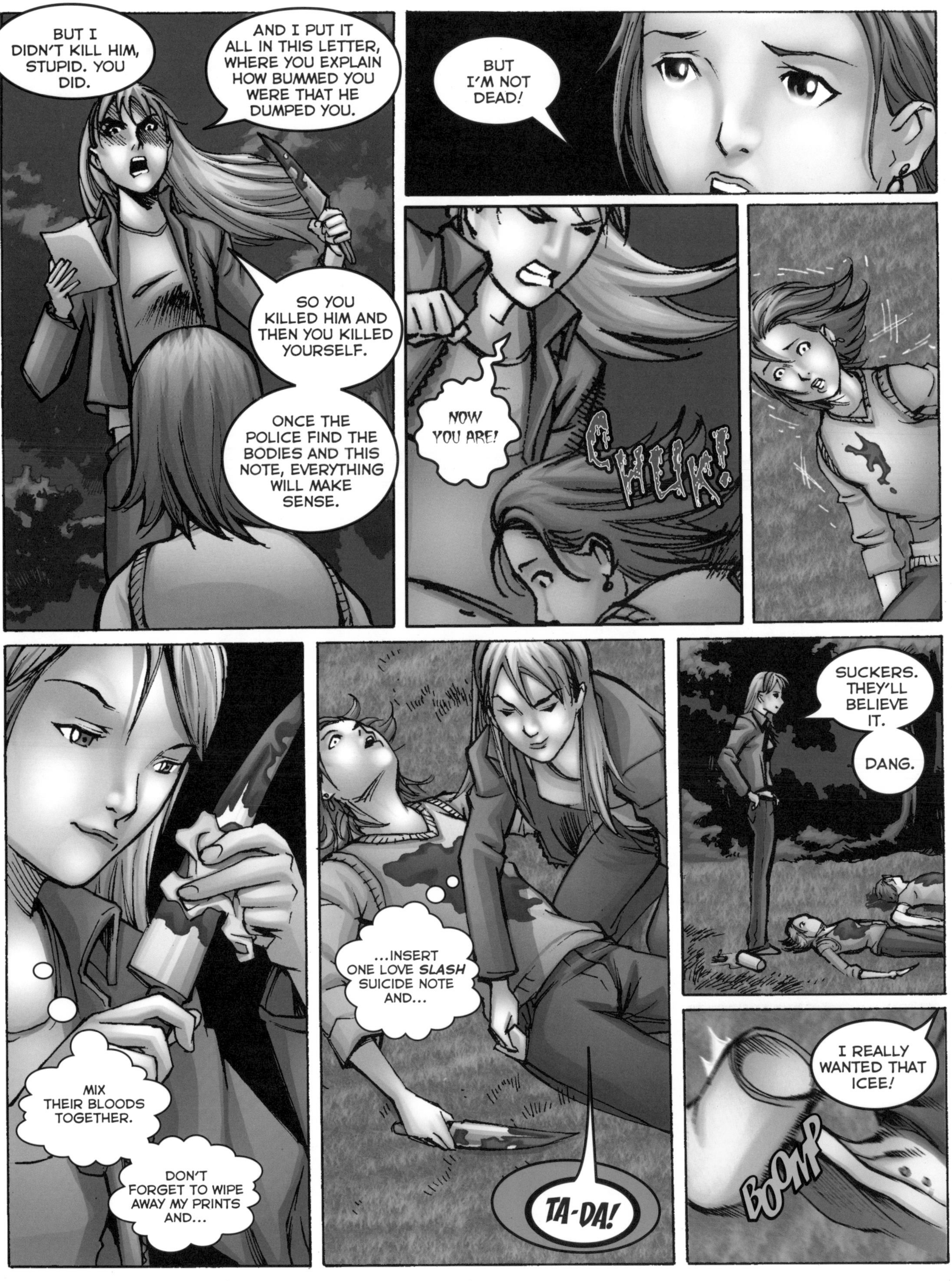

BUT I DIDN'T KILL HIM, STUPID. YOU DID.
AND I PUT IT ALL IN THIS LETTER, WHERE YOU EXPLAIN HOW BUMMED YOU WERE THAT HE DUMPED YOU.
SO YOU KILLED HIM AND THEN YOU KILLED YOURSELF.
ONCE THE POLICE FIND THE BODIES AND THIS NOTE, EVERYTHING WILL MAKE SENSE.
BUT I'M NOT DEAD!
NOW YOU ARE!
CHUK!
MIX THEIR BLOODS TOGETHER.
DON'T FORGET TO WIPE AWAY MY PRINTS AND...
...INSERT ONE LOVE SLASH SUICIDE NOTE AND...
TA-DA!
SUCKERS. THEY'LL BELIEVE IT.
DANG.
I REALLY WANTED THAT ICEE!
BOOMP

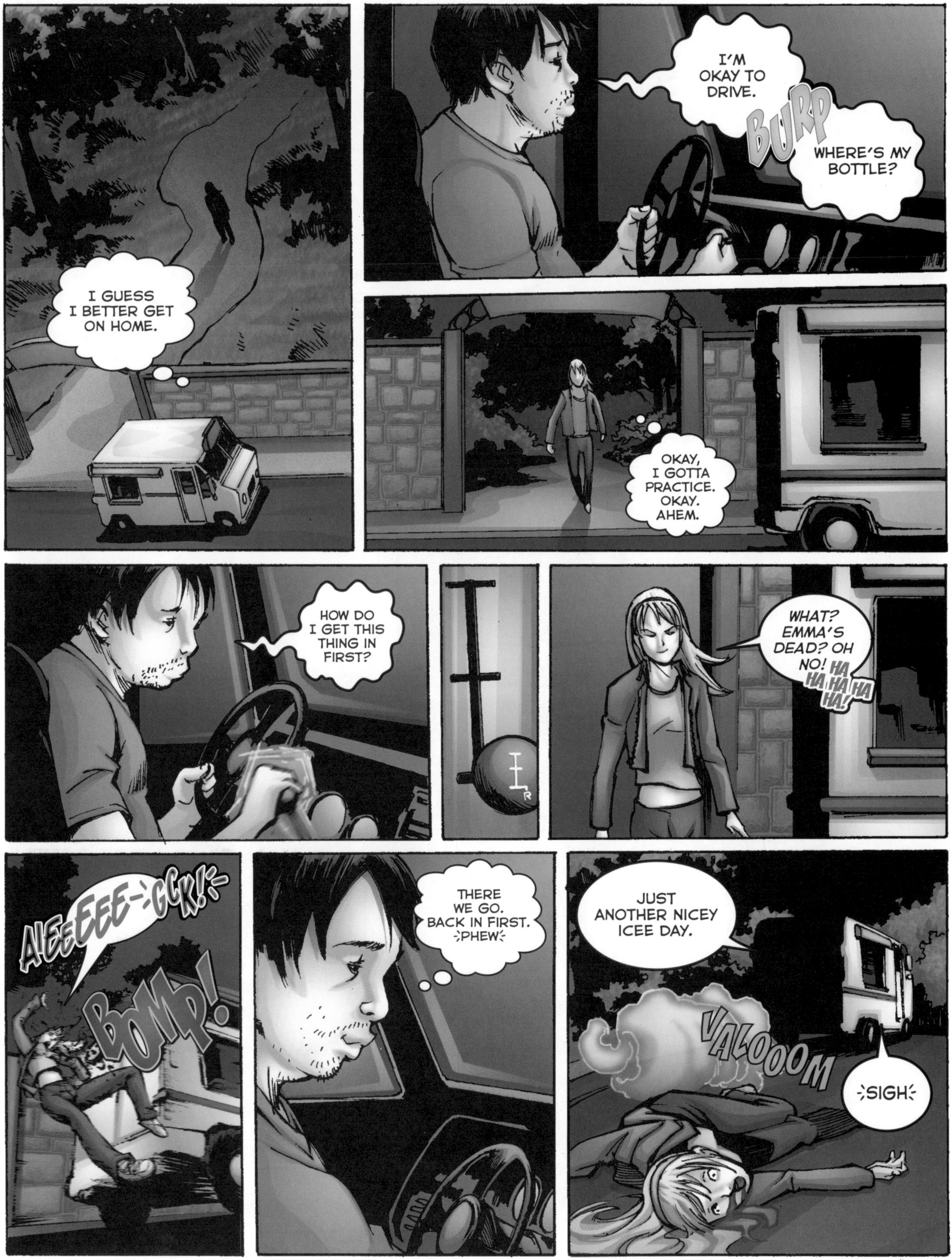
I GUESS I BETTER GET ON HOME.
I'M OKAY TO DRIVE.
BURP
WHERE'S MY BOTTLE?
OKAY, I GOTTA PRACTICE. OKAY. AHEM.
HOW DO I GET THIS THING IN FIRST?
WHAT? EMMA'S DEAD? OH NO! HA HA HA HA HA!
AIEEEEE-GCK!
BOMP!
THERE WE GO. BACK IN FIRST. PHEW
JUST ANOTHER NICEY ICEE DAY.
VALOOOM
SIGH

HAVE A NICEY ICEE LAST DAY

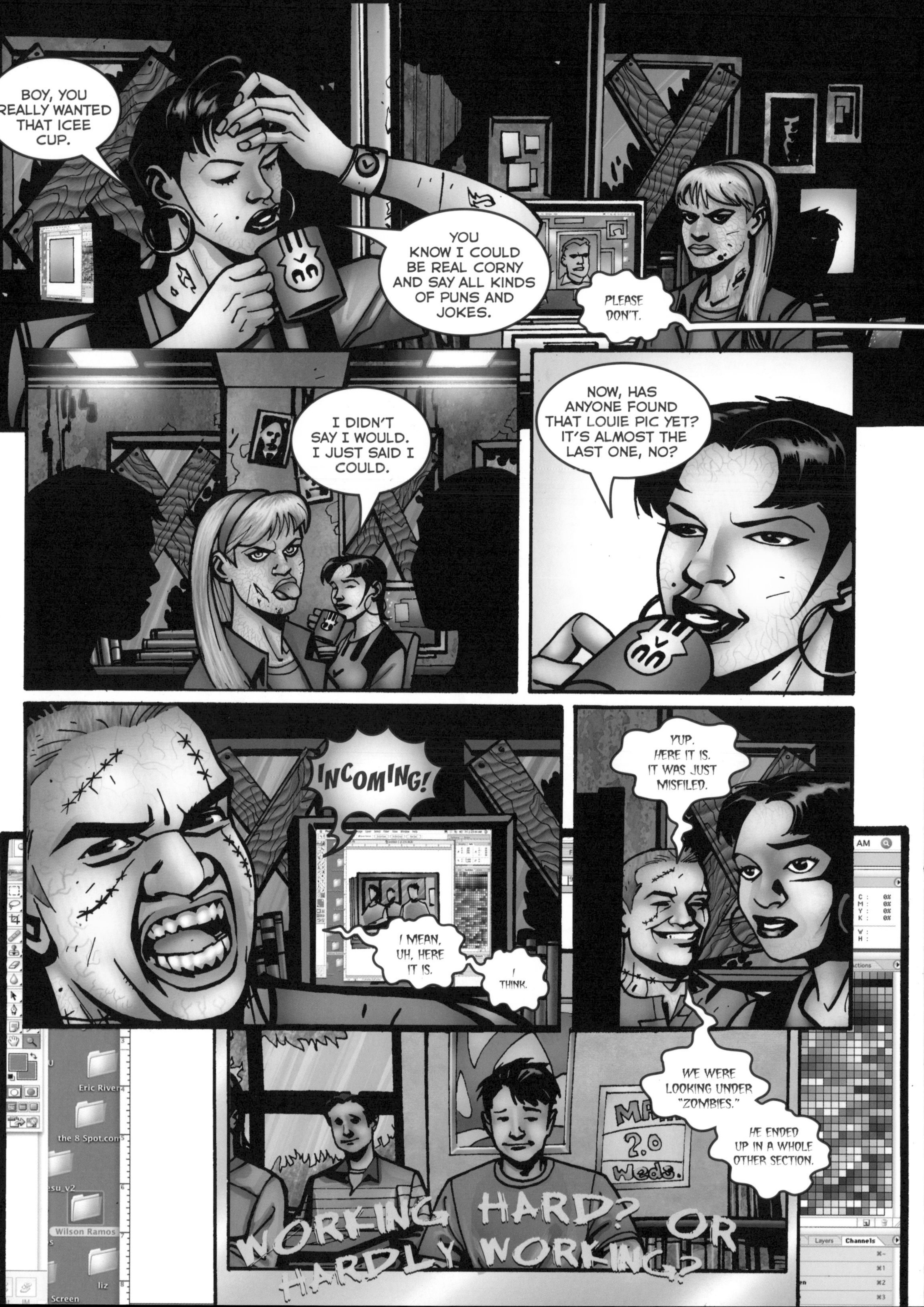
BOY, YOU REALLY WANTED THAT ICEE CUP.
YOU KNOW I COULD BE REAL CORNY AND SAY ALL KINDS OF PUNS AND JOKES.
PLEASE DON'T.
I DIDN'T SAY I WOULD. I JUST SAID I COULD.
NOW, HAS ANYONE FOUND THAT LOUIE PIC YET? IT'S ALMOST THE LAST ONE, NO?
INCOMING!
I MEAN, UH, HERE IT IS.
I THINK.
YUP. HERE IT IS. IT WAS JUST MISFILED.
WE WERE LOOKING UNDER "ZOMBIES."
HE ENDED UP IN A WHOLE OTHER SECTION.
MA
2.0
Weds.
WORKING HARD? OR HARDLY WORKING?
Eric River
the 8 Spot.com
Wilson Ramos
liz
Screen
Layers
Channels

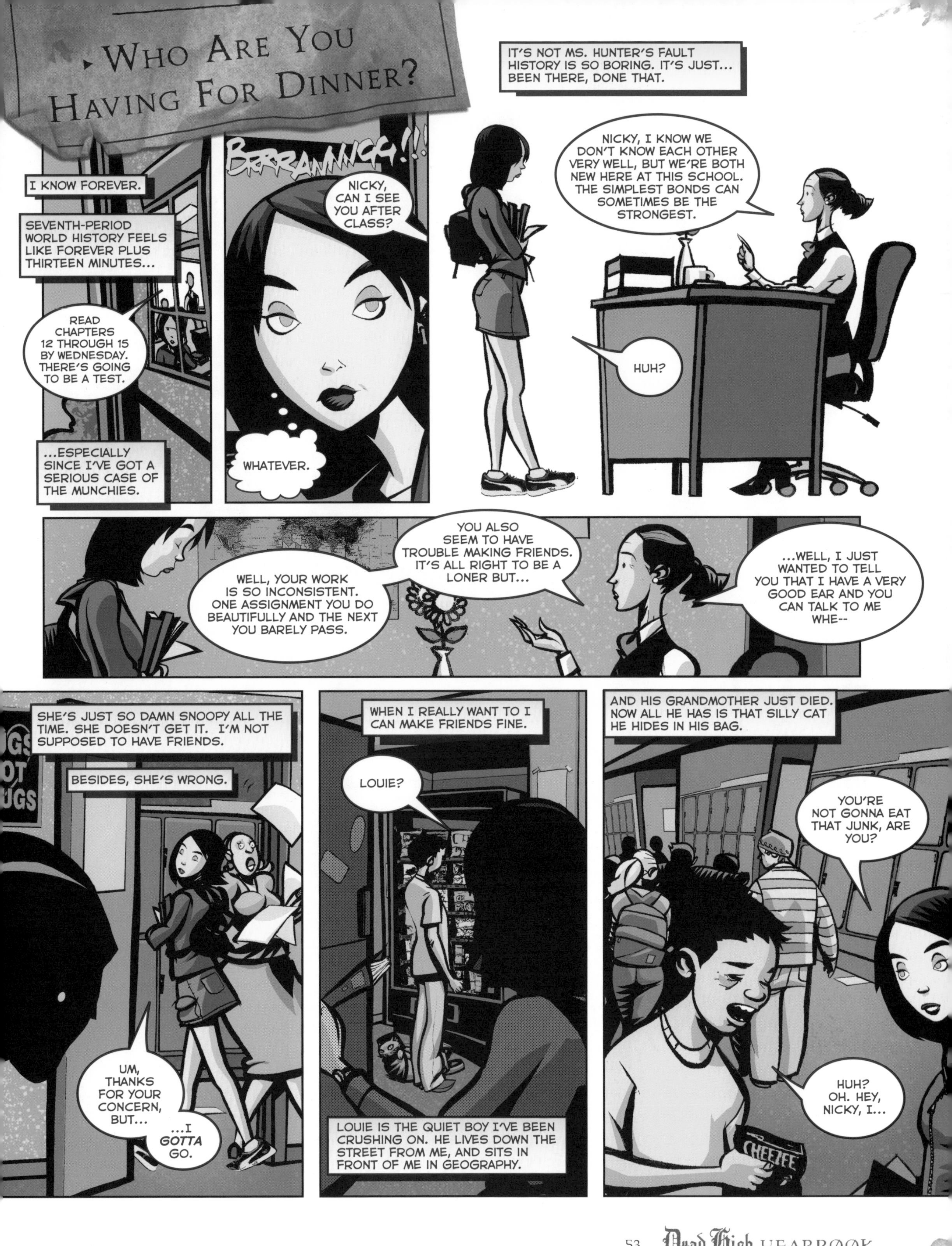
WHO ARE YOU HAVING FOR DINNER?
IT'S NOT MS. HUNTER'S FAULT HISTORY IS SO BORING. IT'S JUST... BEEN THERE, DONE THAT.
I KNOW FOREVER.
SEVENTH-PERIOD WORLD HISTORY FEELS LIKE FOREVER PLUS THIRTEEN MINUTES...
READ CHAPTERS 12 THROUGH 15 BY WEDNESDAY. THERE'S GOING TO BE A TEST.
...ESPECIALLY SINCE I'VE GOT A SERIOUS CASE OF THE MUNCHIES.
BRRRANNNGG!!!
NICKY, CAN I SEE YOU AFTER CLASS?
WHATEVER.
NICKY, I KNOW WE DON'T KNOW EACH OTHER VERY WELL, BUT WE'RE BOTH NEW HERE AT THIS SCHOOL. THE SIMPLEST BONDS CAN SOMETIMES BE THE STRONGEST.
HUH?
WELL, YOUR WORK IS SO INCONSISTENT. ONE ASSIGNMENT YOU DO BEAUTIFULLY AND THE NEXT YOU BARELY PASS.
YOU ALSO SEEM TO HAVE TROUBLE MAKING FRIENDS. IT'S ALL RIGHT TO BE A LONER BUT...
...WELL, I JUST WANTED TO TELL YOU THAT I HAVE A VERY GOOD EAR AND YOU CAN TALK TO ME WHE--
SHE'S JUST SO DAMN SNOOPY ALL THE TIME. SHE DOESN'T GET IT. I'M NOT SUPPOSED TO HAVE FRIENDS.
BESIDES, SHE'S WRONG.
UM, THANKS FOR YOUR CONCERN, BUT...
...I *GOTTA* GO.
WHEN I REALLY WANT TO I CAN MAKE FRIENDS FINE.
LOUIE?
LOUIE IS THE QUIET BOY I'VE BEEN CRUSHING ON. HE LIVES DOWN THE STREET FROM ME, AND SITS IN FRONT OF ME IN GEOGRAPHY.
AND HIS GRANDMOTHER JUST DIED. NOW ALL HE HAS IS THAT SILLY CAT HE HIDES IN HIS BAG.
YOU'RE NOT GONNA EAT THAT JUNK, ARE YOU?
HUH? OH. HEY, NICKY, I...
CHEEZEE

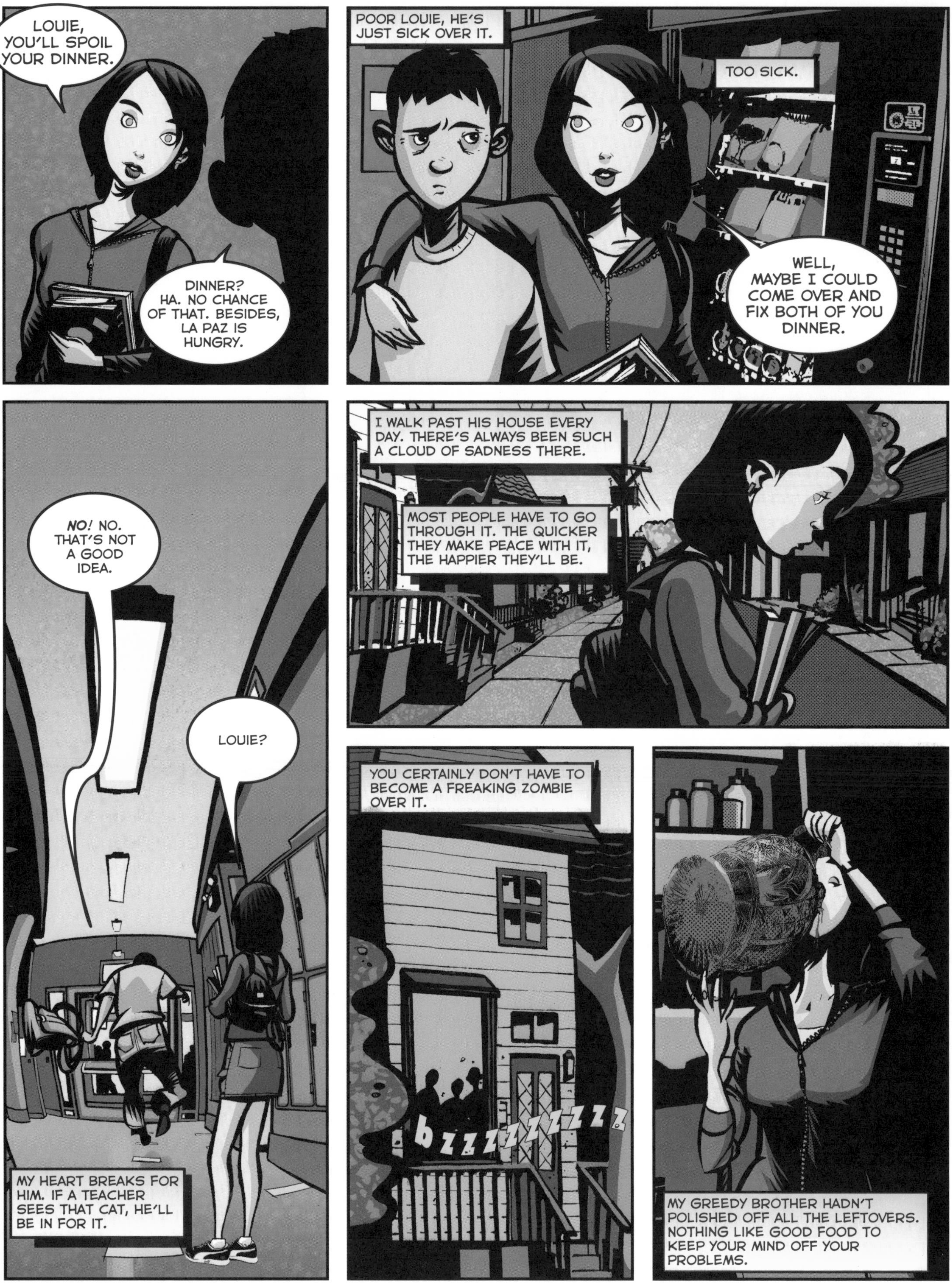
LOUIE, YOU'LL SPOIL YOUR DINNER.
DINNER? HA. NO CHANCE OF THAT. BESIDES, LA PAZ IS HUNGRY.
POOR LOUIE, HE'S JUST SICK OVER IT.
TOO SICK.
WELL, MAYBE I COULD COME OVER AND FIX BOTH OF YOU DINNER.
NO! NO. THAT'S NOT A GOOD IDEA.
LOUIE?
MY HEART BREAKS FOR HIM. IF A TEACHER SEES THAT CAT, HE'LL BE IN FOR IT.
I WALK PAST HIS HOUSE EVERY DAY. THERE'S ALWAYS BEEN SUCH A CLOUD OF SADNESS THERE.
MOST PEOPLE HAVE TO GO THROUGH IT. THE QUICKER THEY MAKE PEACE WITH IT, THE HAPPIER THEY'LL BE.
YOU CERTAINLY DON'T HAVE TO BECOME A FREAKING ZOMBIE OVER IT.
bzzzzzzzzzz
MY GREEDY BROTHER HADN'T POLISHED OFF ALL THE LEFTOVERS. NOTHING LIKE GOOD FOOD TO KEEP YOUR MIND OFF YOUR PROBLEMS.

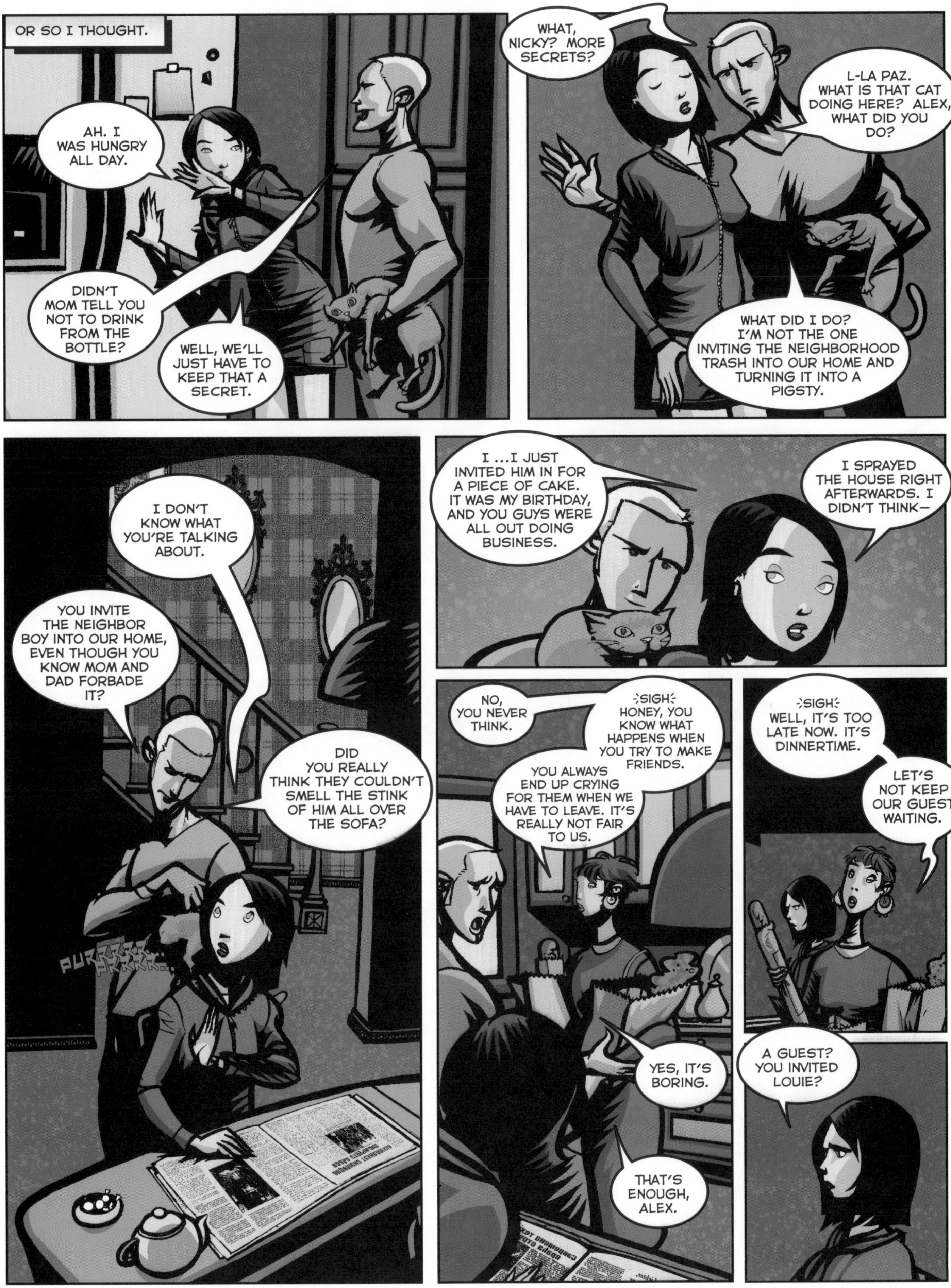
OR SO I THOUGHT.
AH. I WAS HUNGRY ALL DAY.
DIDN'T MOM TELL YOU NOT TO DRINK FROM THE BOTTLE?
WELL, WE'LL JUST HAVE TO KEEP THAT A SECRET.
WHAT, NICKY? MORE SECRETS?
L-LA PAZ. WHAT IS THAT CAT DOING HERE? ALEX, WHAT DID YOU DO?
WHAT DID I DO? I'M NOT THE ONE INVITING THE NEIGHBORHOOD TRASH INTO OUR HOME AND TURNING IT INTO A PIGSTY.
I DON'T KNOW WHAT YOU'RE TALKING ABOUT.
YOU INVITE THE NEIGHBOR BOY INTO OUR HOME, EVEN THOUGH YOU KNOW MOM AND DAD FORBADE IT?
DID YOU REALLY THINK THEY COULDN'T SMELL THE STINK OF HIM ALL OVER THE SOFA?
I ...I JUST INVITED HIM IN FOR A PIECE OF CAKE. IT WAS MY BIRTHDAY, AND YOU GUYS WERE ALL OUT DOING BUSINESS.
I SPRAYED THE HOUSE RIGHT AFTERWARDS. I DIDN'T THINK—
NO, YOU NEVER THINK.
SIGH
HONEY, YOU KNOW WHAT HAPPENS WHEN YOU TRY TO MAKE FRIENDS.
YOU ALWAYS END UP CRYING FOR THEM WHEN WE HAVE TO LEAVE. IT'S REALLY NOT FAIR TO US.
YES, IT'S BORING.
THAT'S ENOUGH, ALEX.
SIGH
WELL, IT'S TOO LATE NOW. IT'S DINNERTIME.
LET'S NOT KEEP OUR GUEST WAITING.
A GUEST? YOU INVITED LOUIE?

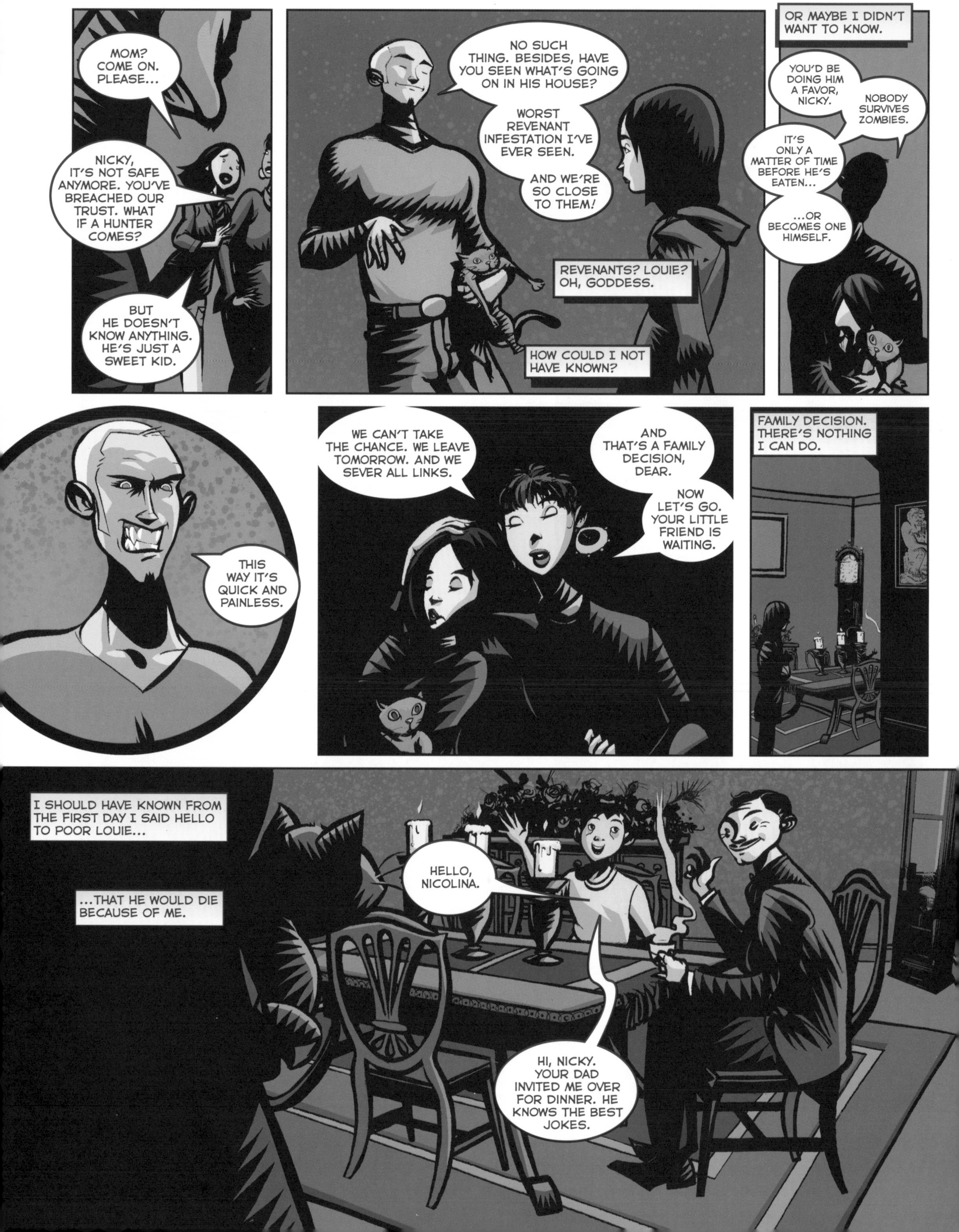

MOM? COME ON. PLEASE...
NICKY, IT'S NOT SAFE ANYMORE. YOU'VE BREACHED OUR TRUST. WHAT IF A HUNTER COMES?
BUT HE DOESN'T KNOW ANYTHING. HE'S JUST A SWEET KID.
NO SUCH THING. BESIDES, HAVE YOU SEEN WHAT'S GOING ON IN HIS HOUSE?
WORST REVENANT INFESTATION I'VE EVER SEEN.
AND WE'RE SO CLOSE TO THEM!
REVENANTS? LOUIE? OH, GODDESS.
HOW COULD I NOT HAVE KNOWN?
OR MAYBE I DIDN'T WANT TO KNOW.
YOU'D BE DOING HIM A FAVOR, NICKY.
NOBODY SURVIVES ZOMBIES.
IT'S ONLY A MATTER OF TIME BEFORE HE'S EATEN...
...OR BECOMES ONE HIMSELF.
THIS WAY IT'S QUICK AND PAINLESS.
WE CAN'T TAKE THE CHANCE. WE LEAVE TOMORROW. AND WE SEVER ALL LINKS.
AND THAT'S A FAMILY DECISION, DEAR.
NOW LET'S GO. YOUR LITTLE FRIEND IS WAITING.
FAMILY DECISION. THERE'S NOTHING I CAN DO.
I SHOULD HAVE KNOWN FROM THE FIRST DAY I SAID HELLO TO POOR LOUIE...
...THAT HE WOULD DIE BECAUSE OF ME.
HELLO, NICOLINA.
HI, NICKY. YOUR DAD INVITED ME OVER FOR DINNER. HE KNOWS THE BEST JOKES.

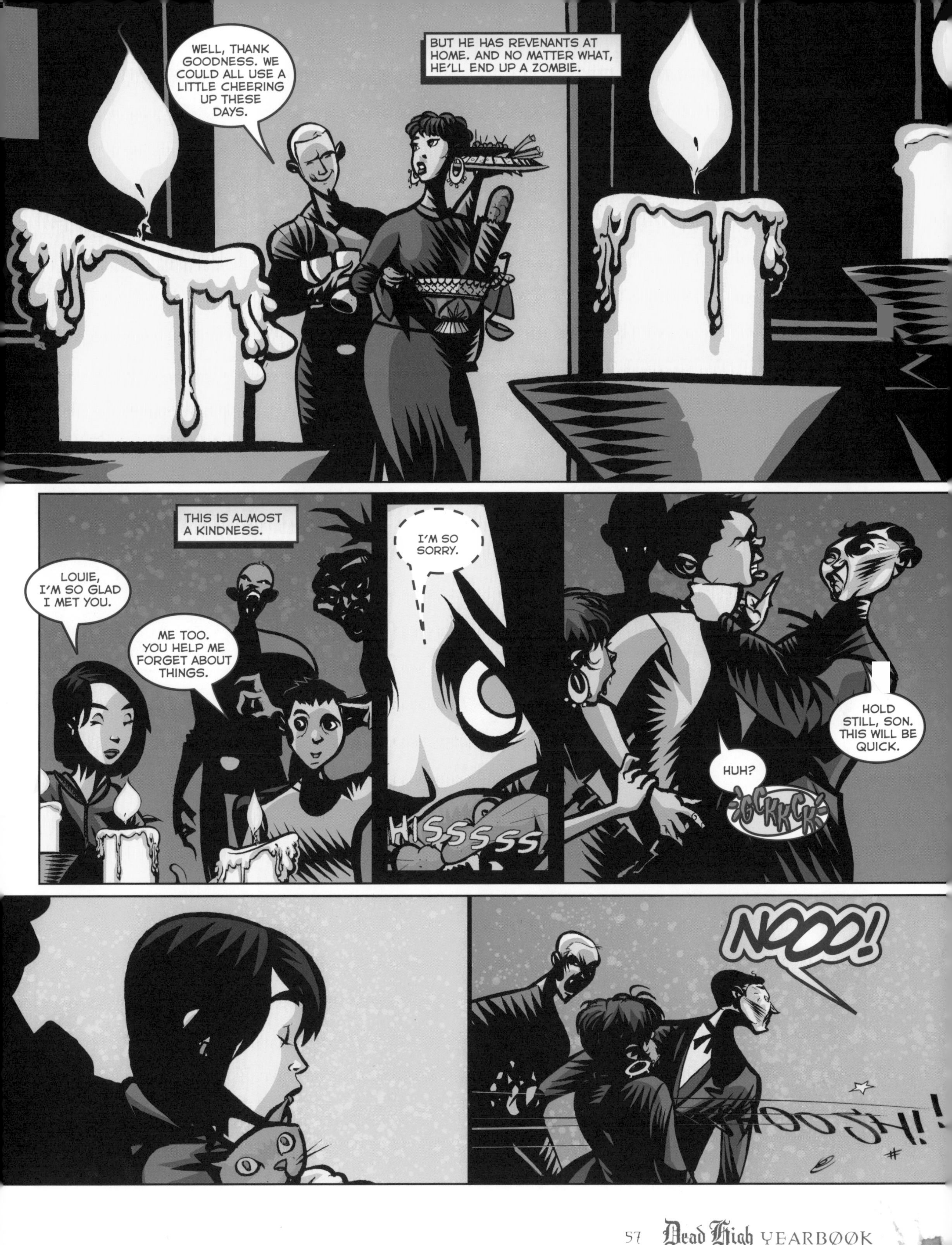
WELL, THANK GOODNESS. WE COULD ALL USE A LITTLE CHEERING UP THESE DAYS.
BUT HE HAS REVENANTS AT HOME. AND NO MATTER WHAT, HE'LL END UP A ZOMBIE.
THIS IS ALMOST A KINDNESS.
LOUIE, I'M SO GLAD I MET YOU.
ME TOO. YOU HELP ME FORGET ABOUT THINGS.
I'M SO SORRY.
HISSSSSS
HOLD STILL, SON. THIS WILL BE QUICK.
HUH?
-GCKKGK-
NOOO!
WOOSH!!

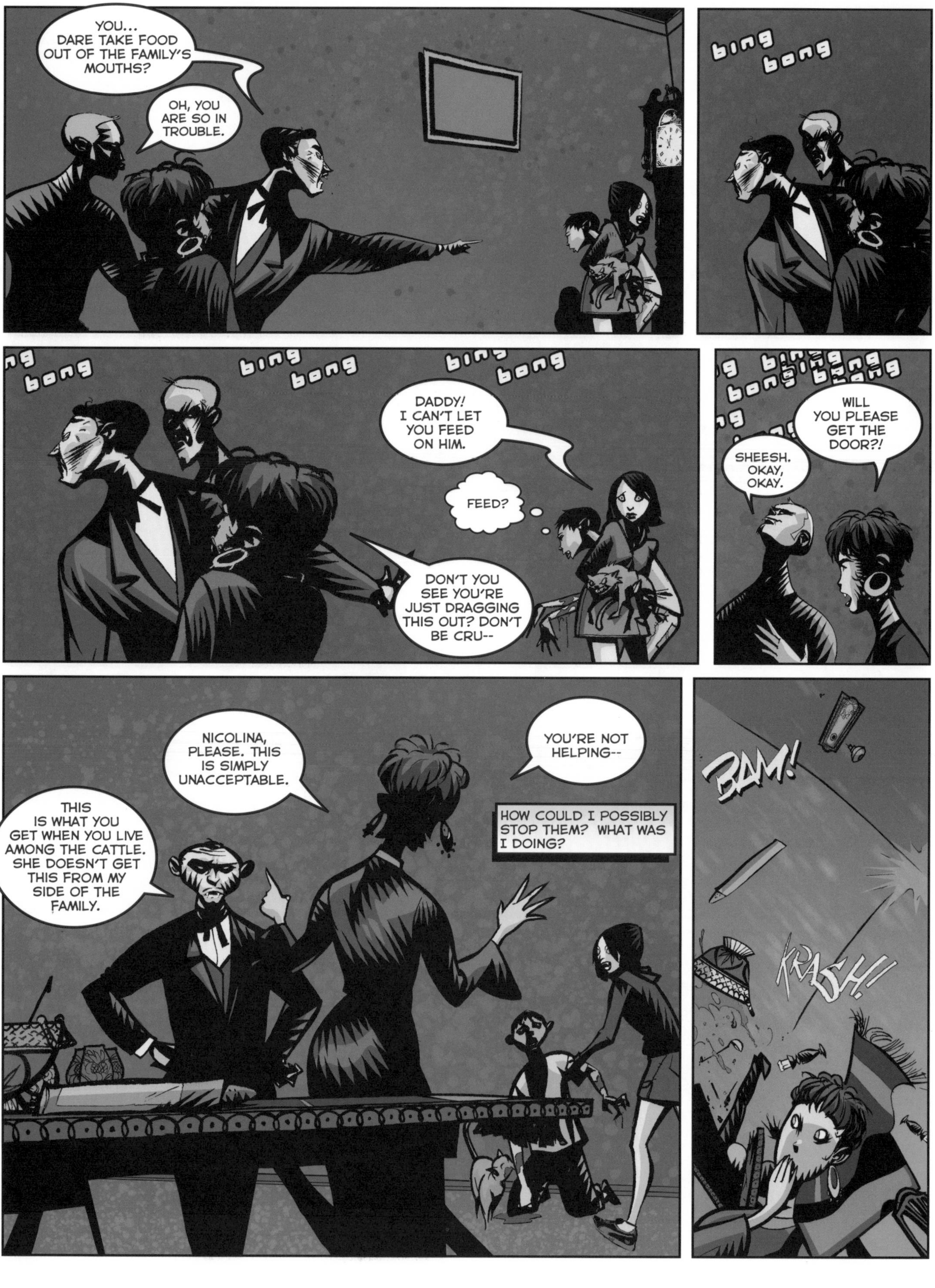
YOU... DARE TAKE FOOD OUT OF THE FAMILY'S MOUTHS?
OH, YOU ARE SO IN TROUBLE.
bing bong
bing bong
bing bong
bing bong
DADDY! I CAN'T LET YOU FEED ON HIM.
FEED?
DON'T YOU SEE YOU'RE JUST DRAGGING THIS OUT? DON'T BE CRU--
WILL YOU PLEASE GET THE DOOR?!
SHEESH. OKAY, OKAY.
NICOLINA, PLEASE. THIS IS SIMPLY UNACCEPTABLE.
YOU'RE NOT HELPING--
THIS IS WHAT YOU GET WHEN YOU LIVE AMONG THE CATTLE. SHE DOESN'T GET THIS FROM MY SIDE OF THE FAMILY.
HOW COULD I POSSIBLY STOP THEM? WHAT WAS I DOING?
BAM!
KRASH!!

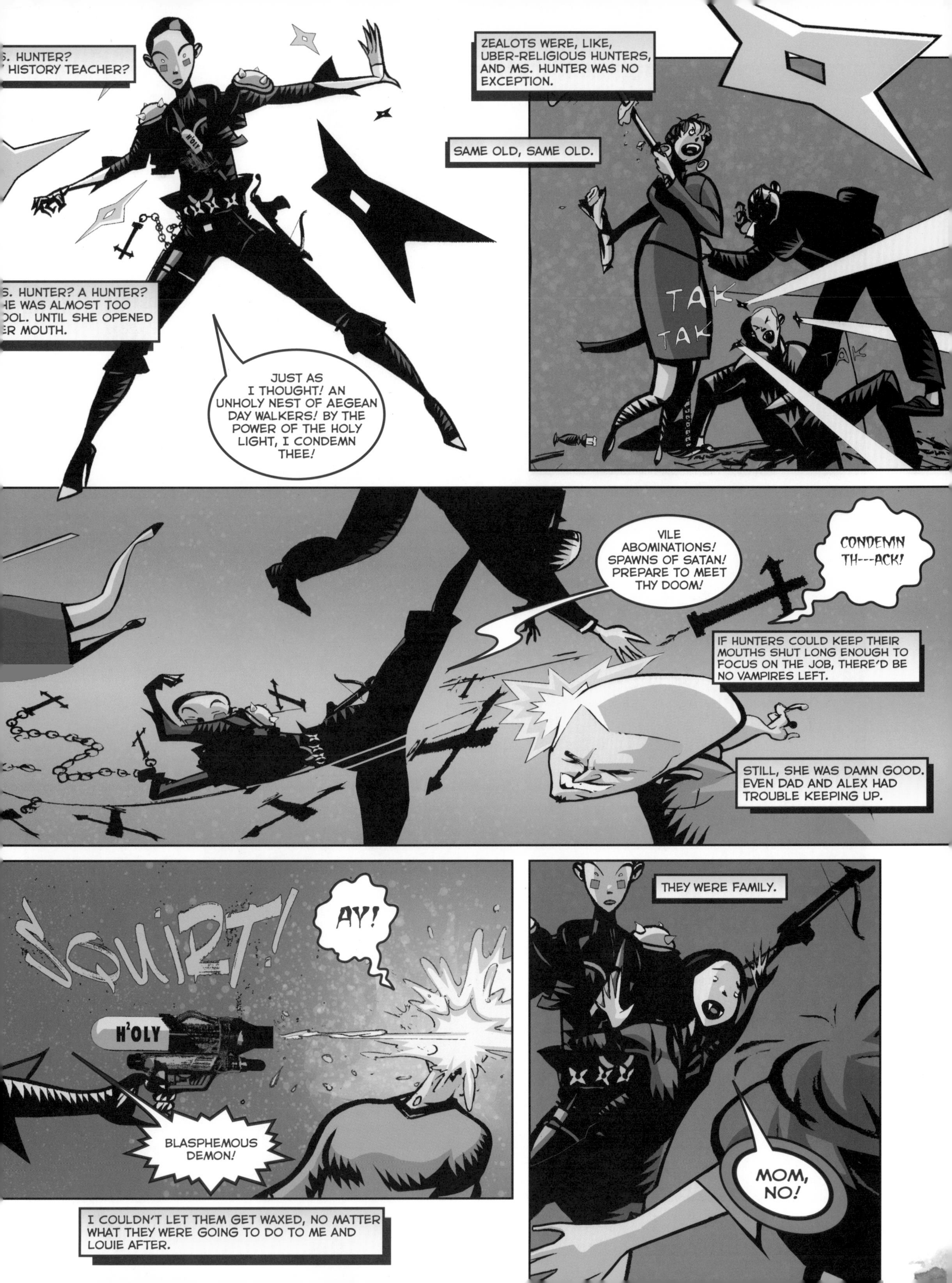

S. HUNTER? HISTORY TEACHER?
S. HUNTER? A HUNTER? HE WAS ALMOST TOO OOL. UNTIL SHE OPENED ER MOUTH.
JUST AS I THOUGHT! AN UNHOLY NEST OF AEGEAN DAY WALKERS! BY THE POWER OF THE HOLY LIGHT, I CONDEMN THEE!
ZEALOTS WERE, LIKE, UBER-RELIGIOUS HUNTERS, AND MS. HUNTER WAS NO EXCEPTION.
SAME OLD, SAME OLD.
TAK
TAK
TAK
VILE ABOMINATIONS! SPAWNS OF SATAN! PREPARE TO MEET THY DOOM!
CONDEMN TH---ACK!
IF HUNTERS COULD KEEP THEIR MOUTHS SHUT LONG ENOUGH TO FOCUS ON THE JOB, THERE'D BE NO VAMPIRES LEFT.
STILL, SHE WAS DAMN GOOD. EVEN DAD AND ALEX HAD TROUBLE KEEPING UP.
SQUIRT!
AY!
H²OLY
BLASPHEMOUS DEMON!
I COULDN'T LET THEM GET WAXED, NO MATTER WHAT THEY WERE GOING TO DO TO ME AND LOUIE AFTER.
THEY WERE FAMILY.
MOM, NO!

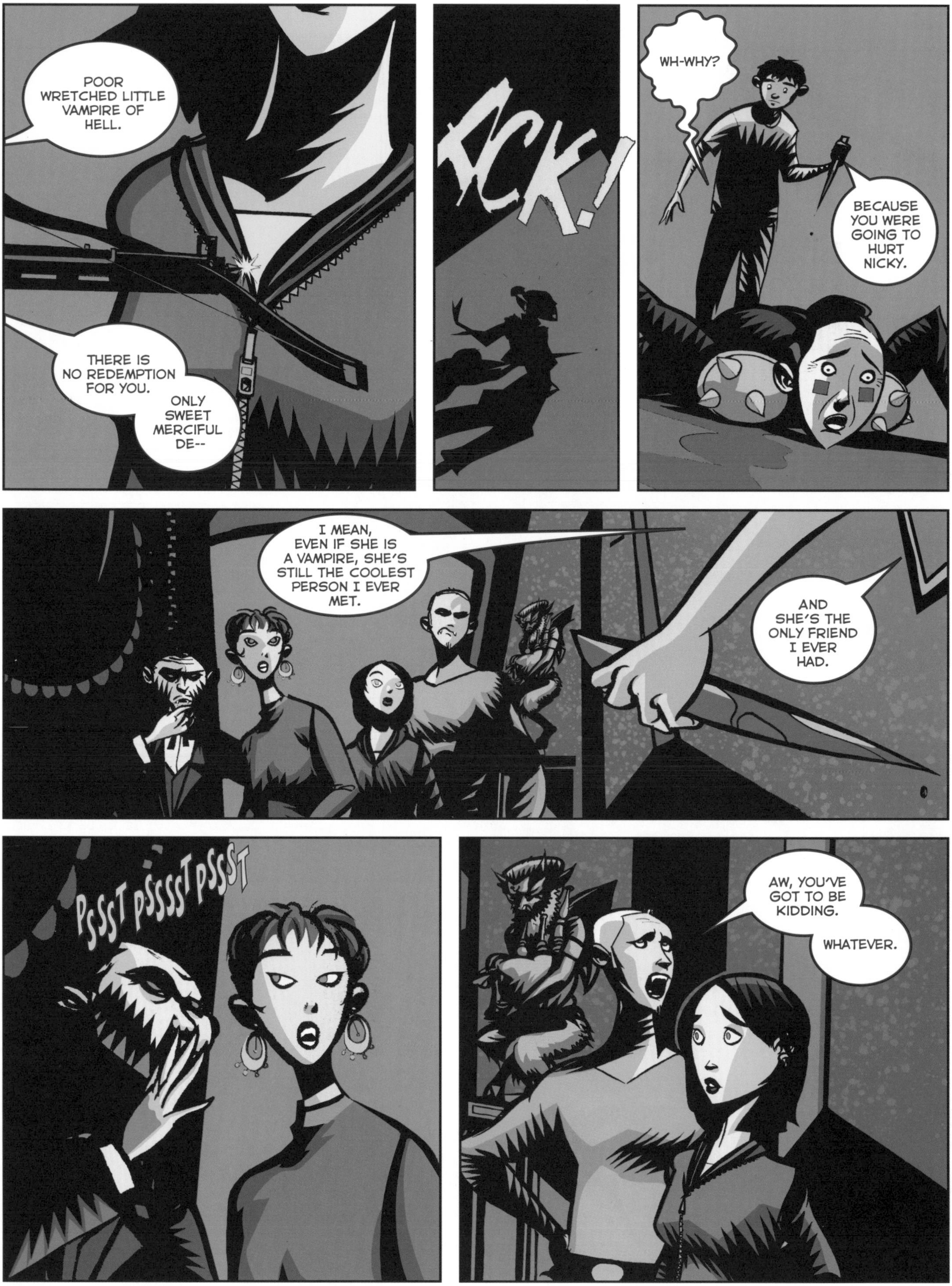
POOR WRETCHED LITTLE VAMPIRE OF HELL.
THERE IS NO REDEMPTION FOR YOU.
ONLY SWEET MERCIFUL DE--
ACK!
WH-WHY?
BECAUSE YOU WERE GOING TO HURT NICKY.
I MEAN, EVEN IF SHE IS A VAMPIRE, SHE'S STILL THE COOLEST PERSON I EVER MET.
AND SHE'S THE ONLY FRIEND I EVER HAD.
PSSST PSSSST PSSST
AW, YOU'VE GOT TO BE KIDDING.
WHATEVER.

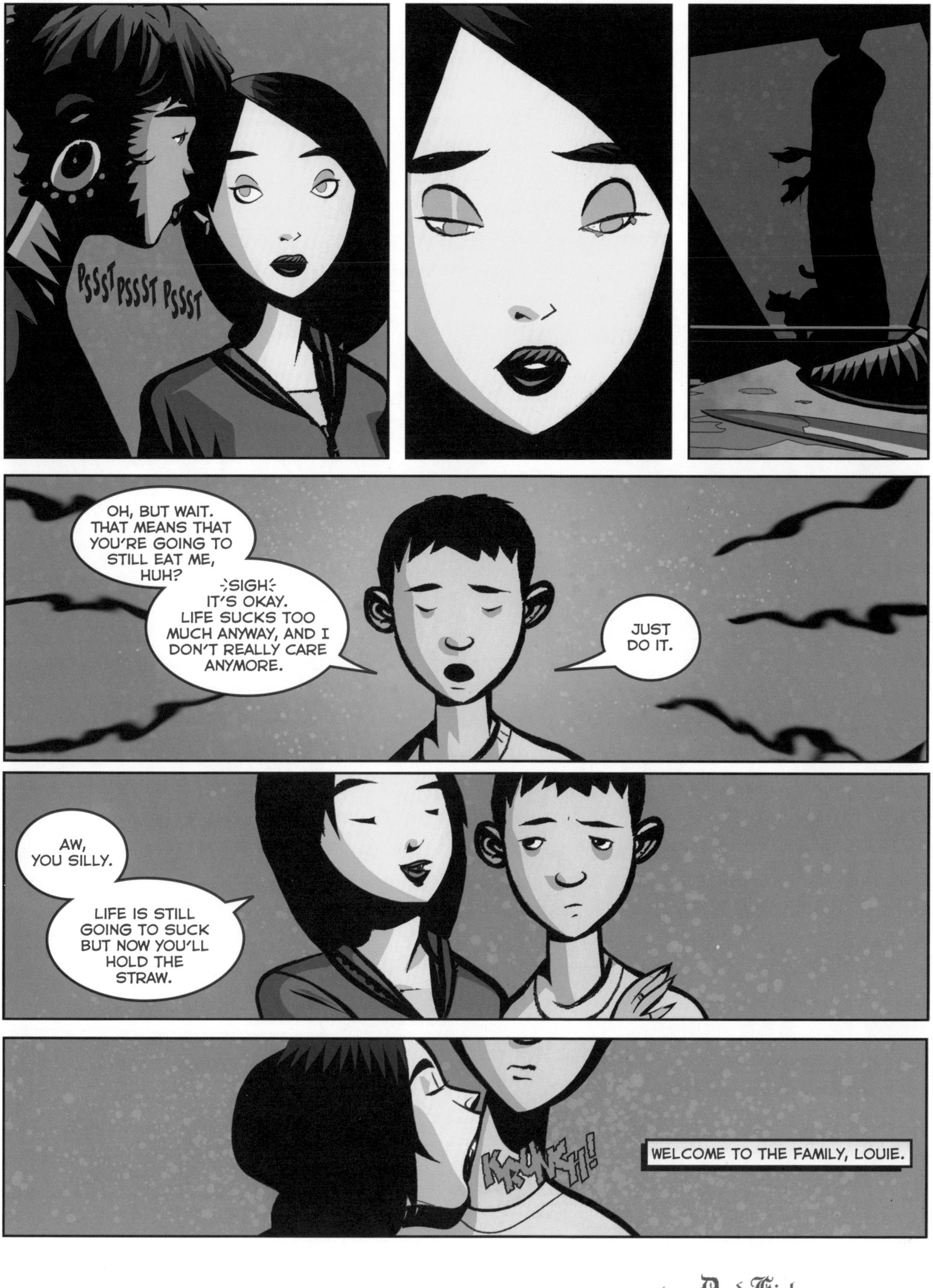
PSSST PSSST PSSST
OH, BUT WAIT. THAT MEANS THAT YOU'RE GOING TO STILL EAT ME, HUH?
-SIGH- IT'S OKAY. LIFE SUCKS TOO MUCH ANYWAY, AND I DON'T REALLY CARE ANYMORE.
JUST DO IT.
AW, YOU SILLY.
LIFE IS STILL GOING TO SUCK BUT NOW YOU'LL HOLD THE STRAW.
KRUNSH!
WELCOME TO THE FAMILY, LOUIE.

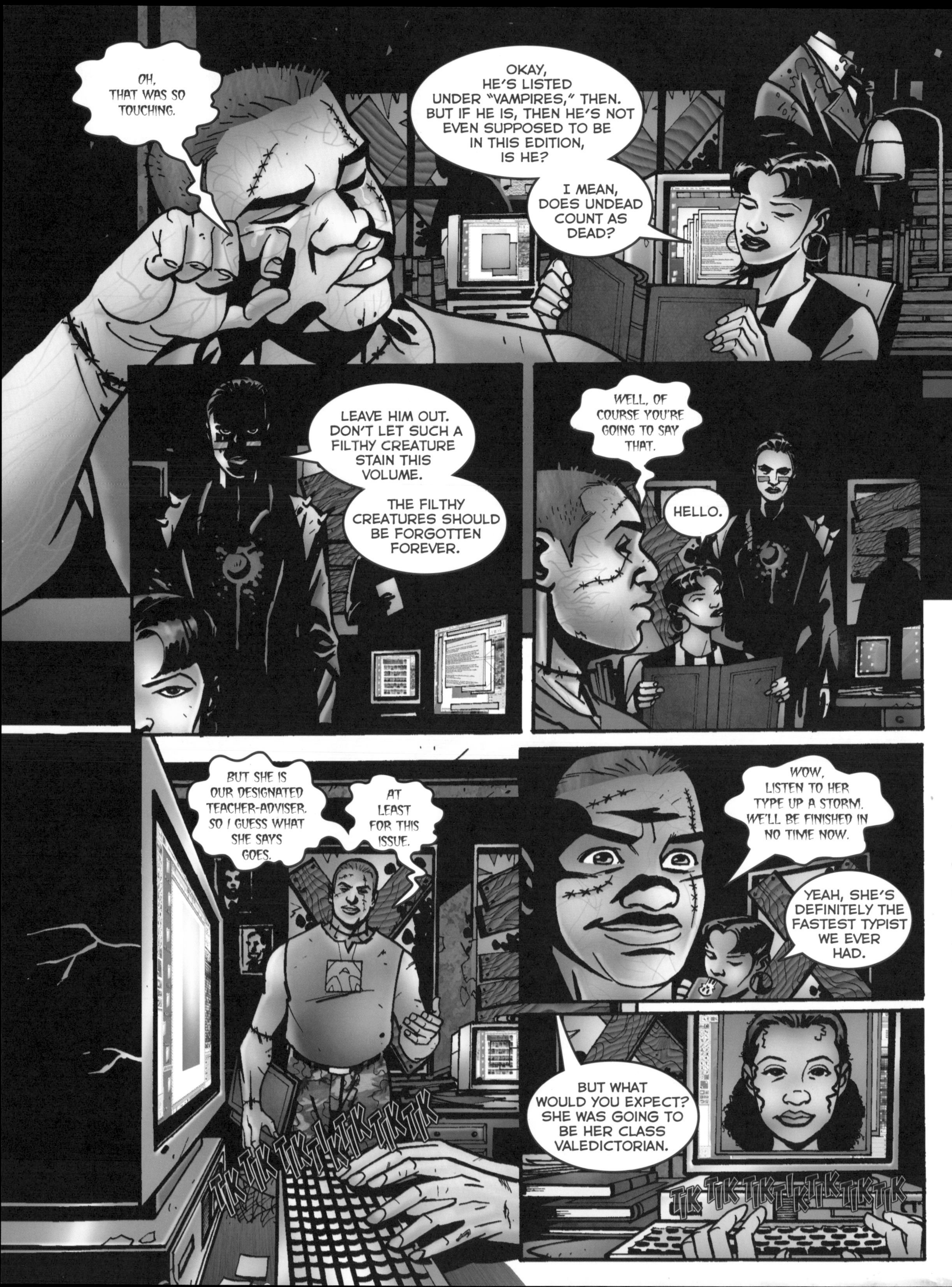
OH, THAT WAS SO TOUCHING.
OKAY, HE'S LISTED UNDER "VAMPIRES," THEN. BUT IF HE IS, THEN HE'S NOT EVEN SUPPOSED TO BE IN THIS EDITION, IS HE?
I MEAN, DOES UNDEAD COUNT AS DEAD?
LEAVE HIM OUT. DON'T LET SUCH A FILTHY CREATURE STAIN THIS VOLUME.
THE FILTHY CREATURES SHOULD BE FORGOTTEN FOREVER.
WELL, OF COURSE YOU'RE GOING TO SAY THAT.
HELLO.
BUT SHE IS OUR DESIGNATED TEACHER-ADVISER. SO I GUESS WHAT SHE SAYS GOES.
AT LEAST FOR THIS ISSUE.
TIKTIKTIKTIKTIKTIKTIKTIK
WOW, LISTEN TO HER TYPE UP A STORM. WE'LL BE FINISHED IN NO TIME NOW.
YEAH, SHE'S DEFINITELY THE FASTEST TYPIST WE EVER HAD.
BUT WHAT WOULD YOU EXPECT? SHE WAS GOING TO BE HER CLASS VALEDICTORIAN.
TIKTIKTIKTIKTIKTIKTIKTIK

Head of the Class

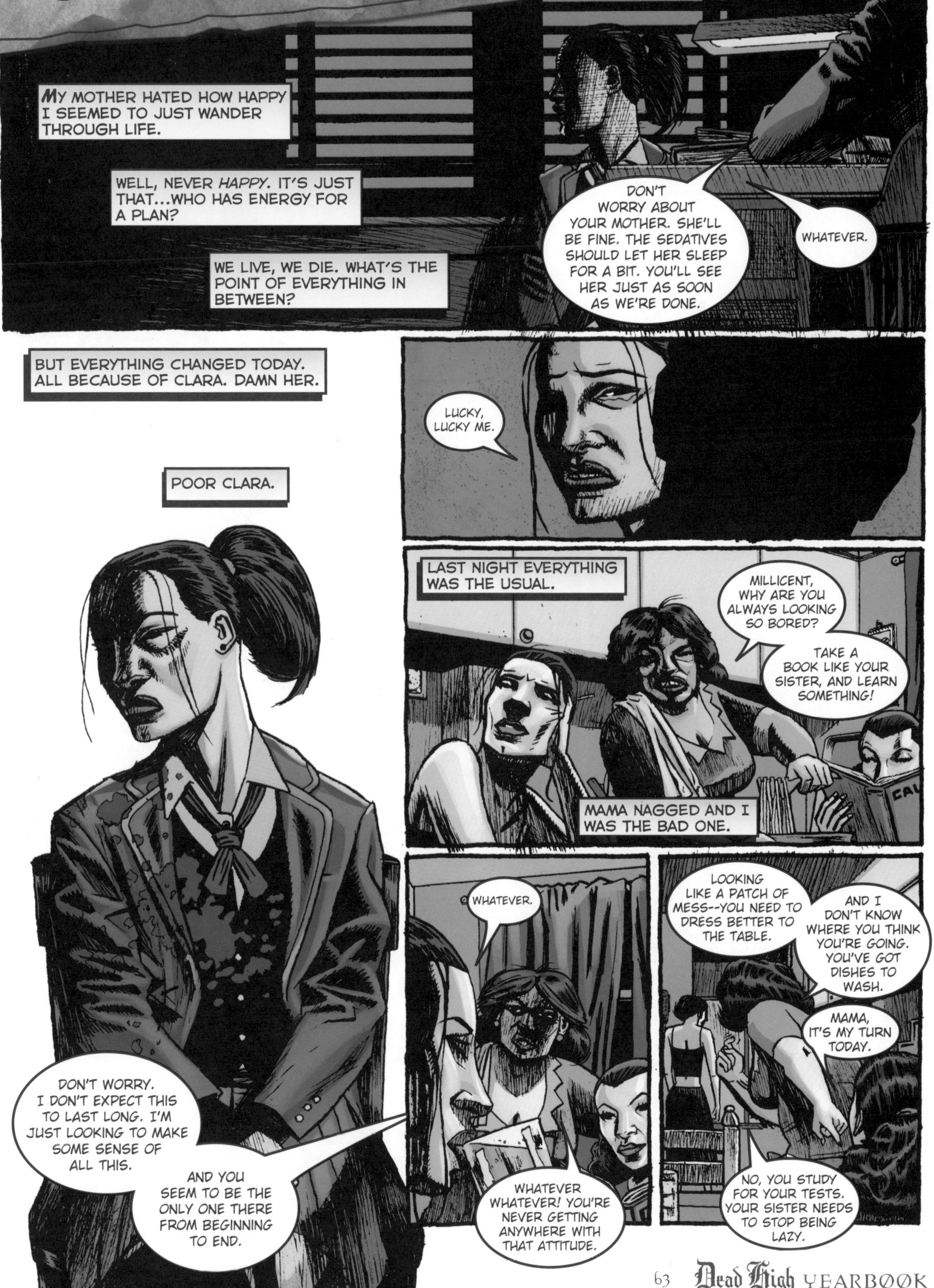
MY MOTHER HATED HOW HAPPY I SEEMED TO JUST WANDER THROUGH LIFE.
WELL, NEVER *HAPPY*. IT'S JUST THAT...WHO HAS ENERGY FOR A PLAN?
WE LIVE, WE DIE. WHAT'S THE POINT OF EVERYTHING IN BETWEEN?
DON'T WORRY ABOUT YOUR MOTHER. SHE'LL BE FINE. THE SEDATIVES SHOULD LET HER SLEEP FOR A BIT. YOU'LL SEE HER JUST AS SOON AS WE'RE DONE.
WHATEVER.
BUT EVERYTHING CHANGED TODAY. ALL BECAUSE OF CLARA. DAMN HER.
LUCKY, LUCKY ME.
POOR CLARA.
LAST NIGHT EVERYTHING WAS THE USUAL.
MILLICENT, WHY ARE YOU ALWAYS LOOKING SO BORED?
TAKE A BOOK LIKE YOUR SISTER, AND LEARN SOMETHING!
MAMA NAGGED AND I WAS THE BAD ONE.
WHATEVER.
WHATEVER WHATEVER! YOU'RE NEVER GETTING ANYWHERE WITH THAT ATTITUDE.
LOOKING LIKE A PATCH OF MESS--YOU NEED TO DRESS BETTER TO THE TABLE.
AND I DON'T KNOW WHERE YOU THINK YOU'RE GOING. YOU'VE GOT DISHES TO WASH.
MAMA, IT'S MY TURN TODAY.
NO, YOU STUDY FOR YOUR TESTS. YOUR SISTER NEEDS TO STOP BEING LAZY.
DON'T WORRY. I DON'T EXPECT THIS TO LAST LONG. I'M JUST LOOKING TO MAKE SOME SENSE OF ALL THIS.
AND YOU SEEM TO BE THE ONLY ONE THERE FROM BEGINNING TO END.

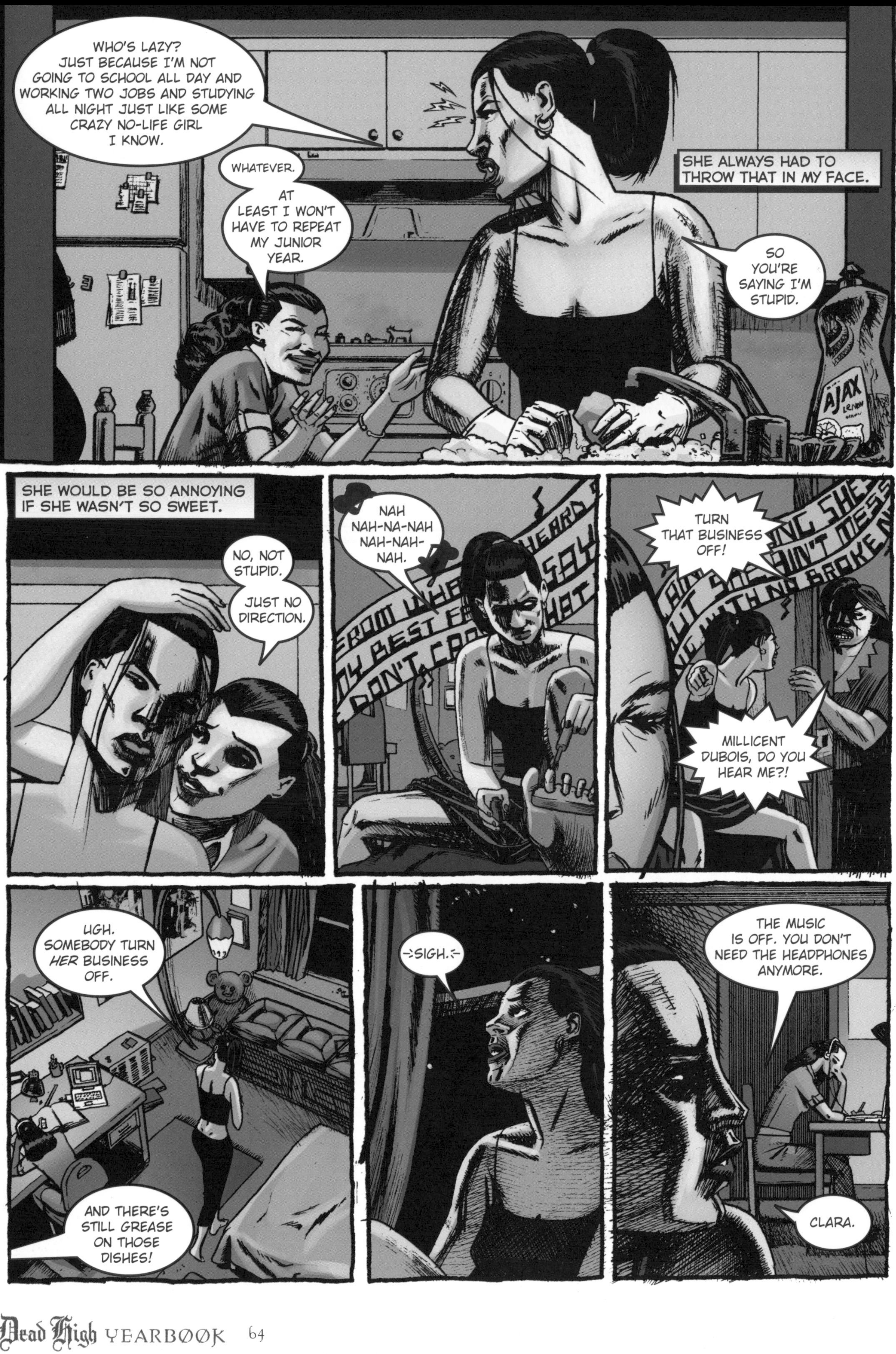
WHO'S LAZY? JUST BECAUSE I'M NOT GOING TO SCHOOL ALL DAY AND WORKING TWO JOBS AND STUDYING ALL NIGHT JUST LIKE SOME CRAZY NO-LIFE GIRL I KNOW.
WHATEVER.
AT LEAST I WON'T HAVE TO REPEAT MY JUNIOR YEAR.
SHE ALWAYS HAD TO THROW THAT IN MY FACE.
SO YOU'RE SAYING I'M STUPID.
AJAX
SHE WOULD BE SO ANNOYING IF SHE WASN'T SO SWEET.
NO, NOT STUPID.
JUST NO DIRECTION.
NAH NAH-NA-NAH NAH-NAH-NAH.
TURN THAT BUSINESS OFF!
MILLICENT DUBOIS, DO YOU HEAR ME?!
UGH. SOMEBODY TURN *HER* BUSINESS OFF.
AND THERE'S STILL GREASE ON THOSE DISHES!
-SIGH.-
THE MUSIC IS OFF. YOU DON'T NEED THE HEADPHONES ANYMORE.
CLARA.

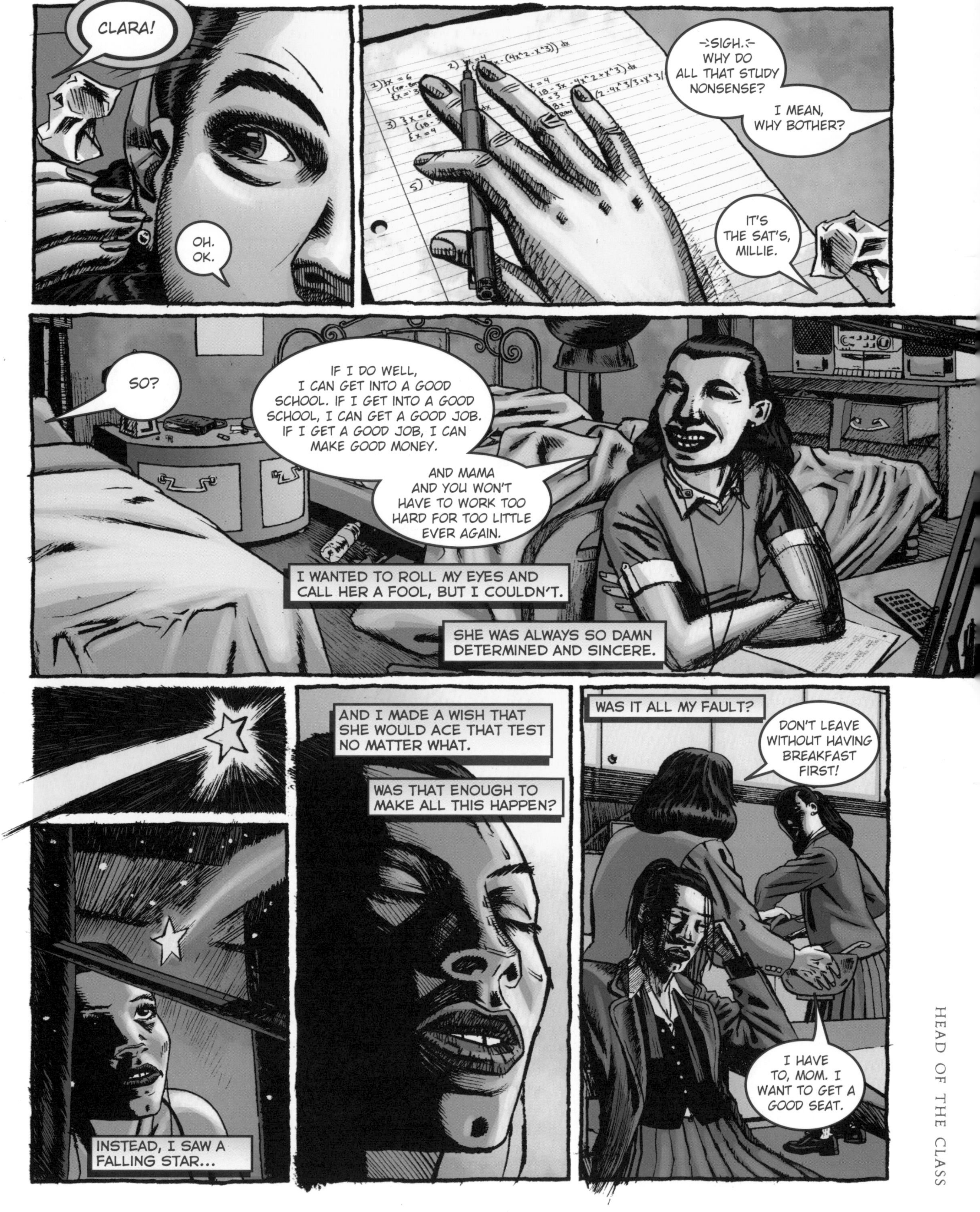
CLARA!
OH. OK.
SIGH. WHY DO ALL THAT STUDY NONSENSE?
I MEAN, WHY BOTHER?
IT'S THE SAT'S, MILLIE.
SO?
IF I DO WELL, I CAN GET INTO A GOOD SCHOOL. IF I GET INTO A GOOD SCHOOL, I CAN GET A GOOD JOB. IF I GET A GOOD JOB, I CAN MAKE GOOD MONEY.
AND MAMA AND YOU WON'T HAVE TO WORK TOO HARD FOR TOO LITTLE EVER AGAIN.
I WANTED TO ROLL MY EYES AND CALL HER A FOOL, BUT I COULDN'T.
SHE WAS ALWAYS SO DAMN DETERMINED AND SINCERE.
INSTEAD, I SAW A FALLING STAR...
AND I MADE A WISH THAT SHE WOULD ACE THAT TEST NO MATTER WHAT.
WAS THAT ENOUGH TO MAKE ALL THIS HAPPEN?
WAS IT ALL MY FAULT?
DON'T LEAVE WITHOUT HAVING BREAKFAST FIRST!
I HAVE TO, MOM. I WANT TO GET A GOOD SEAT.

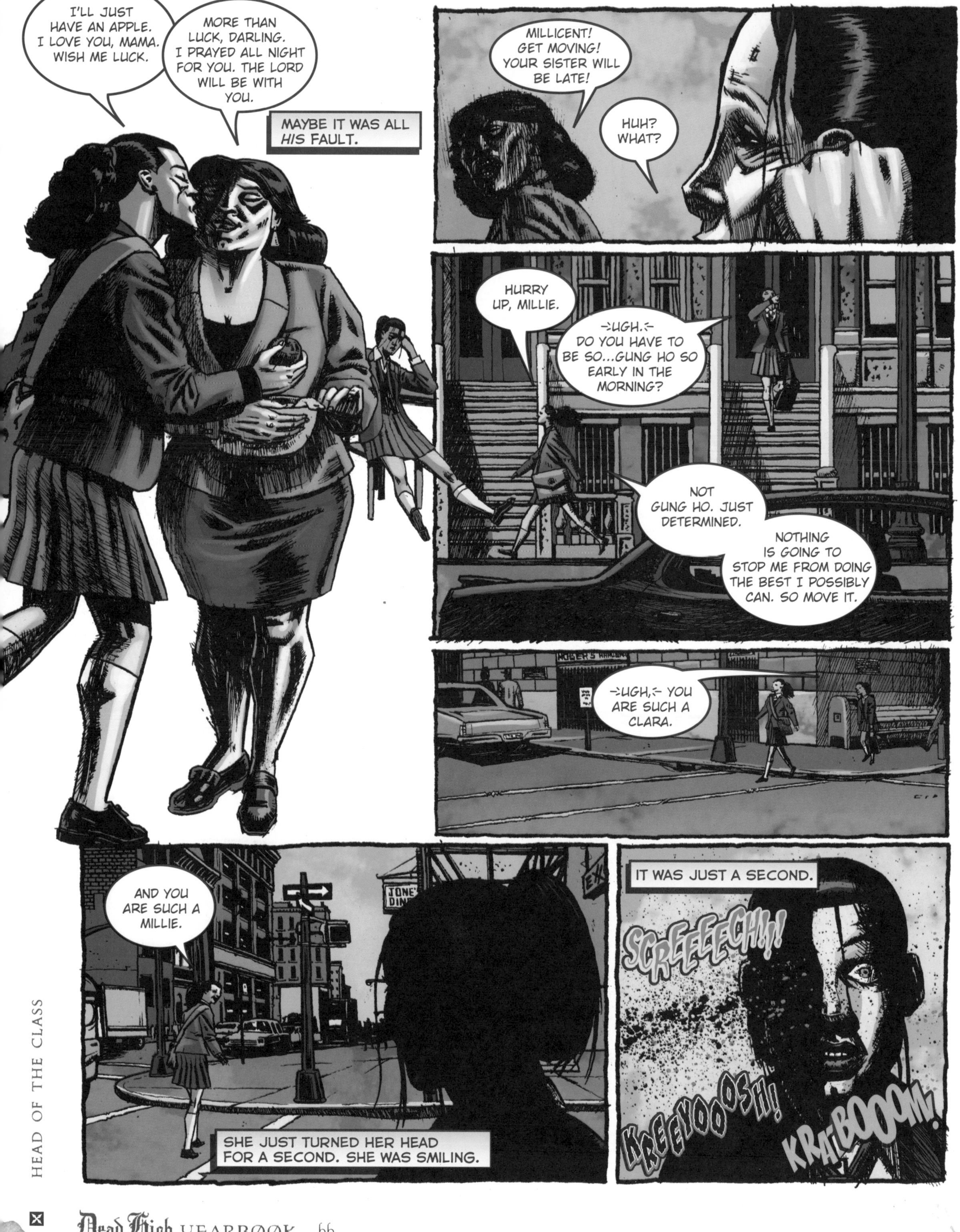
I'LL JUST HAVE AN APPLE. I LOVE YOU, MAMA. WISH ME LUCK.
MORE THAN LUCK, DARLING. I PRAYED ALL NIGHT FOR YOU. THE LORD WILL BE WITH YOU.
MAYBE IT WAS ALL *HIS* FAULT.
MILLICENT! GET MOVING! YOUR SISTER WILL BE LATE!
HUH? WHAT?
HURRY UP, MILLIE.
UGH. DO YOU HAVE TO BE SO...GUNG HO SO EARLY IN THE MORNING?
NOT GUNG HO. JUST DETERMINED.
NOTHING IS GOING TO STOP ME FROM DOING THE BEST I POSSIBLY CAN. SO MOVE IT.
UGH. YOU ARE SUCH A CLARA.
AND YOU ARE SUCH A MILLIE.
SHE JUST TURNED HER HEAD FOR A SECOND. SHE WAS SMILING.
IT WAS JUST A SECOND.
SCREEEECH!!
KREEYOOOSH!
KRA-BOOOM!

HEAD OF THE CLASS

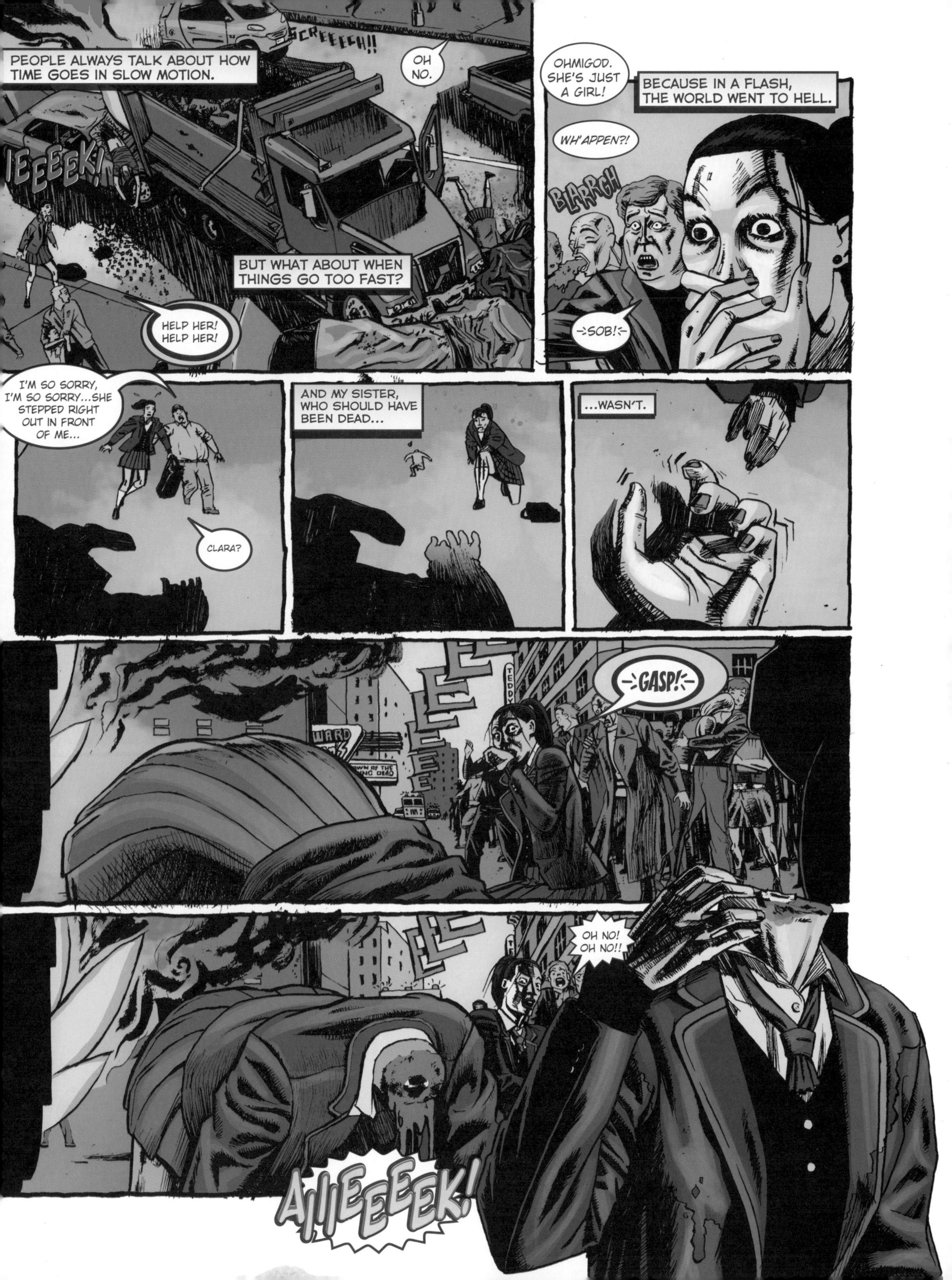
SCREEEECH!!
PEOPLE ALWAYS TALK ABOUT HOW TIME GOES IN SLOW MOTION.
OH NO.
IEEEEK!
BUT WHAT ABOUT WHEN THINGS GO TOO FAST?
HELP HER! HELP HER!
OHMIGOD. SHE'S JUST A GIRL!
BECAUSE IN A FLASH, THE WORLD WENT TO HELL.
WH'APPEN?!
BLARRGH
SOB!
I'M SO SORRY, I'M SO SORRY...SHE STEPPED RIGHT OUT IN FRONT OF ME...
CLARA?
AND MY SISTER, WHO SHOULD HAVE BEEN DEAD...
...WASN'T.
GASP!
OH NO! OH NO!!
AIIEEEEK!

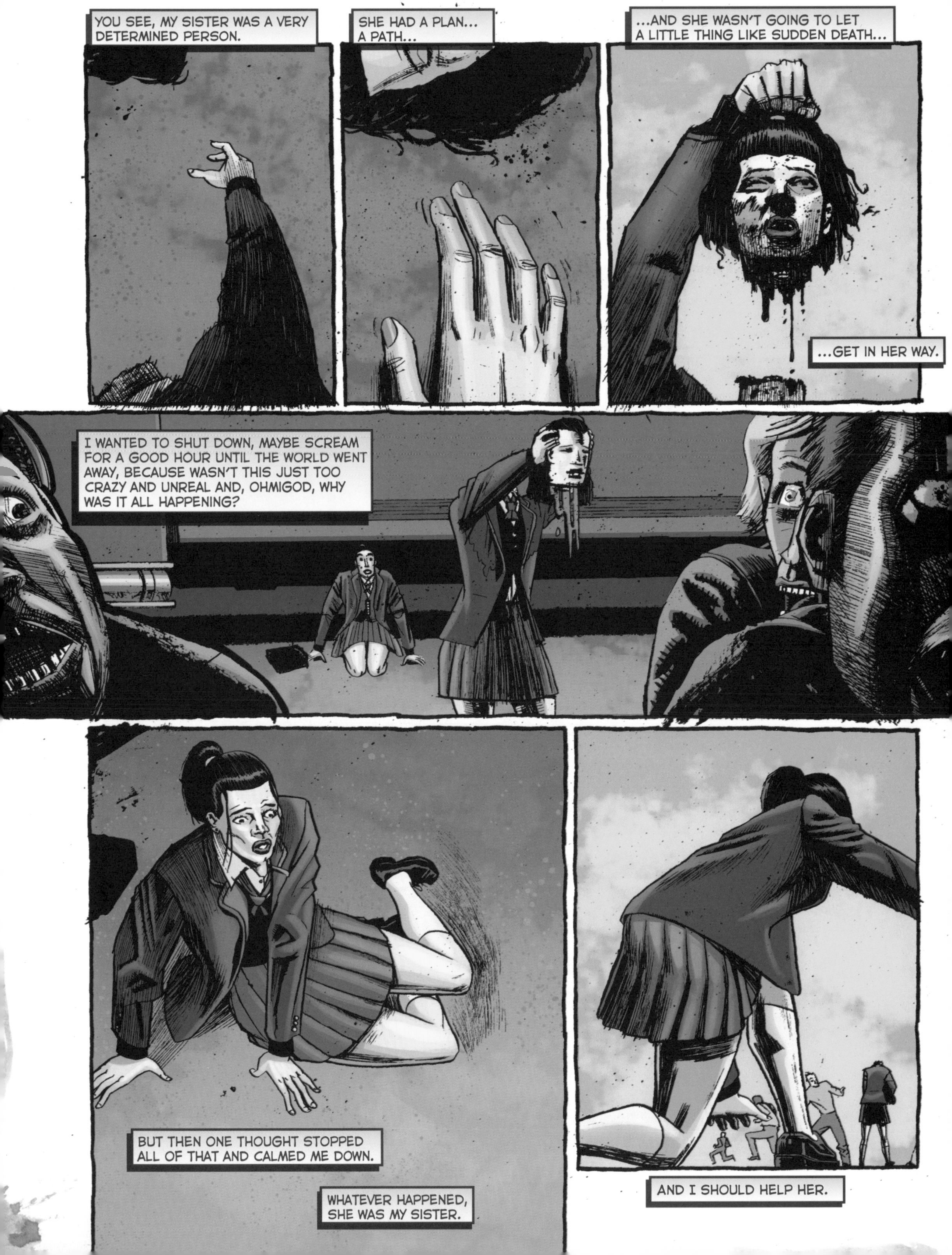
YOU SEE, MY SISTER WAS A VERY DETERMINED PERSON.
SHE HAD A PLAN... A PATH...
...AND SHE WASN'T GOING TO LET A LITTLE THING LIKE SUDDEN DEATH...
...GET IN HER WAY.
I WANTED TO SHUT DOWN, MAYBE SCREAM FOR A GOOD HOUR UNTIL THE WORLD WENT AWAY, BECAUSE WASN'T THIS JUST TOO CRAZY AND UNREAL AND, OHMIGOD, WHY WAS IT ALL HAPPENING?
BUT THEN ONE THOUGHT STOPPED ALL OF THAT AND CALMED ME DOWN.
WHATEVER HAPPENED, SHE WAS MY SISTER.
AND I SHOULD HELP HER.

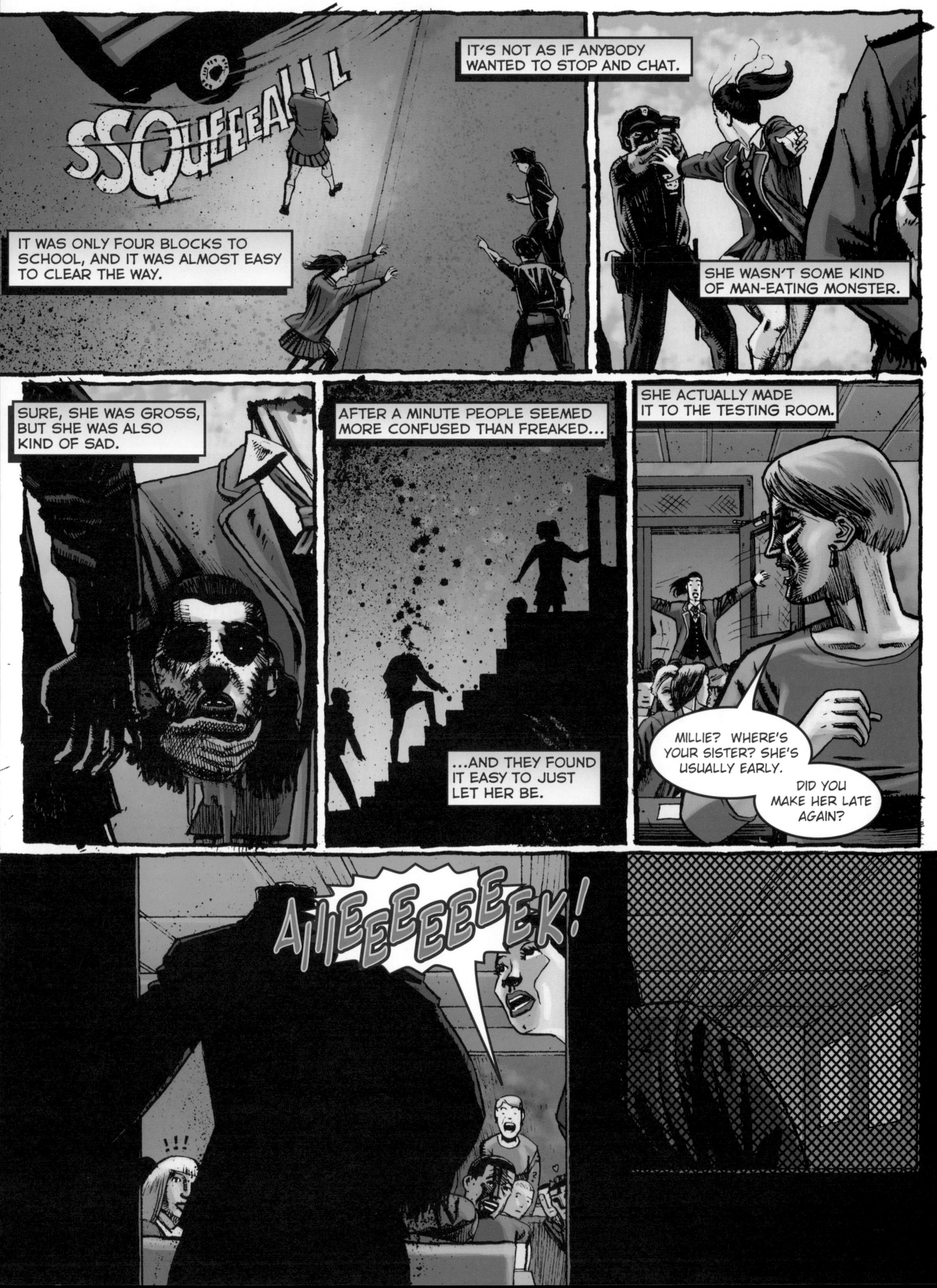

SSQUEEEALLL
IT WAS ONLY FOUR BLOCKS TO SCHOOL, AND IT WAS ALMOST EASY TO CLEAR THE WAY.
IT'S NOT AS IF ANYBODY WANTED TO STOP AND CHAT.
SHE WASN'T SOME KIND OF MAN-EATING MONSTER.
SURE, SHE WAS GROSS, BUT SHE WAS ALSO KIND OF SAD.
AFTER A MINUTE PEOPLE SEEMED MORE CONFUSED THAN FREAKED...
...AND THEY FOUND IT EASY TO JUST LET HER BE.
SHE ACTUALLY MADE IT TO THE TESTING ROOM.
MILLIE? WHERE'S YOUR SISTER? SHE'S USUALLY EARLY.
DID YOU MAKE HER LATE AGAIN?
AIIEEEEEEEK!
!!!

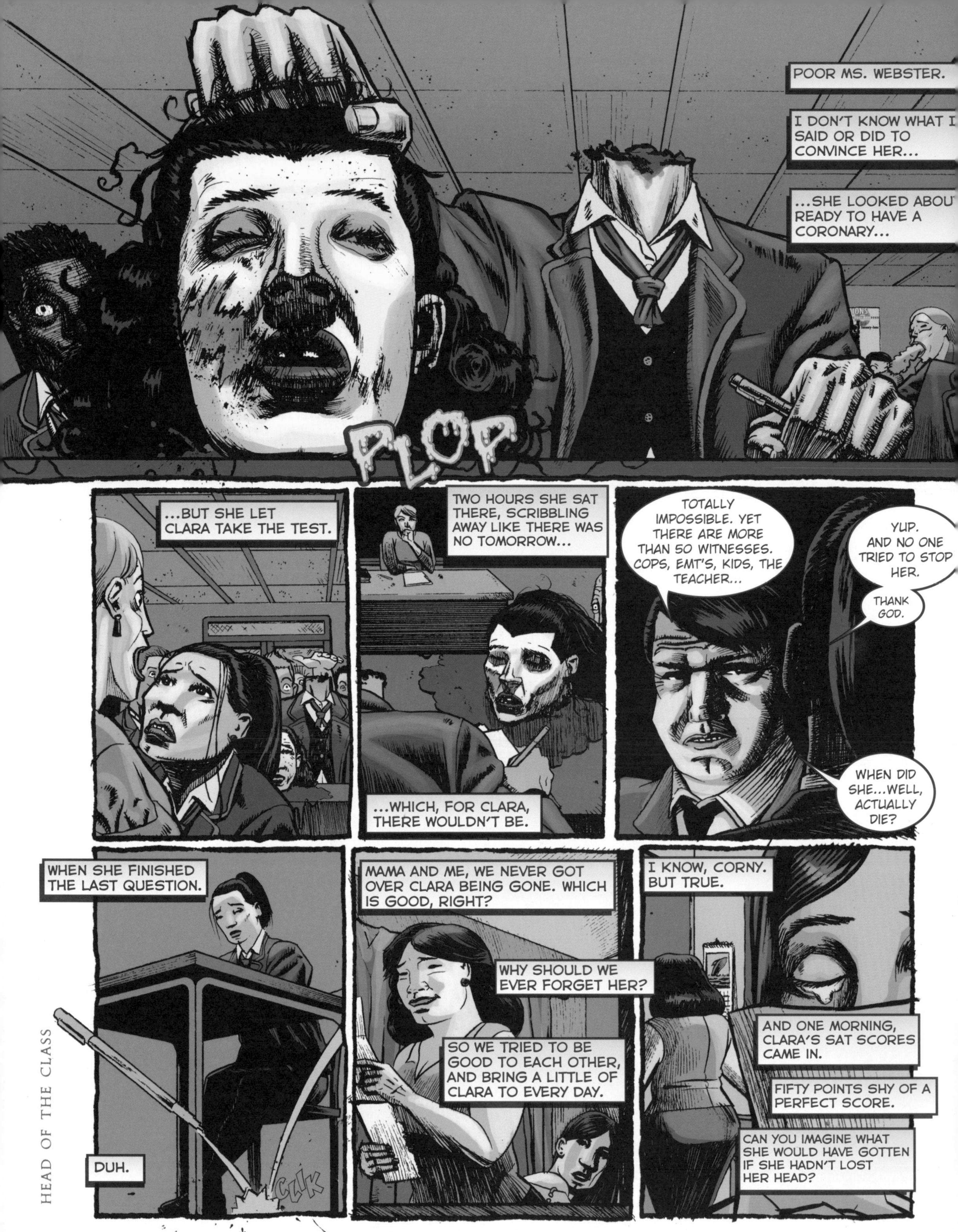
POOR MS. WEBSTER.
I DON'T KNOW WHAT I SAID OR DID TO CONVINCE HER...
...SHE LOOKED ABOU READY TO HAVE A CORONARY...
PLOP
...BUT SHE LET CLARA TAKE THE TEST.
TWO HOURS SHE SAT THERE, SCRIBBLING AWAY LIKE THERE WAS NO TOMORROW...
...WHICH, FOR CLARA, THERE WOULDN'T BE.
TOTALLY IMPOSSIBLE. YET THERE ARE MORE THAN 50 WITNESSES. COPS, EMT'S, KIDS, THE TEACHER...
YUP. AND NO ONE TRIED TO STOP HER.
THANK GOD.
WHEN DID SHE...WELL, ACTUALLY DIE?
WHEN SHE FINISHED THE LAST QUESTION.
DUH.
CLIK
MAMA AND ME, WE NEVER GOT OVER CLARA BEING GONE. WHICH IS GOOD, RIGHT?
WHY SHOULD WE EVER FORGET HER?
SO WE TRIED TO BE GOOD TO EACH OTHER, AND BRING A LITTLE OF CLARA TO EVERY DAY.
I KNOW, CORNY. BUT TRUE.
AND ONE MORNING, CLARA'S SAT SCORES CAME IN.
FIFTY POINTS SHY OF A PERFECT SCORE.
CAN YOU IMAGINE WHAT SHE WOULD HAVE GOTTEN IF SHE HADN'T LOST HER HEAD?

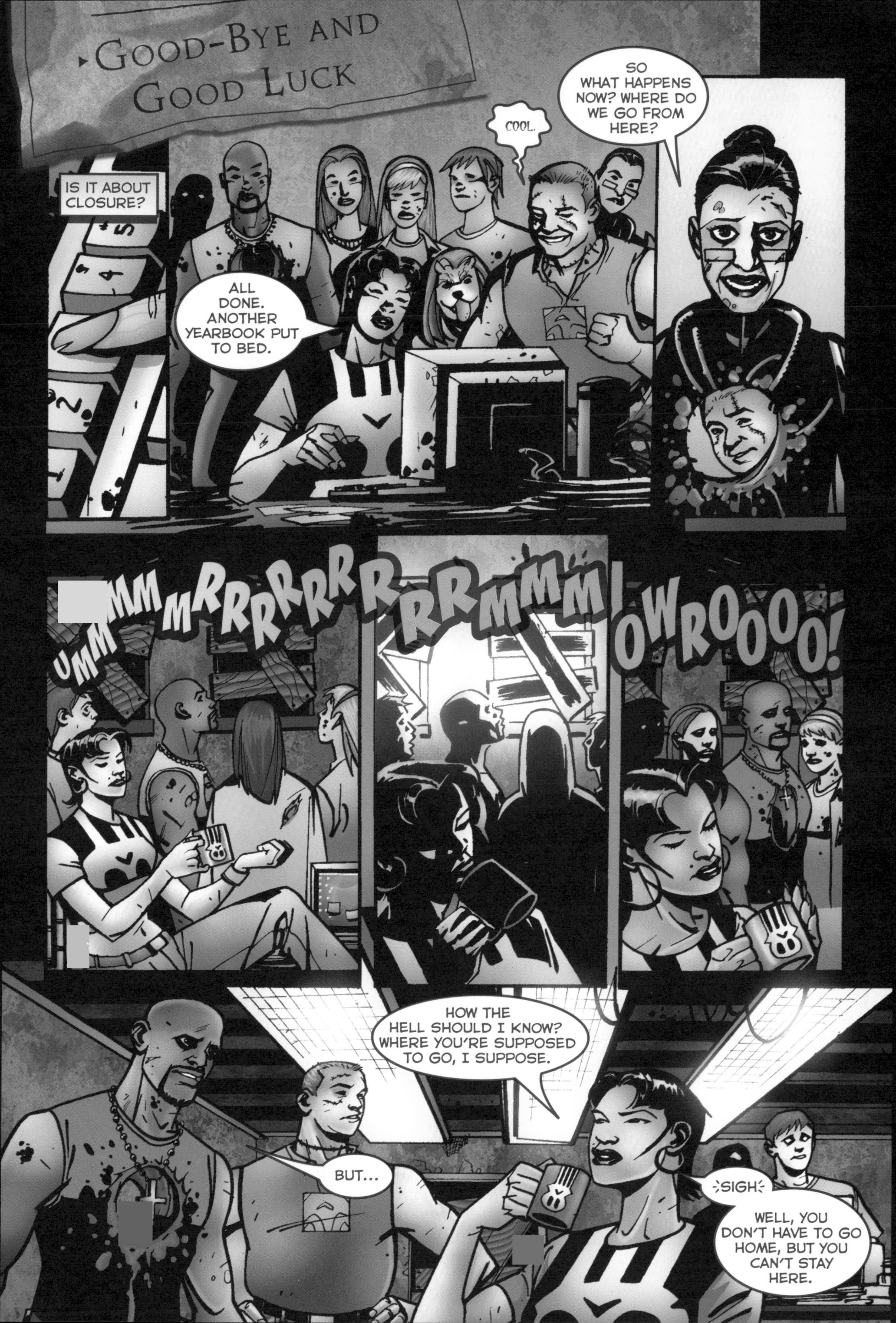
Good-Bye and Good Luck
IS IT ABOUT CLOSURE?
ALL DONE. ANOTHER YEARBOOK PUT TO BED.
COOL.
SO WHAT HAPPENS NOW? WHERE DO WE GO FROM HERE?
UMMMMMMRRRRRRRRRMMMMOWROOOO!
HOW THE HELL SHOULD I KNOW? WHERE YOU'RE SUPPOSED TO GO, I SUPPOSE.
BUT...
SIGH
WELL, YOU DON'T HAVE TO GO HOME, BUT YOU CAN'T STAY HERE.

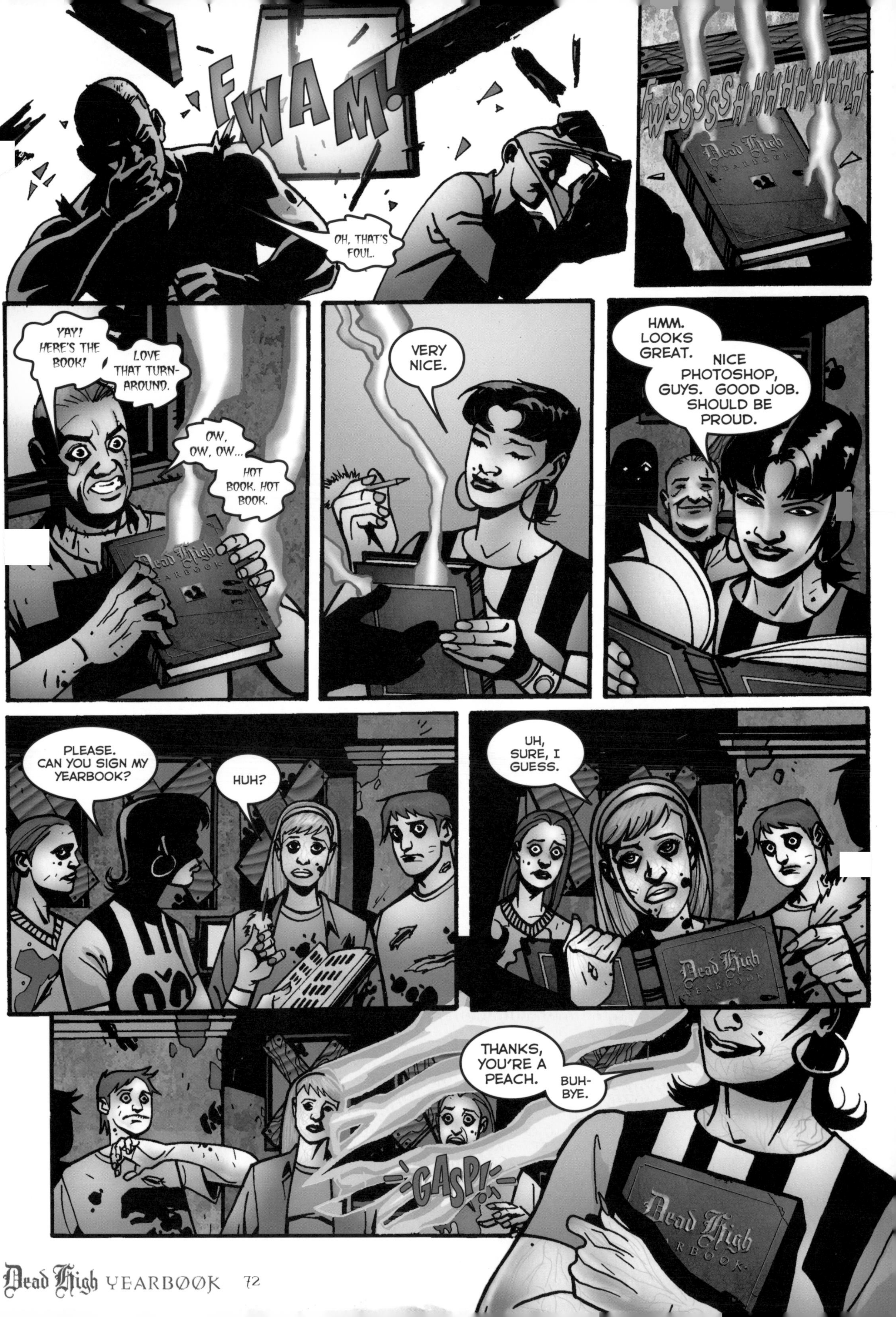
FWAM!
OH, THAT'S FOUL.
FWSSSSSHHHHHHHHH
Dead High YEARBOOK
YAY! HERE'S THE BOOK!
LOVE THAT TURN-AROUND.
OW, OW, OW...
HOT BOOK. HOT BOOK.
VERY NICE.
HMM. LOOKS GREAT.
NICE PHOTOSHOP, GUYS. GOOD JOB. SHOULD BE PROUD.
PLEASE. CAN YOU SIGN MY YEARBOOK?
HUH?
UH, SURE, I GUESS.
THANKS, YOU'RE A PEACH.
BUH-BYE.
GASP!

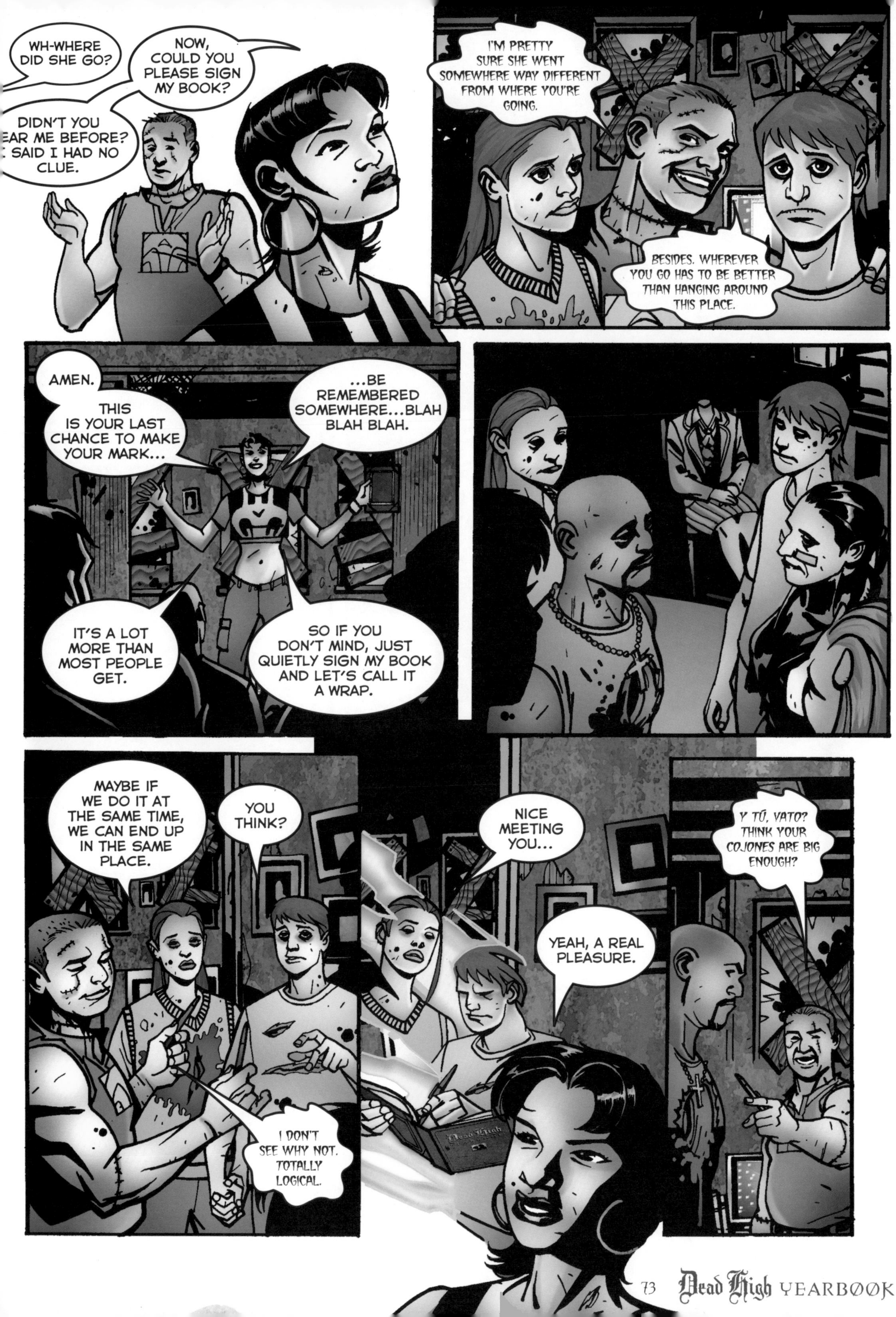

WH-WHERE DID SHE GO?
NOW, COULD YOU PLEASE SIGN MY BOOK?
DIDN'T YOU EAR ME BEFORE? SAID I HAD NO CLUE.
I'M PRETTY SURE SHE WENT SOMEWHERE WAY DIFFERENT FROM WHERE YOU'RE GOING.
BESIDES. WHEREVER YOU GO HAS TO BE BETTER THAN HANGING AROUND THIS PLACE.
AMEN.
THIS IS YOUR LAST CHANCE TO MAKE YOUR MARK...
...BE REMEMBERED SOMEWHERE...BLAH BLAH BLAH.
IT'S A LOT MORE THAN MOST PEOPLE GET.
SO IF YOU DON'T MIND, JUST QUIETLY SIGN MY BOOK AND LET'S CALL IT A WRAP.
MAYBE IF WE DO IT AT THE SAME TIME, WE CAN END UP IN THE SAME PLACE.
YOU THINK?
I DON'T SEE WHY NOT. TOTALLY LOGICAL.
NICE MEETING YOU...
YEAH, A REAL PLEASURE.
Y TÚ, VATO? THINK YOUR COJONES ARE BIG ENOUGH?

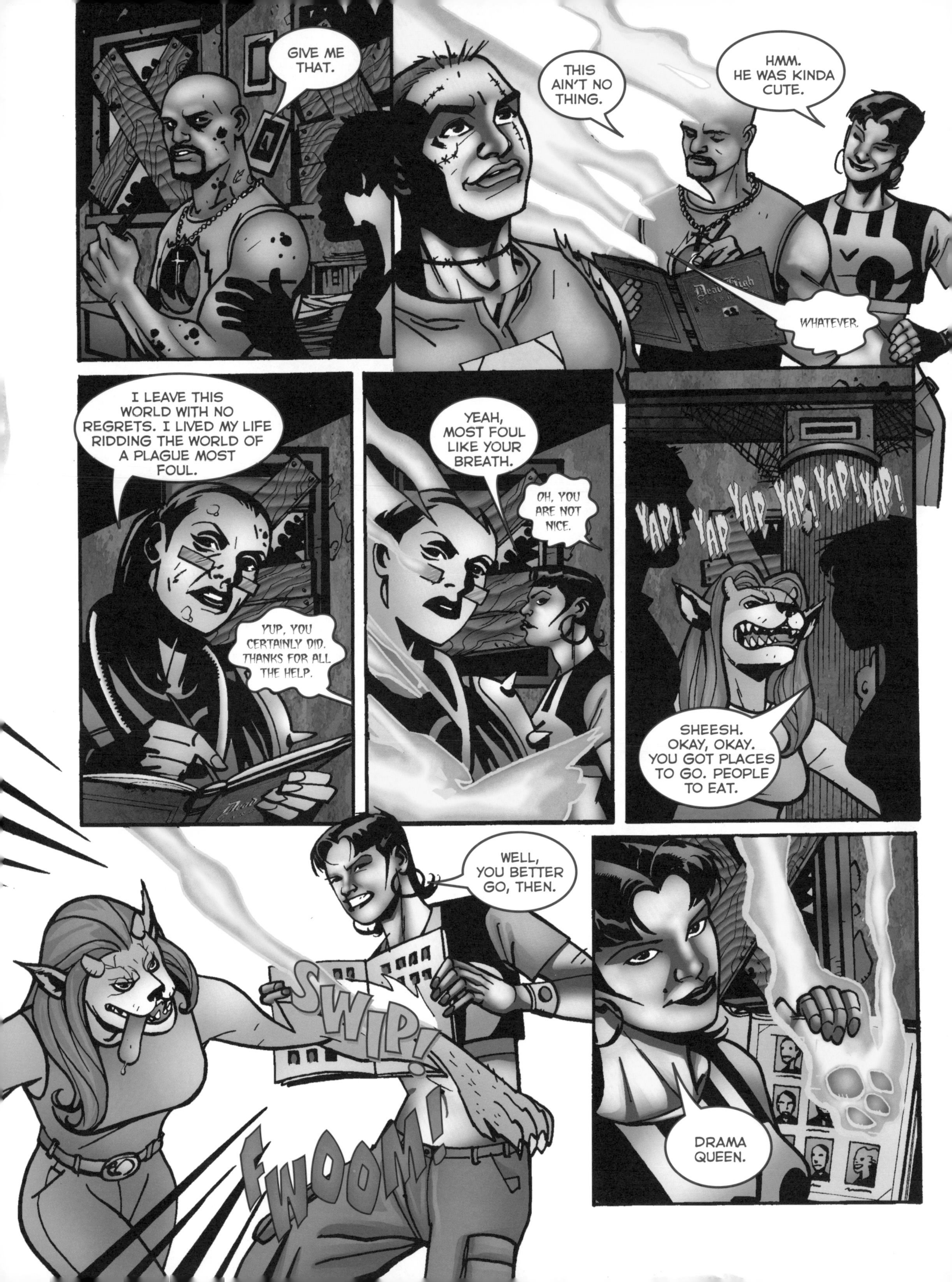
GIVE ME THAT.
THIS AIN'T NO THING.
HMM. HE WAS KINDA CUTE.
WHATEVER.
I LEAVE THIS WORLD WITH NO REGRETS. I LIVED MY LIFE RIDDING THE WORLD OF A PLAGUE MOST FOUL.
YUP, YOU CERTAINLY DID. THANKS FOR ALL THE HELP.
YEAH, MOST FOUL LIKE YOUR BREATH.
OH, YOU ARE NOT NICE.
YAP! YAP YAP YAP! YAP! YAP!
SHEESH. OKAY, OKAY. YOU GOT PLACES TO GO. PEOPLE TO EAT.
WELL, YOU BETTER GO, THEN.
SWIP!
FWOOM!
DRAMA QUEEN.

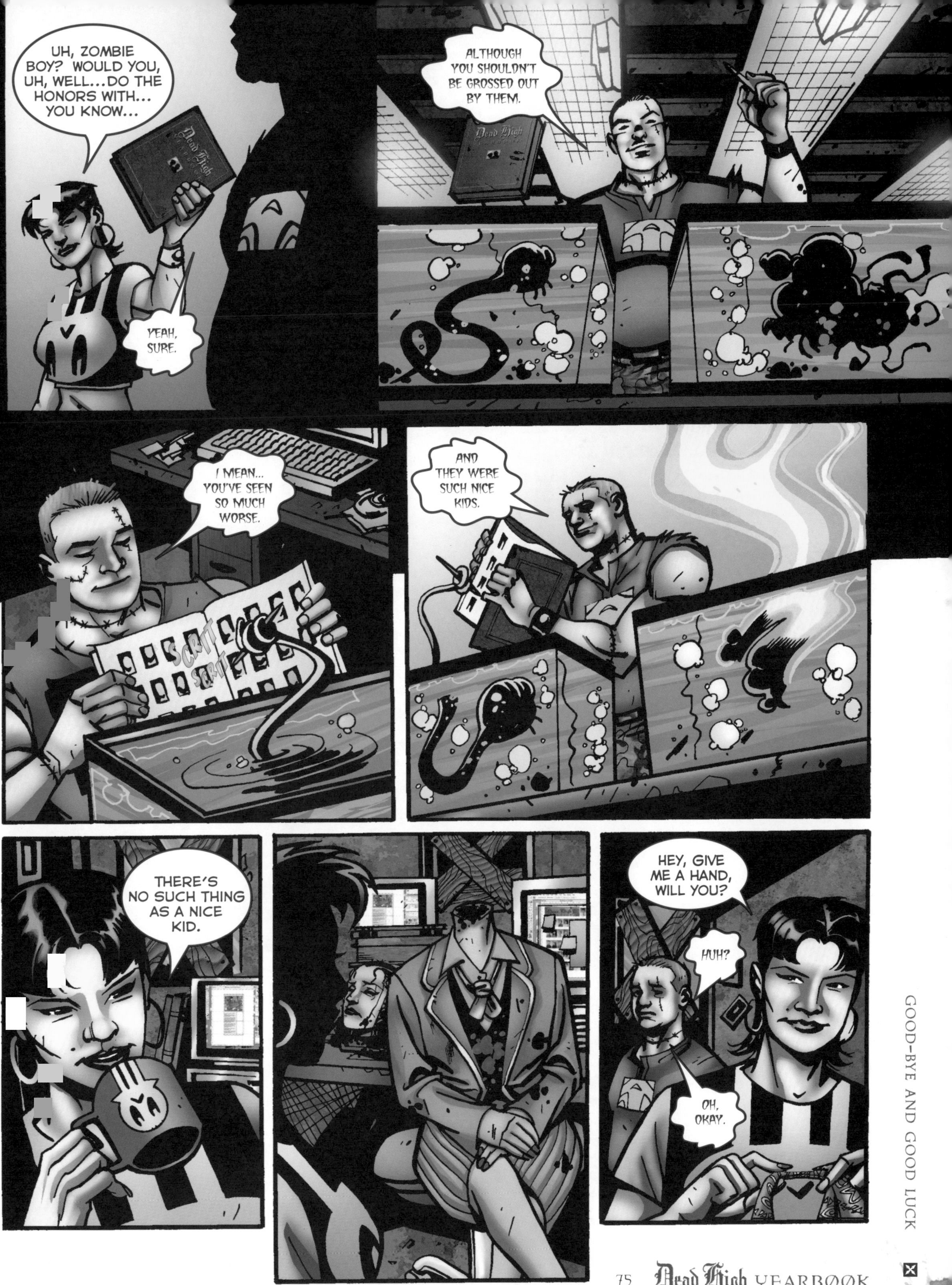
UH, ZOMBIE BOY? WOULD YOU, UH, WELL...DO THE HONORS WITH... YOU KNOW...
YEAH, SURE.
ALTHOUGH YOU SHOULDN'T BE GROSSED OUT BY THEM.
I MEAN... YOU'VE SEEN SO MUCH WORSE.
AND THEY WERE SUCH NICE KIDS.
THERE'S NO SUCH THING AS A NICE KID.
HEY, GIVE ME A HAND, WILL YOU?
HUH?
OH, OKAY.

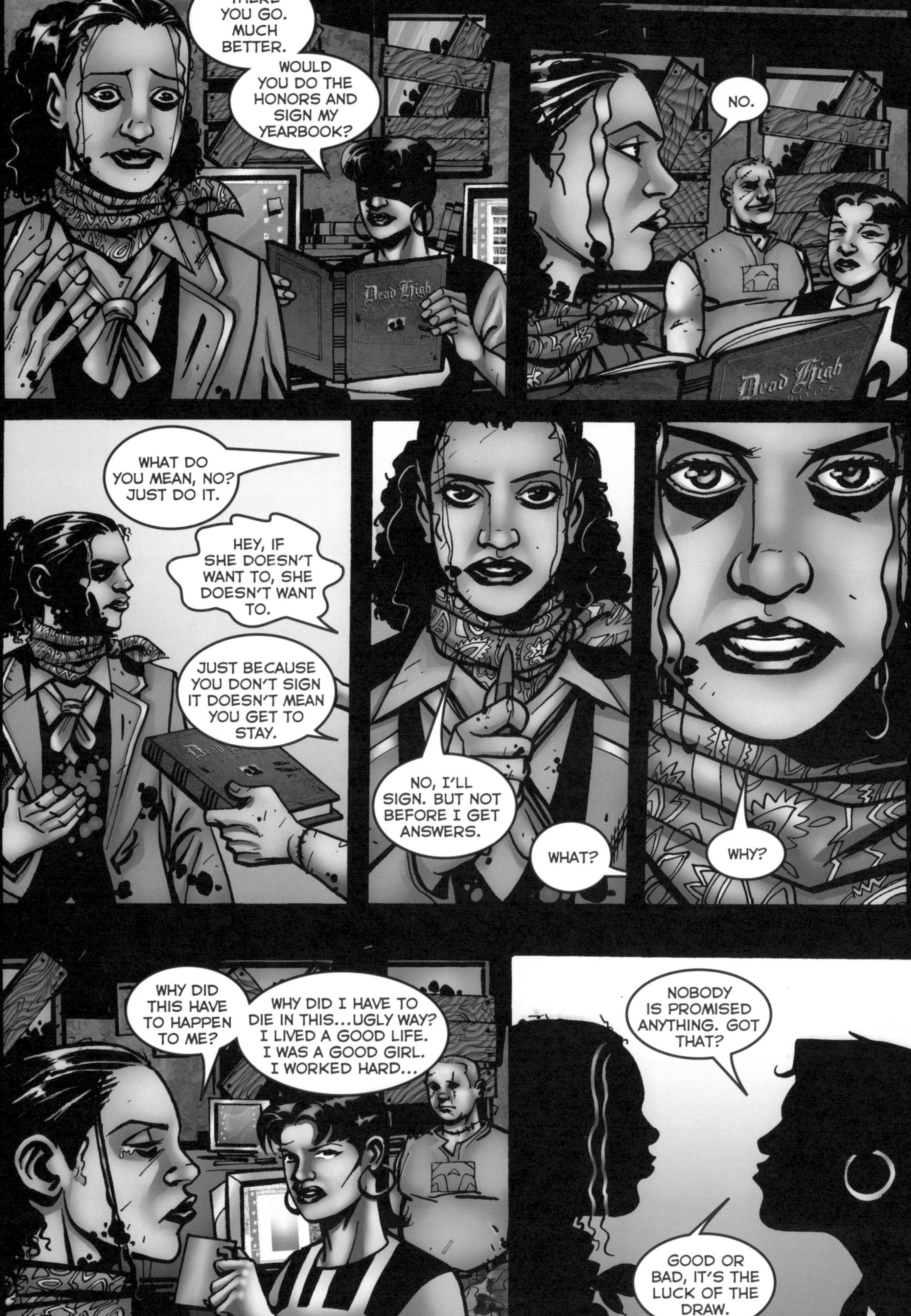

THERE YOU GO. MUCH BETTER.
WOULD YOU DO THE HONORS AND SIGN MY YEARBOOK?
NO.
WHAT DO YOU MEAN, NO? JUST DO IT.
HEY, IF SHE DOESN'T WANT TO, SHE DOESN'T WANT TO.
JUST BECAUSE YOU DON'T SIGN IT DOESN'T MEAN YOU GET TO STAY.
NO, I'LL SIGN. BUT NOT BEFORE I GET ANSWERS.
WHAT?
WHY?
WHY DID THIS HAVE TO HAPPEN TO ME?
WHY DID I HAVE TO DIE IN THIS...UGLY WAY? I LIVED A GOOD LIFE. I WAS A GOOD GIRL. I WORKED HARD...
NOBODY IS PROMISED ANYTHING. GOT THAT?
GOOD OR BAD, IT'S THE LUCK OF THE DRAW.

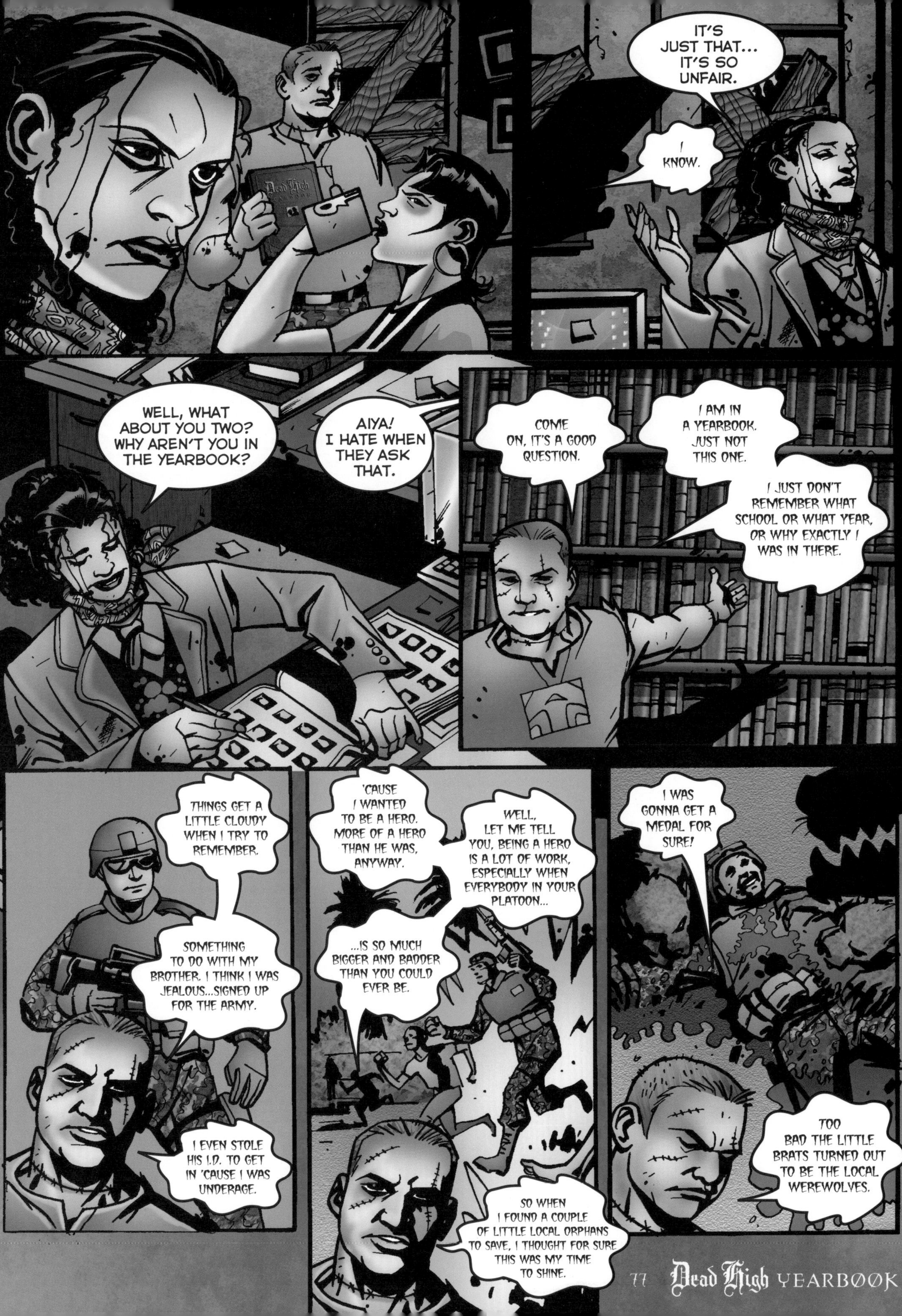
IT'S JUST THAT... IT'S SO UNFAIR.
I KNOW.
WELL, WHAT ABOUT YOU TWO? WHY AREN'T YOU IN THE YEARBOOK?
AIYA! I HATE WHEN THEY ASK THAT.
COME ON, IT'S A GOOD QUESTION.
I AM IN A YEARBOOK. JUST NOT THIS ONE.
I JUST DON'T REMEMBER WHAT SCHOOL OR WHAT YEAR, OR WHY EXACTLY I WAS IN THERE.
THINGS GET A LITTLE CLOUDY WHEN I TRY TO REMEMBER.
SOMETHING TO DO WITH MY BROTHER. I THINK I WAS JEALOUS...SIGNED UP FOR THE ARMY.
I EVEN STOLE HIS I.D. TO GET IN 'CAUSE I WAS UNDERAGE.
'CAUSE I WANTED TO BE A HERO. MORE OF A HERO THAN HE WAS, ANYWAY.
WELL, LET ME TELL YOU, BEING A HERO IS A LOT OF WORK, ESPECIALLY WHEN EVERYBODY IN YOUR PLATOON...
...IS SO MUCH BIGGER AND BADDER THAN YOU COULD EVER BE.
SO WHEN I FOUND A COUPLE OF LITTLE LOCAL ORPHANS TO SAVE, I THOUGHT FOR SURE THIS WAS MY TIME TO SHINE.
I WAS GONNA GET A MEDAL FOR SURE!
TOO BAD THE LITTLE BRATS TURNED OUT TO BE THE LOCAL WEREWOLVES.

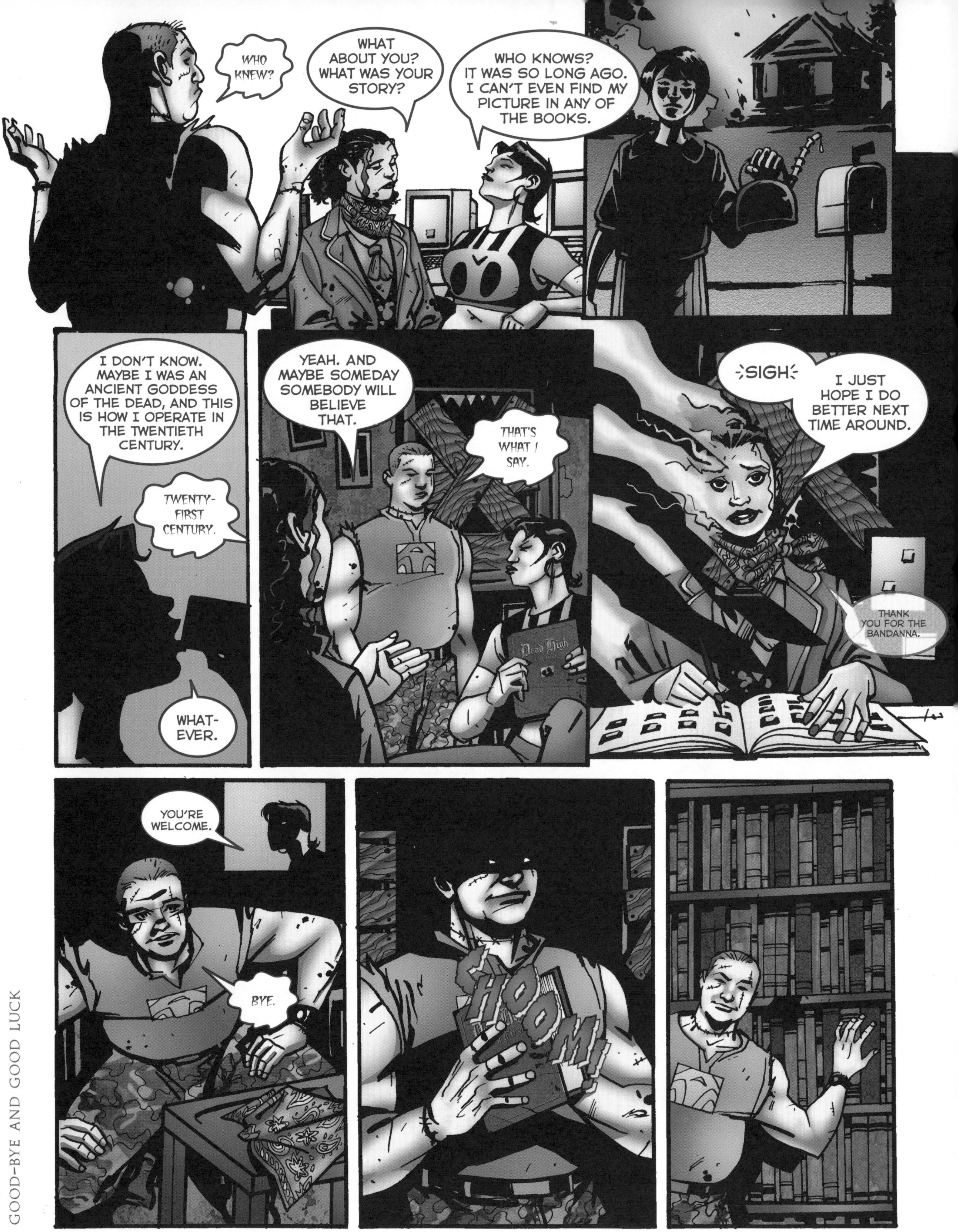
WHO KNEW?
WHAT ABOUT YOU? WHAT WAS YOUR STORY?
WHO KNOWS? IT WAS SO LONG AGO. I CAN'T EVEN FIND MY PICTURE IN ANY OF THE BOOKS.
I DON'T KNOW. MAYBE I WAS AN ANCIENT GODDESS OF THE DEAD, AND THIS IS HOW I OPERATE IN THE TWENTIETH CENTURY.
TWENTY-FIRST CENTURY.
WHAT-EVER.
YEAH. AND MAYBE SOMEDAY SOMEBODY WILL BELIEVE THAT.
THAT'S WHAT I SAY.
Dead High
-SIGH-
I JUST HOPE I DO BETTER NEXT TIME AROUND.
THANK YOU FOR THE BANDANNA.
YOU'RE WELCOME.
BYE.
THOOM!

GOOD-BYE AND GOOD LUCK

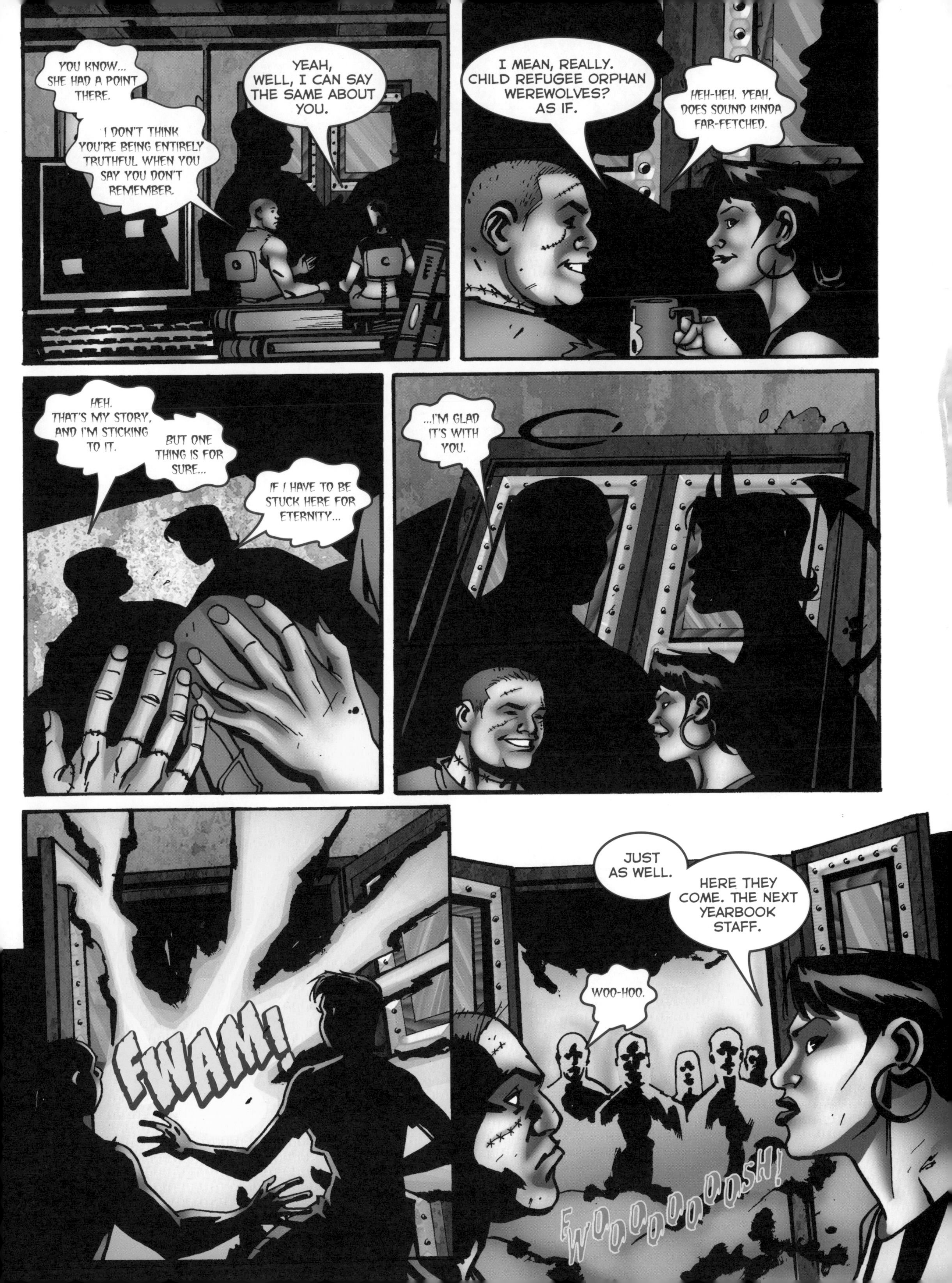

YOU KNOW... SHE HAD A POINT THERE.
I DON'T THINK YOU'RE BEING ENTIRELY TRUTHFUL WHEN YOU SAY YOU DON'T REMEMBER.
YEAH, WELL, I CAN SAY THE SAME ABOUT YOU.
I MEAN, REALLY. CHILD REFUGEE ORPHAN WEREWOLVES? AS IF.
HEH-HEH. YEAH, DOES SOUND KINDA FAR-FETCHED.
HEH. THAT'S MY STORY, AND I'M STICKING TO IT.
BUT ONE THING IS FOR SURE...
IF I HAVE TO BE STUCK HERE FOR ETERNITY...
...I'M GLAD IT'S WITH YOU.
FWAM!
JUST AS WELL.
HERE THEY COME. THE NEXT YEARBOOK STAFF.
WOO-HOO.
FWOOOOOOOOOSH!

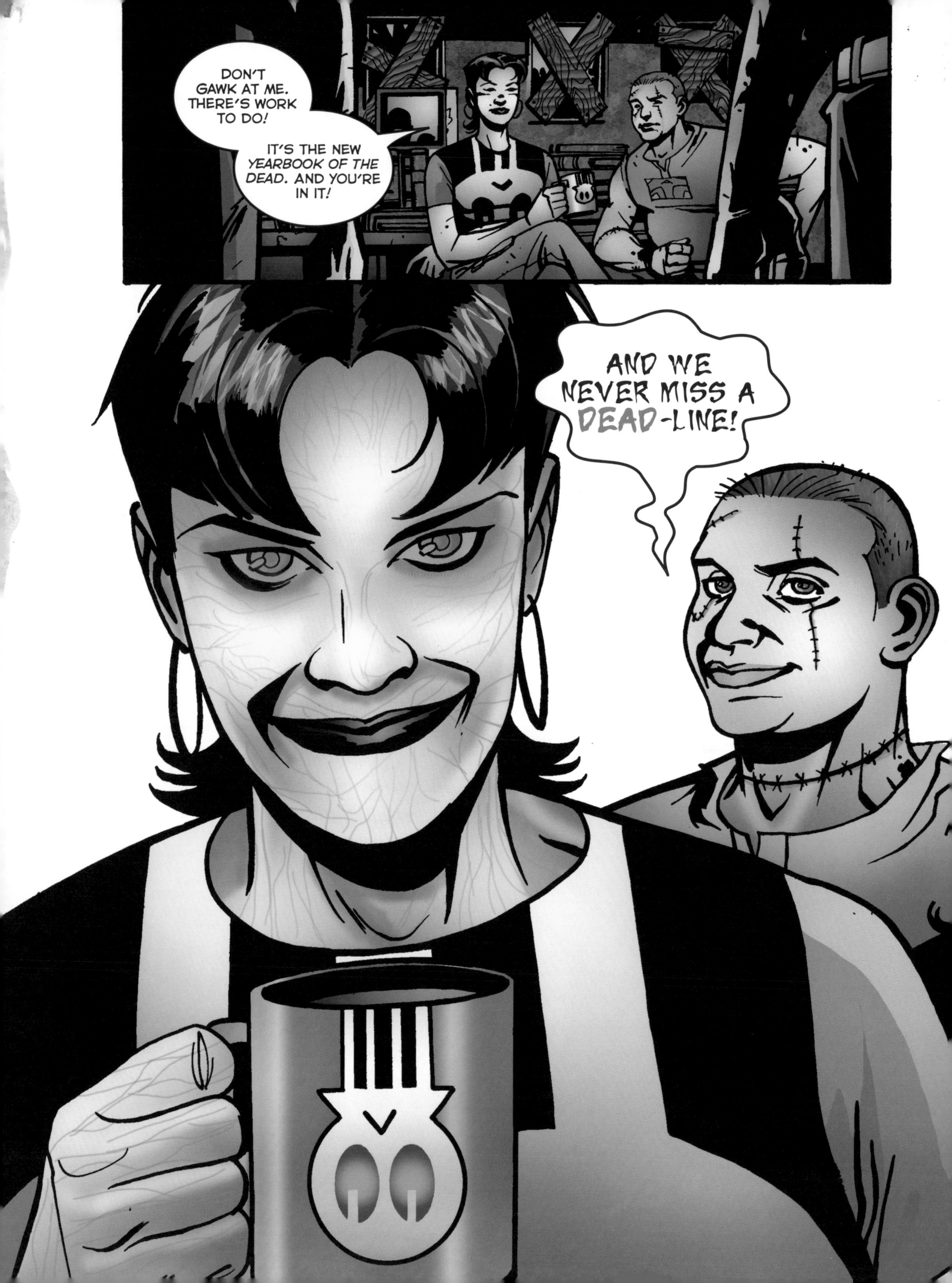
DON'T GAWK AT ME. THERE'S WORK TO DO!
IT'S THE NEW *YEARBOOK OF THE DEAD*. AND YOU'RE IN IT!
AND WE NEVER MISS A DEAD-LINE!

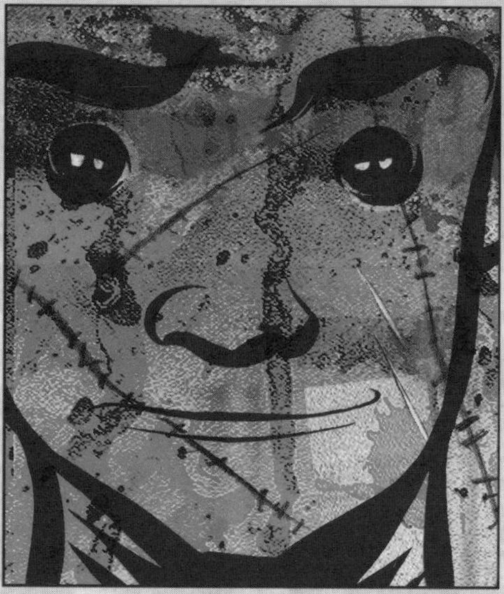
ZOMBIE BOY

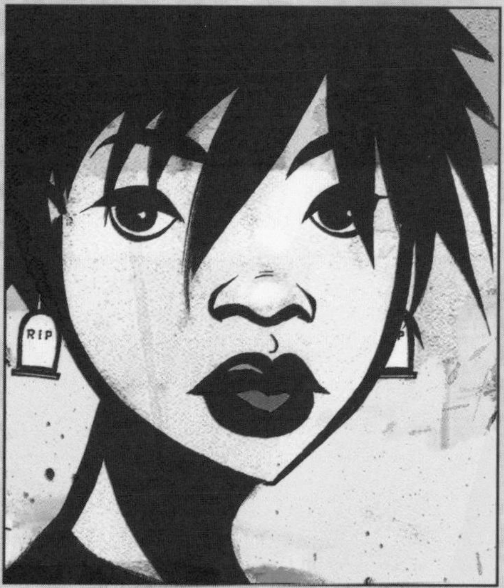
RIP
ZOMBIE GIRL

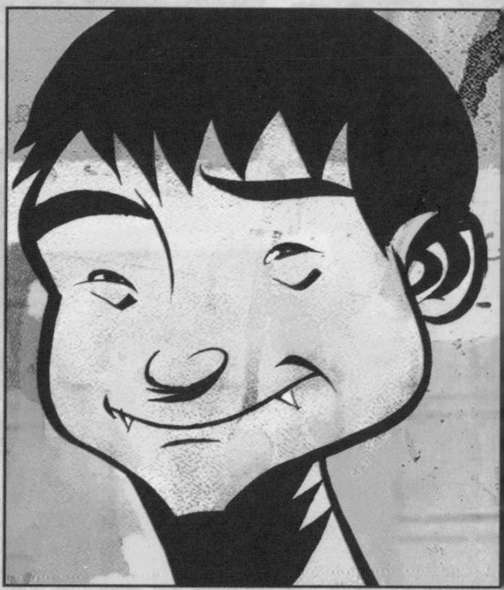
LOUIE

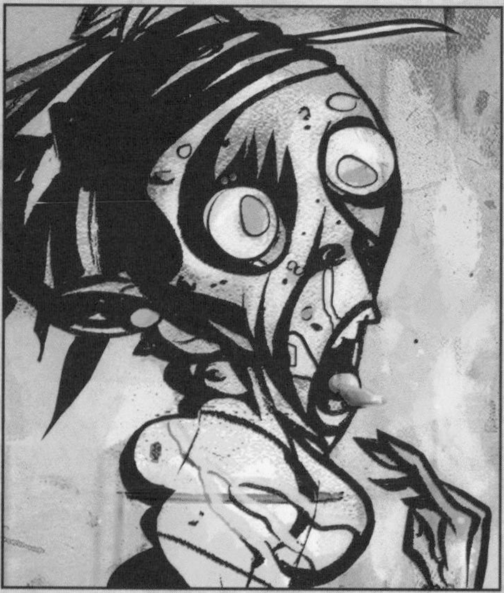
LISA

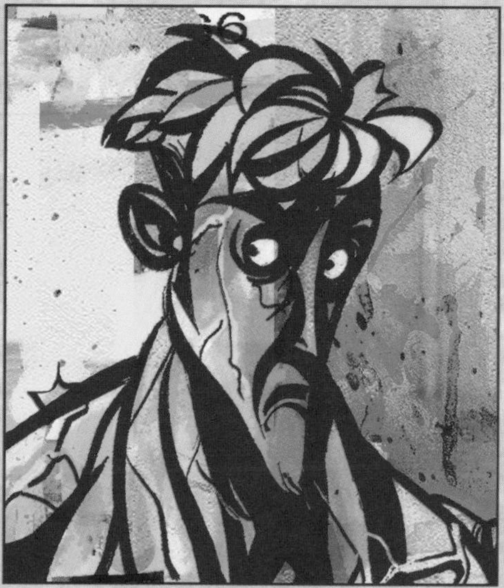
JEFF

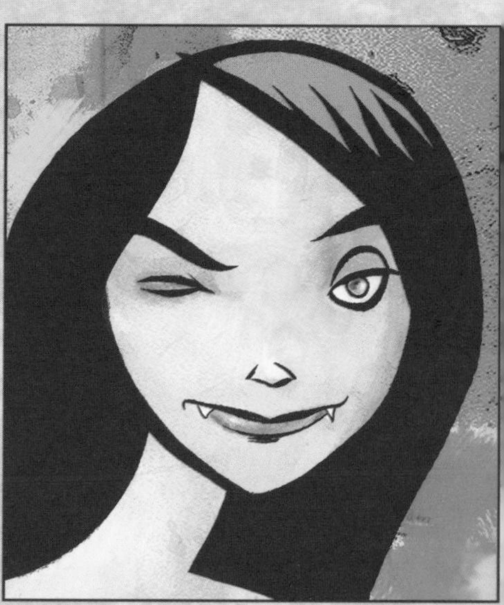
NICKY

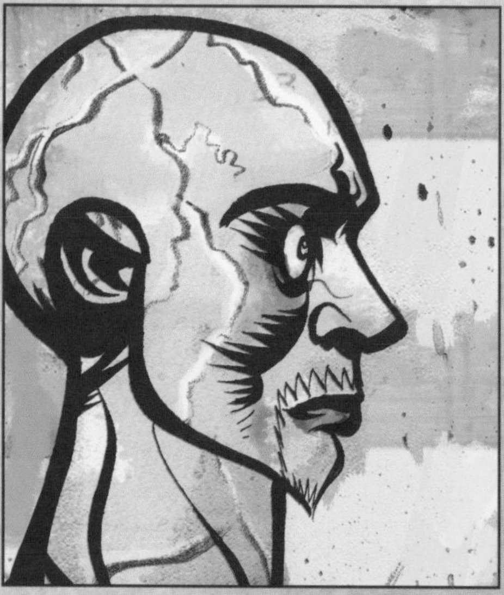
MIGUEL

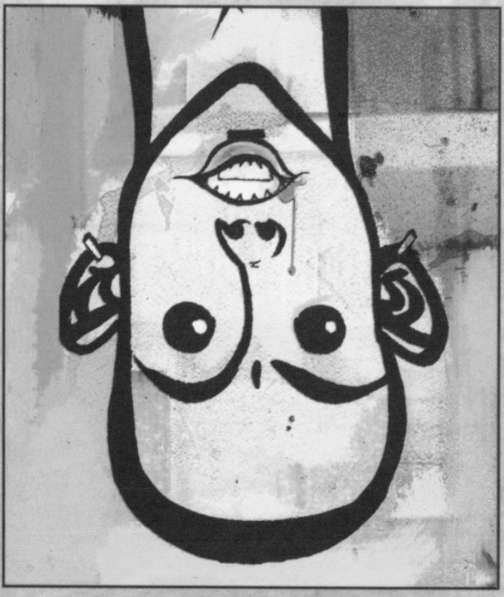
CARLITO

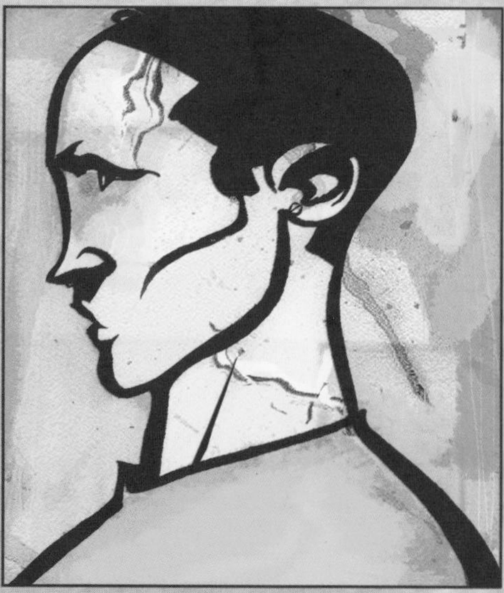
LONNIE